SHAKESPEARE
and the
American Musical

For Barbara,
Warmest regards,
Irene G. Dash

SHAKESPEARE
and the
American Musical

IRENE G. DASH

INDIANA UNIVERSITY PRESS
Bloomington & Indianapolis

This book is a publication of

Indiana University Press
601 North Morton Street
Bloomington, IN 47404-3797 USA

www.iupress.indiana.edu

Telephone orders   800-842-6796
Fax orders   812-855-7931
Orders by e-mail   iuporder@indiana.edu

Manufactured in the United
States of America

Library of Congress Cataloging-
in-Publication Data

Dash, Irene G.
  Shakespeare and the American
musical / Irene G. Dash.
      p.   cm.
  Includes bibliographical
references and index.
  ISBN 978-0-253-35414-3 (cloth : alk.
paper) — ISBN 978-0-253-22152-0
(pbk. : alk. paper) 1. Musicals—United
States—20th century—History and
criticism. 2. Shakespeare, William,
1564–1616—Influence. I. Title.
  ML2054.D37 2009
  782.1'40973—dc22

                    2009026873

1 2 3 4 5   15 14 13 12 11 10

My parents, Samuel Golden and Bella Lasker Golden, created a world where theater was the magic carpet. It could carry you to other wonderful places. It could open a universe of ideas. It could dazzle with its colors and light. They took me there. I never really left. To their memory I dedicate this book.

CONTENTS

ACKNOWLEDGMENTS

Many people helped make this book happen. Among them, perhaps the first were Virginia and Alden Vaughan. On a ride home from the Folger Library they started talking about the American Shakespeare seminar they were going to lead at the International Shakespeare Conference in Japan in 1990. Aware of my great interest in the American theater, they generously invited me to join them, suggesting I write on the American Shakespeare musical. Although I was then working on *Women's Worlds in Shakespeare's Plays,* I acquiesced, delighted to be moving into a new area. Years later, when I was coming to the end of the process of writing *Shakespeare and the American Musical,* the Vaughans once again tapped me. They invited me to contribute an article to the catalogue *Shakespeare in American Life* (2007) for the exhibit they were curating celebrating the Folger Library's seventy-fifth anniversary. My article, "Shakespeare and the American Musical," appears in that catalogue. It helped crystallize my ideas and give me a sense of the overall unity of the whole. I want to thank the Vaughans for their inspiration.

Along the way friends and colleagues encouraged me, patiently listened to me discuss different points, and sought to keep me on the straight and narrow. Elizabeth Hageman was among them. She tried to move me back to my original thesis when I wandered, first on chapter 3, then on the overall book. I greatly appreciate her persistence. Gerald Pinciss worked in subtle ways to have me clarify my ideas through un-adorned, straightforward writing. Much thanks for his brilliant under-standing of content and his sensitivity to language.

One tests out ideas in a variety of places and through multiple devices—in the classroom, in seminars, conference talks, and published papers. CDs of the music and DVDs of the musicals when converted to film can bring them to life, giving them vibrancy and immediacy. In a graduate course on American musical Shakespeare, my students could see how vital music and dance were to understanding these works. In fact, I am indebted to my chair, Sylvia Tomasch, who assigned me this course. The music sparked the students' enthusiasm. They loved watching the musicals and discussing them. My peers too enjoyed hearing the music; however, they reacted on a different level. They were interested in the comparison of Shakespeare's play with its twentieth-century musical adaptation. In the Columbia University Seminar on Shakespeare, where I presented a paper on the musical *Two Gentlemen of Verona,* many remembered the outstanding performance of Raul Julia and the vitality of the rock music that pervaded the show. I want to express my great appreciation to Dr. Robert L. Belknap and the University Seminars at Columbia University for their help in publication. The ideas presented in my book have benefited enormously from discussions in the University Seminar on Shakespeare.

When I presented papers at conferences, the make-up of the participants influenced their reactions. Those from overseas who attended the International Shakespeare Conferences, for example, tended to compare productions in other countries with those in America or to gain new insights about us. Thus at the International Shakespeare Conference in Stratford-upon-Avon my paper "'Even Now a Tailor Called Me in His Shop': *The Boys from Syracuse* and *The Comedy of Errors*" fascinated the audience with its hints of the pre–World War II United States, whereas my talk at the Shakespeare Association of America titled "The Latest Word: *Your Own Thing* (1968) and Trevor-Nunn's *Twelfth Night* (1996)" drew my colleagues to a familiar film. My challenging paper at the Shakespeare Association in 2000 introduced the many borrowings of *Kiss Me, Kate* from Shakespeare's *Taming of the Shrew* while showing how the adaptors revised and rethought their conclusions. I later developed this into "Double Vision: *Kiss Me, Kate*," published in *Shakespeare Newsletter* 55, no. 1 (Spring 2005). Thanks to the editors, Tom Pendleton and John Mahon, for their careful editing. Finally, in 2006 I discussed "American Musical Tragedy: *Romeo and Juliet* and *West Side Story*" for members of the Society for the Study of Women in the Renaissance seminar.

Until I finally retired from teaching, extended research and writing were primarily confined to the summers, when I worked mainly at the Library of Congress, where two skilled and knowledgeable librarians, Walter Zvonchenko and Mark Eden Horowitz, guided me. They introduced me to the library's riches, especially the Leonard Bernstein and Cole Porter collections. During that time, I also occasionally relied on the resources of the Folger Shakespeare Library for backup material. Thanks to Betsy Walsh, Jean Miller, Barbara Mowat, Gail Paster, Richard Kuchta, Laetitia Yaendle, and Harold Batie. When, however, full-time work on the American musicals became possible, I settled in at the New York Public Library for the Performing Arts. Once again librarians ungrudgingly helped me, no matter how ephemeral the item I needed. My special thanks to Christine Karatnytsky and Jeremy Megraw in the Billy Rose Theatre Division, whose familiarity with scripts and the library's holdings was special, as well as to Bob Taylor, the division's curator, who assisted me with the difficult business of rights to the Danny Apolinar collection. His quiet style and answers as he guided me through the difficulty of other permissions was invaluable. My thanks, too, to Barbara Knowles, the archivist, who accompanied me as I went through boxes of the then uncatalogued Danny Apolinar papers. I also appreciate the help of Louise Matzinek and Dr. Bladel. Since my work crossed several disciplines, I drew on the expertise of Charles Perrier and Pat Rader of the Jerome Robbins Dance Division, whose knowledge of the ins and outs of the Jerome Robbins Collection is vast. Bob Kosovsky of the Music Division helped me with some of the hard questions on music. I greatly appreciate their help.

Other friends and colleagues, too, provided important support for me over the years. Among these was Bernice Kliman, who most recently put me in touch with Robert Hapgood. His multimedia presentation of films, slides, and commentary at the 1976 centenary meeting of the Shakespeare Association in Washington, D.C., provided an invaluable resource. My friendship with Gloria Beckerman extends to a love of the theater and a concern for one another's lives. Her warmth and caring are palpable. Lois Schwoerer, in a different discipline but also a scholar, shared a deep concern for the accuracy of research, understanding some of the challenges I faced. Phyllis Rackin, a leading concerned feminist, has always extended a hand to me when I needed it. Carol Carlisle has been an inspiration from the time I read her first book, *Shakespeare from the Greenroom,* to her dynamic presence as I later grew to know her. A meticulous scholar, she led a seminar on *Two Gentlemen of Verona* and generously shared her findings with me. Georgiana Ziegler often drew on her special skills as a librarian to help me out with answers to difficult questions.

Russell Jackson, with his extensive background in Shakespeare and the staging of the plays, offered a new vision. Patricia Lennox taught me the value of a telephone call now that I was out of the Renaissance and the eighteenth century. I discovered how accessible people are when I called Lois and Arthur Elias, who owned the copyright on Bella and Samuel Spewack's material at the Manuscript and Special Collections Library of Columbia University. After that call, the Eliases generously permitted me to examine the many drafts of *Kiss Me, Kate,* to note the material Bella Spewack and Cole Porter discarded, and to read her correspondence with him as the scriptwriter and composer slowly worked through the multiple drafts of what would eventually become *Kiss Me, Kate.* A telephone call also elicited the gracious response of John Guare, who explained some of the theatrical techniques used in his musical *Two Gentlemen of Verona.* David Lobenstine brought a new pair of eyes and editorial expertise to my work. At a distance, he gave a fresh perspective and fine insightful comments that spurred me on. At Indiana University Press, Janet Rabinowitch, Jane Behnken, and Katherine Baber have been most helpful in guiding me through the maze of turning the manuscript into a book. Thanks, too, to my copyeditor, whose sharp and critical eye saved me from errors.

Most of all, my family has been unusual and caring. My daughter Deborah has read and reread every chapter as it slowly came into focus. Willing to speak with me at length and to explore ideas I sometimes expressed unclearly, she has pushed me on when I was discouraged. My son-in-law MacDonald, a perfectionist, would modestly point out holes in sentences where my meaning was obscure. My daughter Deena, listening to me struggle over my introduction, offered me the key. "Why don't you personalize it and write from your own experience?" It was a brilliant notion. I followed it. My son-in-law Sidney, although in another field, sympathetically understood the pressures I was under. Finally, of course, the one person always there for me even when I pretend not to notice is my husband, Martin. To him I owe a tremendous debt of gratitude and love.

I send this book out into the world hoping it provides a new look at familiar territory and that it once again confirms the amazing greatness of a sixteenth-century artist, William Shakespeare, to speak to the modern world.

PERMISSIONS ACKNOWLEDGMENTS

Boys from Syracuse

Book of *Boys from Syracuse* by George Abbott used by permission of Joy Abbott. Music by Richard Rodgers, lyrics by Lorenz Hart.

"Opening Fanfare," "Dear Old Syracuse," "Falling in Love with Love," "This Can't Be Love," "The Shortest Day of the Year," "You Have Cast Your Shadow on the Sea," and "Sing for Your Supper" copyright © 1938 by Chappell & Co., Inc. Copyright Renewed and assigned to Williamson Music (for the extended renewal period) and WB Music for the USA. International Copyright Renewed. All Rights Reserved.

"What Can You Do with a Man," "Ladies of the Evening," "He and She," and "Come with Me" copyright © 1954 by Chappell & Co., Inc. Copyright Renewed. International Copyright Renewed. All Rights Reserved.

"Let Antipholus In" copyright © 1986 by The Estate of Richard Rodgers and the Estate of Lorenz Hart. International Copyright Renewed. All Rights Reserved.

"Big Brother" copyright © 1965 by Chappell & Co., Inc. Copyright Renewed. International Copyright Renewed. All Rights Reserved.

Kiss Me, Kate

Book of *Kiss Me, Kate* by Bella and Samuel Spewack used by permission of Lois and Arthur Elias. Music and lyrics by Cole Porter.

"Another Op'nin, Another Show" Words and music by Cole Porter. © 1949 by Cole Porter. Copyright renewed, assigned to John F. Wharton,

Inc. owner of Publication and Allied Rights throughout the World. All Rights Reserved. Used by Permission of Alfred Publishing Co., Inc.

Two Gentleman of Verona

Excerpts used by permission of John Guare, Mel Shapiro, and Galt MacDermot. Book adapted by John Guare and Mel Shapiro; Music by Galt MacDermot; Lyrics by John Guare. All Rights Reserved.

West Side Story

Conception by Jerome Robbins. Excerpts from the Jerome Robbins papers are used by permission of the Jerome Robbins Foundation and the Robbins Rights Trust. All rights reserved.

Book of *West Side Story* © 1956, 1958 Arthur Laurents. Used by generous permission of Arthur Laurents.

Excerpts from "Something's Coming," "America," "Cool," "One Hand, One Heart," "Tonight," "Gee, Officer Krupke," "A Boy Like That" Music by Leonard Bernstein, lyrics by Stephen Sondheim. © 1956, 1957, 1958, 1959 by Amberson Holdings LLC and Stephen Sondheim. Copyright Renewed. Leonard Bernstein Music Publishing Company LLC. International Copyright Secured. Reprinted by Permission of the Leonard Bernstein Office, Inc.

All excerpts from the Leonard Bernstein Papers are used by permission of the Leonard Bernstein Office, Inc. © Amberson Holdings LLC. Used by permission of the Leonard Bernstein Office, Inc.

Your Own Thing

Music and Lyrics by Danny Apolinar and Hal Hester. Book by Donald Driver. Excerpts of the papers of Danny Apolinar are used by permission of John Britton.

Photos reproduced in chapter 4 of *Your Own Thing* were taken by Frank Derbas and kindly shared with me by Robert Hapgood, Professor Emeritus, University of New Hampshire. I was unable to locate Derbas during research for this book, but wish to credit the photos to him. I also thank Professor Hapgood for his generosity.

SHAKESPEARE
and the
American Musical

Shakespeare's Enchantment

Never absent from the American stage, Shakespeare took on a new guise in the twentieth century. He danced and sang and helped to shape American musical theater. Whereas dance, song, and story had often been part of Shakespeare productions, never before had they all been united in a concerted effort to propel the plot forward. During the twentieth century, a growing new genre, adaptations of Shakespeare's plays incorporating techniques from the American musical, revealed the importance of the dramatist's perceptions of women, power, relationships between the sexes, and societal mores. Five of Shakespeare's plays were particularly conducive to this new form and successfully made the transfer: *The Boys from Syracuse* grew out of *The Comedy of Errors*; *Kiss Me, Kate* owed its origin to *The Taming of the Shrew*; *West Side Story* evolved from *Romeo and Juliet*; *Your Own Thing* transformed *Twelfth Night*; and *Two Gentlemen of Verona*, retaining its title, metamorphosed into a rock musical.

Sometimes Shakespeare scared people, especially those writing about the American musical. They didn't know what to do with him. Despite Shakespeare's texts being in the forefront of the development of the organic musical and being popular, these adaptations were basically overlooked. But they shouldn't have been. Right from the start, from the time that Richard Rodgers and Lorenz Hart decided to turn to a Shakespeare play rather than write their own story, his works were central. Rodgers and Hart knew they were in the business of composing music and writing lyrics, not creating plot, so they turned to stories that were tried and true: the stories of Shakespeare.

The Boys from Syracuse was a bold adventure for its creators, since they told Shakespeare's story primarily through song and dance, transposing the play into the vernacular of everyday speech and drawing on the contemporary world. In song and costume *The Boys from Syracuse* picked up reverberations from a Europe on the verge of the Second World War. Moreover, Rodgers, Hart, and George Abbott, who wrote the book, engaged the talents of George Balanchine, the ballet master of the Metropolitan Opera, even acceding to his wish to be listed as choreographer, a first in the theater. Ballet was no longer unusual; now it was an organic part of the whole. The dancing in *The Boys from Syracuse* was integral to the story. It usually illustrated or interpreted a song, as for example occurred with "Ladies of the Evening in the Morning." The women sang of their trade in the morning. Again the dance "Looking for an Honest Man," sung by another woman, had Diogenes as the central figure while policemen, whose costumes resembled those of storm troopers, captured the troopers' movements in their dance.[1] Balanchine brought a new vision to the American musical, one that would blossom in the subsequent choreography of Hanya Holm and Jerome Robbins. Rodgers and Hart also wrote songs that were integral to the plot and advanced its development.

With the exception of *The Boys from Syracuse,* I have seen all the musicals I discuss in this book, and my first-hand impressions of their staging inform my work. However, my memory of Shakespeare on stage goes back to an unforgettable production that preceded the musicals discussed here. I can recall Alfred Lunt and Lynn Fontanne in *The Taming of the Shrew* with vivid clarity. Although the show was not my first experience of theater, Shakespeare was comparatively new to me, and that production was magical. For the first time in many years, Lunt and Fontanne brought back a frequently eliminated character, Shakespeare's Christopher Sly. In a framing action, a drunken tinker is thrown out of an alehouse by a woman barkeeper. He is tricked into believing he is a lord and watches a traveling company present the play of Kate and Petruchio. I was enchanted. But when the curtain came down on Kate and Petruchio at the play's end, I wanted to know what happened to the guy for whom they were performing. I was totally involved in the play.

0.1. A drunken Christopher Sly (Richard Whorf) sits in the balcony of the theater, waiting to be entertained by traveling players, in the 1935 production of *The Taming of the Shrew*. Shakespeare's incomplete frame to the play both enchants and entices the audience, challenging it to understand this enigmatic play. *Vandamm Studio, Billy Rose Theatre Division, New York Public Library for the Performing Arts, Astor, Lenox, and Tilden Foundations.*

It was an experience I never forgot and one I used in class every time I taught the play. The audience needed to have a double vision—an ability to absorb the message of the play, if it had one, to follow the story, and to look for Shakespeare's character development to see how it supported a complex plot. "Double vision" describes the greatness of Shakespeare's artistry. He has you seeing the story of Kate and Petruchio through the lens of a play-within-a-play. Thus the audience is uncertain whether the story of the taming of Kate is the theme of the story or whether it is a fiction created for a character who has been thrown out of an alehouse by a woman and is dreaming of his revenge.

In a recent talk at Lincoln Center, Arthur Laurents was asked whether *West Side Story* was the first musical to integrate the music and dancing with the plot. He answered, "Oh no, the integrated musical began with *On Your Toes*" (1936). According to Brooks Atkinson, *On Your Toes* was "a pioneering show that had an independent style. It included a genuine ballet, 'Slaughter on Tenth Avenue,' staged by George Balanchine and danced by Ray Bolger and Tamara Geva, at a time when ballet on Broadway was a couterie art-form."[2] But Ethan Mordden notes that "Slaughter on Tenth Avenue" was actually a ballet-within-a-play and did not move the plot forward at all.[3] Thus *On Your Toes* really didn't fall into the category of the integrated or organic musical. Atkinson writes that Rodgers and Hart's "standards were high in all departments of the theater. In 1938, their *Boys from Syracuse* was an uproarious fantastification of Shakespeare's unactable *The Comedy of Errors*."[4] Mordden acknowledges that it has both "a lot of Shakespearean storyline" and "one of the decade's most narrative and characterful scores."[5] That was exactly what the composer and lyricist were aiming for, the integration of all the dances with the story line. And here's where George Balanchine's role was important. His contribution was a first.

What *On Your Toes* lacked—a through plot with dance clearly linked to that plot—was only barely present in the early musicals. But *The Boys from Syracuse* had that plot, a complex story from Shakespeare. The musical enhanced it with song, dance, lyrics, and character development.

By the time I saw *Kiss Me, Kate,* I was a young woman in love with the theater, in love with Shakespeare, and in love with a new husband just returned from three years at sea. I was a woman with a career about to unfold, feeling the pressures and aftereffects of a war that had interrupted our lives. The conflicts in that play were real to me. The musical spoke to me. I could recognize the double vision of *The Taming of the Shrew* transposed to *Kiss Me, Kate*. I also reveled in the appearance of African American performers singing "Too Darn Hot," meaning just too tired for sex, and noted the simplicity and ease with which Bill, the white hoofer character, joined them in this dance number following intermission. This was very new in the theater, where black performers were normally limited to stereotyped roles. As I point out in chapter 2, this song was totally changed in the movie, where no Blacks appear. In its original stage production, *Kiss Me, Kate* was ahead of its time.

Research material, promptbooks, correspondence among principals, biographies, autobiographies, and reviews of performances supplement my first reactions to the performed musical but have never supplanted it. The Bella and Samuel Spewack Collection at Columbia University's Rare Book and Manuscript Library opened the world of collaboration for me. The owners of the Spewack copyright, Lois and Arthur Elias, generously permitted me to peruse letters and the multiple typescripts. Through them I learned a great deal about the evolution of *Kiss Me, Kate*. I also examined the letters in the Cole Porter Collection and learned how the organic musical was developed when the choreographer, Hanya Holm, became involved in planning and design. I observed how women, even those who were part of the creative process, worked and weighed their relationships with men into their evaluation of their own work. Hanya Holm continued her career, unlike other creative women who retired to being homemakers. I also saw the scraps of paper where Cole Porter brainstormed a series of related words until he hit on the exact combination for the song "I Hate Men." This too I discuss in a note to chapter 2.

In 1957 I sat in the audience of *West Side Story*, enthralled by its excitement, its tragic vision, and especially its dances. Where did this combination come from? How had these artists managed to create such a new vision of the familiar tale of Romeo and Juliet? With other members of that audience, I was surprised by Maria's survival and wondered whether there was another answer to the ending, rather than having her survive. There wasn't. When I turned to writing *Shakespeare and the American Musical*, I began looking at all the background material—the letters, the proposals, the sketches for the sequence of scenes and incidents within them. I found much of what I was looking for at the

Library of Congress. The Leonard Bernstein collection introduced me to the personalities of Bernstein, Jerome Robbins, and Arthur Laurents as well as the newcomer to that collaboration, Stephen Sondheim. The Bernstein trust was most generous in permitting me to examine its holdings: typescripts, partial typescripts, and correspondence. Letters have a way of making the past fresh and contemporary. This material also sent me back to the New York Library of the Performing Arts with its rich dance, drama, and music divisions.

As I point out in chapter 3, *West Side Story* had a history that began with *East Side Story* and with a copy of *Romeo and Juliet* where Bernstein noted that this was "an out and out plea for racial tolerance."[6] Or was that notation an indication of the direction he was heading? Both he and Robbins were Jewish. Both were aware of the racial intolerance of the Nazis and of the plight of Jews during the Second World War. Indeed, after the war, Bernstein had gone to Palestine to help shape the Palestine Symphony Orchestra. Robbins, we learn in Amanda Vaill's biography, went as a child to Rozhanka, Poland, for a summer, where he met his grandfather, whom he loved and never saw again.[7] The land was unrecognizable after the war; the Nazis had erased the entire Jewish community. This destruction strongly affected Robbins. In his recent talk about the making of *West Side Story*, Arthur Laurents mentioned Jerome Robbins's instruction to his dancers; after separating them into Jets and Sharks, he said, "Make believe you're the Jews and you're the Nazis." "Of course," observed Laurents, "this was 1957 and these kids didn't know what he was talking about."[8] But Robbins knew.

Between 1957 and 1968, the year of the production of *Your Own Thing*, American musicals changed. Although they still retained the original shape of the organic musical, where all the elements in a production worked together to propel the plot forward, the music itself had altered. Rock and rock 'n' roll had invaded the form. However, Shakespeare still offered the grounding with his wonderfully sly comedy of twins, *Twelfth Night*, with its homoerotic implications.

I remember my own excitement at seeing that musical. How new and fresh it was, and how inventive was the use of film and slides with the primary plot running in another dimension on the stage! *Twelfth Night* is a complicated play, full of scholarly challenges. I wondered how these adaptors would address the questions of the women's roles. When I looked for additional material documenting their work, however, I was surprised at the Library of the Performing Arts' meager holdings. It had a clipping file and a photo file but not much else. As I stood at the desk only half waiting my turn, I blurted out, "Don't you have anything else on *Your Own Thing?*" "*Your Own Thing!*" the man standing beside me at the desk nearly shouted. "My wife worked on that show for three years." Serendipity. He gave me her phone number, insisting I call her at once.

Unfamiliar with the art of the interviewer, I began by asking Janet Sovey questions that were not very well thought out. I persevered by phone and email, however, and soon discovered that although Danny Apolinar, the major creative force behind this musical, was dead, as were his collaborators, his friend and companion of many years, John Britton, was alive. He had contributed Apolinar's papers to the Billy Rose Theatre Division of the Library for the Performing Arts several years earlier. There they sat in the archives in seven boxes, untouched and uncatalogued. Through the good offices of the Lincoln Center Curator of the Billy Rose Theatre Division, Robert Taylor, and the archivist, Barbara Knowles, I was permitted to view their contents. There I discovered the range of Apolinar's output.

He too was working to create an American musical—this time, a rock musical. From Janet Sovey I discovered that there had been a lucrative screen offer, but no film had ever been made. Overseas companies had performed in Montreal, Stockholm, Berlin, Tel Aviv, Oslo, and Copenhagen, and others had traveled throughout the States. Built on the theme of homophobia and insisting on the right of a person to do his or her own thing, this musical had been tremendously successful. It also moved further from Shakespeare's play than did some of the other adaptations discussed in this book. The adaptors had substituted the members of a rock group for Shakespeare's secondary characters. They also interwove the plot with commentaries by characters projected on slides. These projected images argue about the goings-on of the main characters. Moreover, they are unrelated to Shakespeare's play. John Wayne, a Buddha who hands out calling cards, Shirley Temple, Humphrey Bogart, and religious figures such as the pope, Jesus Christ, and God (as he is painted on the Sistine Chapel ceiling) appear on these screens, along with the two Renaissance giants Queen Elizabeth and Shakespeare himself. In many ways the presentation was a mixed-media collage, and it worked.

By the time I went to Shakespeare in the Park in 1971, I was taking my children with me. A family romp with a picnic supper preceded the magic of Shakespeare. That was how we saw the rock musical *Two Gentlemen of Verona* for the first time. Everything about it was new. It was the first time an American musical adaptation of Shakespeare had retained the title of the original. John Guare, Galt MacDermot, and Mel Shapiro transported the audience into a world they knew but had never realized they knew. The people of the city, the ones who sat across the aisle or beside me in the subway, were coming alive onstage in *Two Gentlemen of Verona*. And here were the city's people.

I saw *Two Gentlemen of Verona* three times. First came its exciting opening in Central Park in the summer of 1971, a major breakthrough in both its multiracial casting and its use of rock music. Joe Papp moved it to Broadway that winter, where I saw it again, this time bringing my class along. Being inside, instead of outside in the large amphitheater in the park, meant the adaptors had to alter the production slightly, as I discuss in chapter 5. Alone, I went to its revival in 2005 in Central Park. Much as I describe its original opening on a wet evening in 1971, the weather in 2005 also was wet. We waited for the ushers to wipe the seats in this vast space, then finally entered, anticipating a great show. While fun to watch, the production lacked the excitement of the original, which had been the first to have a completely racially mixed cast, as well as the first time I had seen the hijinks and skill of that wonderful performer, Raul Julia, who went on to become a star in the movies. As John Guare said to me over the phone, "I was most proud of that review that said 'the score sounded like walking down a street in El Barrio with all the windows open and a different radio blaring out of each one.'"[9]

The merging of dramatic traditions that began with *The Boys from Syracuse* was nearing completion in the 1970s. The voyage that began with my going to the theater as a kid and ended with my becoming a mature adult and teacher paralleled the development of the American Shakespeare musical. During that time, a band of instrumentalists live on stage replaced the large orchestra working from the pit. Microphones supplemented the players' voices, altering their sound. The rock musical now dominated the theater. And for the most part, it came from across the ocean; but then so did Shakespeare. Joe Papp's dedication to the Renaissance playwright's work had contributed to the last step in this synthesis. According to Guare, "Terry Hands said that our use of the different peoples of the city was a real inspiration. His production of *The Comedy of Errors* with Trevor Nunn in 1976 [in Stratford and London] was inspired by our *Two Gentlemen of Verona*."[10] In fact, the critics compared that production, whether consciously or not, with the American musical.

As Hands's production demonstrates, stagings of Shakespeare's plays often add new dimensions, incorporating music and dance inspired by twentieth-century American musical theater into their performances. The distinguished critic Philip Edwards called theater the "interpretation centre of Shakespeare study," observing that "each national culture transmutes what it receives and enhances the totality in which it shares."[11] Completely organic in their fusion of dance, words, music, and design, the American Shakespeare musicals of the twentieth century drew on the dramatist's works to give us a new perspective even as they enhanced the totality of his vision. The essential theatrical ingredients—play texts from the late sixteenth and early seventeenth centuries and musicals from the twentieth—fused to provide a new view of the earlier works and to increase our understanding of the subtleties of Shakespeare's texts and the organic musicals. *Shakespeare and the American Musical* tells the story of how American culture transmuted these Renaissance plays into a vibrant new experience in the modern theater.

ONE

A Bold Adventure
The Boys from Syracuse and
The Comedy of Errors

Responding to the blast of a trumpet, two characters tap-dance sedately to center stage. Adorned with Greek comic and tragic masks, they brusquely announce,

> This is a drama of Ancient Greece. It is a story of mistaken identity.
> If it's good enough for Shakespeare, it's good enough for us. (1.1, p. 1)[1]

The American adaptors of *The Comedy of Errors* thus proclaim their aim: to upstage Shakespeare and offer a populist version of *The Comedy of Errors*. They go beyond the confusion of identities that lies at the heart of Shakespeare's play by placing that confusion within the context of 1938. This was a time when Hitler was striding through Europe and Stalin was triumphing in the east. Two dictators with different ideologies but similar techniques seemed to be dominating the world. At home, the Depression was taking its toll on American feminism. Although earlier women had won the right to vote, in 1938 jobs were still scarce and many women stayed home. As a result, many traditional attitudes toward women prevail in *The Boys from Syracuse*. And yet the adaptors also develop women characters only sketched in by Shakespeare. Their outspoken lines and songs reveal another side of the twentieth century. This Shakespeare romp excels as an example of the new organic American musical comedy even as it explores gender relationships and captures echoes of the ominous sounds heard in Europe.

When the tap-dancers part the stage curtains to reveal the public square of the city of Ephesus, people are yelling. "Be quiet," shouts the

Sergeant of Police from his perch on the sill of an open window in the rear. Through the window, two old men—Aegean and the Duke—can be seen arguing inside the courthouse. Music underlies the scene. Rodgers and Hart have employed the new form of the organic musical. Through song, the Sergeant reports the courthouse conversation to the crowd below and guides the plot forward. A bass clarinet imitates the movement of the Duke's mouth, capturing the officious tone of his inquiry, and when the aged Aegean responds, a plaintive E-flat clarinet pleads as his voice. The Sergeant translates the sounds for the crowd.

> Sergeant: "He says No!"
>
> Crowd: "Hurrah, Hurroo!" (1.1, p. 2)

Dressed mockingly like a Nazi storm trooper—his arms widespread, his waist belted, and wearing a helmet—the Sergeant reports musically on the exchange as the two men debate the fate of Aegean, the old Syracusan who has unwittingly landed on hostile shores.[2] Thus begins *The Boys from Syracuse.*

Far less raucously, Shakespeare's early play, *The Comedy of Errors,* opens with an old man, Egeon, a merchant of Syracuse, being haled before the duke of Ephesus as an enemy of his city.[3] Syracusans are forbidden to enter Ephesus, but Egeon, unaware of the edict, has come to the city in search of his son, Antipholus, and the youth's servant, Dromio.[4] When commanded by the Duke to tell why he came to Ephesus, Egeon presents a long explanation of his woes. He tells how in a distant land his wife gave birth to twins long ago. At the same time a poor woman also gave birth to twins. Egeon and his wife bought the twins as servants for their sons, then headed home to Syracuse. Their ship went down when a storm overtook them at sea. Although they survived, each parent then taking one of the pair of twins, further misfortune befell them when they were separated in that storm. He and his wife never saw one another again.

Even worse, seven years ago, his one remaining son, Antipholus, along with his servant, Dromio, having long heard tales of the lost half of the family, left home in search of them. They never returned. Searching for them, Egeon has wandered the neighboring lands, without success, until finally landing in Ephesus. Moved, but unwilling to alter his original edict—the death sentence—the Duke allows Egeon a day to raise a thousand marks, the price of freedom for a Syracusan trespasser. So Shakespeare begins his comedy.

Having given the exposition, the dramatist then introduces the two sets of twins, who, unbeknownst to one another, happen to be in Ephesus at this moment. The two Syracusans, master and servant, wanderers and strangers, are searching for their long-lost brothers. As it turns out, the other pair, unaware that they have brothers, reside in Ephesus and bear the same names as their Syracusan brothers. Antipholus of Ephesus is a wealthy man, haughty, self-centered, and vain, who flaunts his status. Nonetheless, he is married and highly respected. His servant, Dromio, seems to mimic his boss but yet appears less independent than does Dromio of Syracuse. Antipholus of Syracuse is more introspective than his twin and is aware of his loneliness. And yet, physically, the pairs of brothers exactly resemble one another. That resemblance leads to the servants not recognizing their own masters and even Antipholus's wife not recognizing her husband—mistaken identity carried to an extreme, thus *The Comedy of Errors.*

Shakespeare fashions this story, derived from Plautus's *The Menaechmi,* into a Renaissance entertainment, complete with jugglers, magic, and hexing by a schoolmaster. Since the pairs of brothers have the same names, texts of the play identify them by their cities of origin—"S" and "E" for Syracuse and Ephesus. Onstage, of course, their speech, their responses to the environment—familiar or hostile—and their places in society all reveal their identities to the audience, even while those around them mistake one for the other because of their complete physical resemblance.

After Egeon's opening narrative, Shakespeare shifts his focus to the wanderers from Syracuse: Dromio S. and Antipholus S. In the second scene, they meet a "merchant of Ephesus," a friend of Antipholus S. who, by prearrangement, is returning the traveler's gold, having long held it in safekeeping. The merchant warns them that they should pretend to be from Epidamnum, as this is a hostile environment for Syracusans. That gold, immediately passed from Antipholus S. to his Dromio with instructions to take it to the Centaur—the inn where they are staying—is soon disputed in the first of many instances of mistaken identity.

Dromio S. departs with it for the inn; Dromio E. shortly enters with a message for Antipholus E. from his wife.

In the brief interim, Shakespeare provides a portrait of Antipholus S. through a soliloquy. Invited to accompany him on a stroll through town, the merchant refused, saying as he left, "I leave you to your own content." But content eludes the wanderer. Alone onstage, he muses, "He that commends me to mine own content, / Commends me to the thing I cannot get" (1.2.33–34). In soliloquy, he compares himself to a drop of water "that in the ocean seeks another drop" (36). Wistful, thoughtful, and somewhat depressed, having searched for his and Dromio's twins for seven years, Antipholus S. realizes that his search is fruitless despite his persistence.

When Dromio E. enters, the servant and the man he believes to be his master speak at cross purposes. "Where have you left the money that I gave you?" asks Antipholus S. (1.2.54). "O—sixpence that I had a' We'n'sday last," Dromio E. replies mournfully (55), explaining where it was spent. His present mission has nothing to do with gold; he was sent to bring his master home to supper. "To me, sir? Why, you gave no gold to me" (71). He then asserts, "My charge was but to fetch you . . . home . . . to dinner" (74–75). The master becomes furious at his seeming slave's response and begins to beat him. Fleeing Antipholus S.'s fury, Dromio E. returns home to report to his mistress, Adriana, and her sister, Luciana, that his master has gone mad, having denied both home and wife.

Insulted by her husband's response, Adriana storms into town looking for him. Her unmarried sister, Luciana, accompanies her, drumming in the lesson that a husband's role is one of master. "O, know he is the bridle of your will" (2.1.13). But Adriana rejects such a premise. "There's none but asses will be bridled so," she swiftly replies (14). Both are expressing a Renaissance concept of marriage. According to Lawrence Stone, the eminent historian, on the one hand, women were the property of their fathers or husbands, but on the other, the concept that a good marriage was a union with "goodly consent of them both" had also won acceptance. Shakespeare exploits both conventions in this comedy, assigning the sisters opposite viewpoints and then creating a real problem for them when they, especially the unmarried Luciana, discover that marriage isn't quite that simple.

Arriving at the town square, Adriana rails at Antipholus S.: "Ay, Ay, Antipholus look strange and frown, / Some other mistress hath thy sweet aspects: / I am not Adriana, nor thy wife" (2.2.110–12). And of course she isn't, but her hold on him is so strong and convincing that he almost believes her:

Shouldst thou but hear I were licentious,
And that this body, consecrate to thee,
By ruffian lust should be contaminate?
Wouldst thou not spit at me, and spurn at me? (131–34)

she asks, addressing the wrong man. Contemporary ideas of marriage as a partnership infuse her speech, overwhelming Antipholus S. He wonders, "What, was I married to her in my dream? / Or sleep I now, and think I hear all this?" (182–83). His man Dromio S. shivers, "O, for my beads! I cross me for a sinner," certain that they have found themselves in fairyland (188). What is particularly interesting is the acceptance of her role and her dismissal by her husband in the twentieth-century update as compared with Shakespeare's presentation of a woman who insists that they are as one. If she were to transgress, it would affect him.

Centering his play around the Syracusans, Shakespeare does not introduce Antipholus E. until act 3, when the local pair reinforce his theme: the pairs of twins' complete physical resemblance to one another, and the importance of appearance over speech patterns, actions, and emotional expression. The "errors" then multiply. Antipholus E. negotiates with Angelo, the goldsmith, to buy a gold chain for his wife, Adriana, and invites Balthazar, the merchant, to dinner. But the host finds himself locked out of his own home. In this scene, the dramatist develops the character of Antipholus E. as he calls on a list of people—his wife, his sister-in-law, his servants—of whom he demands, "Let Antipholus in." They refuse, ordering the intruders away. The Ephesian bangs at the gate, threatening to break it in, but finally listens to his guest's advice. There must be an error. Later referred to as the "lockout scene," this marks the dramatic center of the comedy.

Shakespeare's complex plot continues to develop. Antipholus E. is arrested for failing to pay for the chain. Antipholus S. attempts to convince Luciana that he is not her brother-in-law: "But if that I am I, then well I know / Your weeping sister is no wife of mine, / Nor to her bed no homage do I owe" (3.1.41–43). Luciana remains unconvinced. Other errors include the Courtesan's insistence that Antipholus S. return her ring to her, since he refuses to give her the gold chain that he had promised her in its place (a promise actually made, of course, by Antipholus E.), and the confusion of Luce, the "greasy kitchen maid," of the two Dromios; she mistakes Dromio S. for her husband, Dromio E., and runs after the Syracusan.

Only after one pair of twins seeks protection in a sanctuary and the abbess comes out to protect them does the end of the tale unfold, as the other pair waits in the town square for the governor to appear. Their incontrovertible resemblance startles Adriana. "Which of you two did dine with me to-day?" she asks, hoping it was her husband. "I, gentle mistress," offers the Syracusan. "And are you not my husband?" she continues. "No, I say nay to that," the Ephesian swiftly responds (5.1.370–73). Meanwhile, the Dromios, looking at one another, note their uncanny physical similarity. "Methinks you are my glass and not my brother," insists Dromio E., then continues, "I see I am a sweet faced youth" (418–19). As they debate who should enter the house first, they agree to "go hand in hand, not one before another" (426). So ends Shakespeare's comedy, offering a wonderful challenge to its twentieth-century adaptors intent on creating an organic musical with its integration of plot, lyrics, music, and dance.

Fashioning their musical adaptation of this play, Richard Rodgers, Lorenz Hart, and George Abbott in 1938 created *The Boys from Syracuse*. For the first time, the new American organic musical, which was to dominate the Broadway theater for a long time, was married to a Shakespeare play. This new musical adaptation picks up theatrical ideas that had first emerged in *Show Boat* in 1927 and develops them into a single work, integrating music, story, plot line, and dance. The opening number by the Sergeant of Police signals the importance of the new organic form. As the songs and dances told the story or commented on it, Rodgers and Hart were opening new territory.

These two young New Yorkers were well qualified to transpose Shakespeare into the new musical idiom. Lorenz Hart knew not only this play, but most of Shakespeare's work. His love for the bard dated back to his childhood. The story goes that when he went to camp, his trunk was so heavy his counselor couldn't lift it. No wonder: Shakespeare's *Complete Works* had replaced his clothes.[5] That summer, Hart earned the nickname "Shakespeare." He carried his love of the plays into adulthood. In 1938, when he and Rodgers were looking for new ideas for a musical, Shakespeare was a natural choice. Eliminating the histories and the tragedies, they settled on a comedy. The specific choice of *The Comedy of Errors* may also have been due to other factors. Among these was the close resemblance between Hart's brother, Teddy, and the great comic actor Jimmy Savo; the two men eventually played the Dromio twins.

Writing later of their approach to their work, Rodgers recollected their conscious decision not to write their own stories but "stick with what we do best—song writing."[6] He and Hart immediately hit it off because they agreed about how the old forms for musicals should be changed. They were not about to follow the standard methods of Tin Pan Alley, where composers wrote songs on demand that had no particular relevance to the plot. Nor were they adopting the "European" model of operettas. They were striving to do something new, something that they saw as American, something they found in the music of Jerome Kern.

Although different ages, the two men shared similar backgrounds, interests, and enthusiasms, along with the determination to alter the form of the musical. Rodgers's primary concern with the sound of the music complemented Hart's focus on the lyrics. Hart wanted more than rhyming "shush" with "mush" and sought to bring new ideas into the songs as well as to introduce complex patterns of rhyme. He saw the possibilities "inherent in double and triple rhymes, slant rhymes, fragmented rhymes, false rhymes, interior rhymes, feminine rhymes—but most of all witty rhymes."[7] Moreover, he was aware of the multiple literary forms open to him. Schooled at Columbia College, he had tested these forms in some of Columbia's varsity shows.

In fact, it was through work on the varsity shows that he and Rodgers met. Prior to *The Boys from Syracuse,* the two young men had collaborated on a number of musicals, including the successful *A Connecticut Yankee* in 1928 and *Babes in Arms* and *On Your Toes* in 1936. They had written musical revues and were always on the lookout for new material. Their turn to Shakespeare gave them a broader vision.

They wired George Abbott, an important and well-known writer and director, asking him if he would write the script. When Abbott agreed, the three began assembling a team. By July 22, 1938, Jo Mielziner, the famous scenery and lighting designer, headed that team, having signed a contract with Abbott to work on a play to be called *Mixed Company.*[8] Later renamed *The Boys from Syracuse,* it opened on Broadway on November 24, 1938, to rave reviews and ran until June 1939, when the new World's Fair skimmed off the show's talents. Performers left Broadway for jobs on the fairgrounds in Queens.

Not only music but dance as well played a major role in the development of this new form. It is difficult for us today to realize how revolutionary this integration of dance with plot was. Until this time, dances, like songs, had been introduced into shows at the behest of the producer. Now, for the first time, dance would grow out of the plot and propel it forward. George Balanchine, trained in the Russian Ballet and brought to the United States in 1933 by Lincoln Kirstein to help found the School of American Ballet, was to choreograph *The Boys from Syracuse.* He would create dances that were integrated with the plot and helped to advance it. Balanchine hoped to win a new audience for ballet. He believed that "many who might be awed by a performance at the Metropolitan Opera, where [he] was maitre de ballet," could be lured to dance if they were exposed to it in lighter doses. He also showed a new attitude toward the Broadway musical comedy and revue, refusing to discriminate against these popular forms. Rather, he sought to incorporate them. In a 1939 interview, Balanchine spoke of his great admiration for American musical films, particularly those of Fred Astaire and Ginger Rogers, which he had seen in his native Russia. "I can watch them dance again and again," he observed.[9]

Although his earliest attempts at choreographing a musical dated back to his time in London before coming to the United States and his first work on Broadway was for Florenz Ziegfeld, the famous producer of the *Ziegfeld Follies,* Balanchine's initiation into American musical Shakespeare occurred with *The Boys from Syracuse.* He astonished the critics. "George Balanchine," wrote Burns Mantle in the *New York Daily News,* "has done more with the dances than you would expect a ballet master to do. . . . [He] has combined art as he knows it from his better ballet training with tap dancing interludes that have a true Broadway swing."[10] Besides the tap-dance numbers, where he was assisted by David Jones and Duke McHale, experts in the field, Balanchine choreographed the rest, including the "Big Brother Ballet" and the famous "Ladies of the Evening," in which whores sing of the work of the evening and the fatigue in the morning, when they give their favors to officers of the law. Their dance reflects both their vocation and their fatigue. Ultimately, he achieved his aim: to popularize ballet and integrate it into the American musical.

Not only did Balanchine come from Europe because of the political situation in his native Russia, but all of Europe was teeming with the uproar and enmity that eventually led to the Second World War. Appearing as it did in 1938, *The Boys from Syracuse* was poised between the Great Depression that began in 1929 and the entry of the United States into the Second World War in 1941. Franklin Delano Roosevelt had been elected president in 1932 and in his inaugural address had told the nation, "Let me assert my firm belief that the only thing we have to fear is fear itself."[11] He then introduced the National Recovery Act. Later the government would introduce the Federal Theatre Project, with its support for the arts. This was a time when the Germans were burning books; Hitler and Mussolini had signed a treaty of friendship that created a Rome-Berlin axis; and Americans were going to Spain to fight for the Loyalists. Radio was still a major medium of public communication. Indeed, it was in 1938 that Orson Welles broadcast his fictive "Invasion from Mars," and many people believed it was real.

Inevitably, the adaptors were working within the context of their own time. Thus, while they were aware of the threat of war across the ocean, they were also drawing on the richness of theater, dance, and film that surrounded them. In addition, they were responding to contemporary ideas about women and their roles. For instance, Adriana, Antipholus E.'s wife, who is briefly visible as an independent, thoughtful character in *The Comedy of Errors,* was reduced to a stereotype. The adaptors also adopted the conventions of the theater and the movies. They developed a love story that had been only marginal in Shakespeare's play. And they superimposed the mores of early twentieth-century American society on that love story. Moreover, they developed the lower-class woman character to express the more blatant ideas on sexuality denied to Shakespeare's heroines. Again adopting a theater convention of the time, that of restricting the conventional roles of women to conventional behavior, the adaptors permitted lower-class women more freedom. Finally, and most importantly, *The Boys from Syracuse* demonstrated that a Shakespeare text could be transformed into a specifically American form—the twentieth-century organic musical. It was a bold undertaking.

The works differ in their underlying structure, Shakespeare's play having five acts in contrast to the modern musical's two. But this difference masks the similarities between the comedy and its musical reinvention. At times, these similarities emerge in characterization or in the duplication of specific dramatic incidents. At other times, the adaptors transpose the sequence of events, scenes, or even add new scenes. In still other examples, the language of Shakespeare's play may be slightly altered into twentieth-century American vernacular. Nevertheless, *The Boys from Syracuse* clearly derives from *The Comedy of Errors* and offers insights into Shakespeare's play even as the musical boldly transforms the Renaissance work for twentieth-century audiences. While other adaptations had previously appeared, none had incorporated the original plot with other media. Rather, music or dance had merely supplemented those earlier adaptations. Here was something different.

Starting with Egeon's tale to the Duke, the adaptors invent a new presentation of his opening monologue by having two policemen take over when the old man falters. Moreover, the policemen sing most of the exchange. In addition the scene, filled with men and women dancers, focuses on those policemen (the singing policemen of the cast list), who stand on a raised platform on the left of the stage singing Rodgers and Hart's "I Had Twins" but also interspersing their own comments, assisted by the chorus. "I had twins, who looked alike," sings the first policeman, evoking his buddy's response: "He had twins—for them he'd give his life / He had twins—to say nothing of his wife!" (1.1, p. 5). But the song doesn't end here. Rather, the crowd takes over, celebrating the forthcoming execution of the Syracusan who landed on their shore.

Thematically, the opening number also differs from Shakespeare's, where the whole concern is the story of Egeon and the twins. On the other hand the adaptors were stressing the indifference of European

1.1. The singing policeman relays the fate of Aegean to the waiting crowd, in the opening scene of *The Boys from Syracuse.* They are joyously singing, "Hurrah, Hurroo," hoping he'll be hanged. Through costumes, the adaptors are tapping into the explosive 1938 world of dictators while drawing on Shakespeare's *Comedy of Errors.* *Vandamm Studio, Jerome Robbins Dance Division, New York Public Library for the Performing Arts, Astor, Lenox, and Tilden Foundations.*

dictators and their people, who were striding ruthlessly through countries. "Hurrah! Hurroo! There'll be an execution!" the populace sings. The adaptors then raise the question "What did he do?" But there is no answer. Basically, he did nothing. He only came from the wrong place, as we discover when the song continues: "He came from Syracuse" (1.1, pp. 2–3). That is Aegean's crime, as Hart notes, rhyming "hurroo" with "do" and as a slant rhyme with "cu" in "exe*cu*tion" as well as with "cuse" in "Syra*cuse*" in the seemingly joyous song.

> Sergeant: "So let him plead,
>   For what's the use?
>   The sap's from Syracuse!" (p. 3)

The alliterative last line, with its repeated "s" sound, confirms the crowd's opinion of the "sap" who has ventured onto their territory. The unreasonableness of mob action becomes apparent here. Hitler had already marched into Austria, annexing it in the Anschluss. Hate abounded, and it did not need to be explained. Rodgers and Hart were inserting their observations on human behavior into the drama, taking the material of Shakespeare's comedy and giving it the imprint of their own culture.

As well as translating the play's language into the modern vernacular, the adaptors, or perhaps George Abbott singly, introduced a new scene, the tailor scene, based on the slimmest reed of material. Its aim was to reinforce the uncanny resemblance between the brothers. In Shakespeare's *Comedy of Errors,* an astonished Antipholus of Syracuse, overwhelmed by the attention he is receiving, observes, "Even now a tailor call'd me in his shop / And show'd me silks that he had bought for me, / And therewithal took measure of my body" (4.3.7–9). In *The Boys from Syracuse,* this encounter is depicted in a scene that takes place immediately after Aegean's sentencing. Moreover, this new material is linked to Antipholus S.'s precarious situation. And here we see the skill with which the adaptors related their musical to the political situation in Europe. In order to convince Antipholus S. to change his clothes, the merchant notes the hostility of the crowd in the marketplace. The cheers sound ominous. Hearing them, the Syracusan merchant advises his friend, "You must leave the city. . . . No citizen of Syracuse is safe in Ephesus." Protesting, Antipholus S. explains, "But I've spent years searching for my mother and my brother and for poor Dromio's little brother." Nevertheless, the merchant insists: "You'd be condemned to death. You're not safe here. Even now I notice that your clothes have a strange cut . . . you'd better change them." He then offers help in evading detection. "If any one asks you any questions, say you're my cousin and live in the country" (1.1, p. 8). Is there a hint here of protecting the friend although risks lie ahead? Are we in Ephesus or pre–World War II twentieth-century Europe? Undoubtedly the parallel occurred to the adaptors. With the repetition of the joyous song anticipating an execution, Antipholus of Syracuse changes his mind. He'll leave in the morning.

To bolster the logic of the tailor scene, the adaptors introduce Antipholus and Dromio of Ephesus early in the musical. They visit the tailor before the Syracusans do. "Good evening, Sir Antipholus. Would you care to try on the other suit now?" the tailor asks the Ephesian, who is wearing his new clothes when he swaggers in with his Dromio. "I only ordered this one suit—and that for Dromio," the master asserts. "I made two suits—you told me—" the tailor begins, but is quickly cut off by Antipholus E. "One suit." Aware that he can do little, the tailor changes the subject: "And also in the matter of pay." Antipholus E. dismisses him with "I'll take care of that later. But just now I'm in a hurry. Come on, Dromio—Phff!—I hate pests." With that, he leaves the stage. Copying his master, Dromio E. asserts, "Phfft! I hate pests, too" (1.1, p. 6). The adaptors have painted a portrait of the hometown boy. They have captured Antipholus E.'s personality, highlighting his fame in town, his wealth, and his cavalier attitude toward people and money. Like his model in Shakespeare's play, he seems unconcerned about others.

Moments after he leaves, his brother appears. Artfully, George Abbott combines the new tailor scene with Shakespeare's scene 2 of act 1, in which the merchant gives Antipholus back the gold his friend had entrusted to him. Antipholus S., his Syracusan merchant friend, and Dromio S. enter. The sounds of that hostile crowd joyously anticipating an execution greet them. Then suddenly the Syracusan observes a tailor-shop sign hanging on the far right wall: a large pair of scissors, cut out of metal. (The audience, of course, had already seen his twin in conversation with the tailor.) "Tailor, I might need a little . . ." Antipholus S. begins, but the tailor's apprentice blanches. Antipholus had just departed in his new clothes, yet here he is again, differently dressed. "What!" the apprentice asks, interrupting the Syracusan. "What do you mean . . . what? I haven't finished my sentence," Antipholus indignantly replies. Quickly trying to explain himself, the apprentice stammers, "Why I thought at first, you were. . . . I mean you look like. . . . and him too. Why, Sir Antipholus, I don't understand." Calling his master, the young man rushes off into the shop. Equally confused, Antipholus notes, "He knows me. . . . called me by name" (1.1, p. 9).

Having added this extra element and provided a story line for the absolute resemblance between the two pairs of men—in clothing as well as physical features—the adaptors give their play a new twist. They also connect the musical to the events exploding in Europe even as they construct this new scene. "Everything is ready for you. Lad, the other suit," the tailor says to his apprentice, who runs ahead. "And you wish one for Dromio too, sir?" he queries. Bewildered, Dromio S. exclaims, "Dromio? Hey Boss! We're haunted." They rush into the shop. When they emerge, they are dressed exactly like their twins who just left (1.1, p. 10). The tailor outfits both Antipholus S. and Dromio S. In addition,

Antipholus S. pays him, even though only for one set of clothes each for himself and Dromio. Delighted at this change in behavior, the tailor accepts its oddness and drops the subject.

Once out of the tailor shop, Dromio S., feeling the fabric, observes, "Just the same, it's a nice piece of goods we've got here, Boss. It's a little tight around the neck," he notes as he pulls at the seat of his pants. Turning to Antipholus S., Dromio S. asks, "How does it hang, Boss?" modeling the costume (1.1, p. 11). Thus Abbott gave a nod to those members of the audience in the cloak and suit business, a major New York industry at the time. Surely this little byplay must have evoked laughter. They all knew that kind of customer who pulled at the pants and was concerned with the fit.

The addition of the tailor scene leads to a theatrical change. Whereas in Shakespeare's play, Antipholus S. expresses his despair at the futility of his search in a soliloquy, comparing himself to "a drop of water that in the ocean seeks another drop," these lines disappear from the adaptation. Instead, the lyricist and composer transfer the melancholy of the original soliloquy to several of the love songs, particularly "You Have Cast Your Shadow on the Sea," a song of unrequited love. Nor is Dromio S. given money to safeguard, the excuse for his exit in Shakespeare's comedy. And yet he must leave the stage for his twin to appear. The adaptors therefore introduce a dance number.

As Antipholus S. and his Dromio begin sight-seeing, they find themselves accosted by "ladies of the evening." The set adds luster to the women's dance; they move against a blue sky and the muted orange-brown of the columns of the Temple of Justice. Master and servant react differently to the women, their calling cards, and their dance. Whereas Dromio follows one of them offstage, Antipholus, shocked at the calling cards they are passing out, thinks longingly of home, singing a song called "Dear Old Syracuse." It begins, "This is a terrible city. / The people are cattle and swine." He is reacting to the crowd psychology that puts him on the run for no apparent reason. Then, looking around, he observes, "There isn't a girl I'd call pretty / Nor a friend that I'd call mine." Momentarily alone onstage, he picks up the poetic thread from the sixteenth-century play and transforms it into just a cry of loneliness: "You can keep your Athens, / You can keep your Rome, / I'm a home-town fellow / And I pine for home. / I want to go back—go back— / To dear old Syracuse"

(1.1, p. 12). Rodgers and Hart have again converted an idea into a song advancing the plot. Meanwhile, the ladies of the evening, as well as the Courtesan, have drifted in, finally engaging Antipholus of Syracuse in a dance. And as this scene develops, the organic musical begins taking shape. Lyrics, music, plot, dance, and the emotional elements work together to create a whole.

A policeman joins the women's dance only long enough to distract Antipholus S. and allow Dromio E. to arrive in the place of his twin, who has left. Like Shakespeare's character, Dromio E. in the musical also speaks of Antipholus E.'s wife and home. Confusion reigns. Although rooted in Shakespeare's *Comedy of Errors,* the scene as newly created reflects the work of the adaptors of *The Boys from Syracuse.*

> Dromio E.: Hey, Maestro. Oh, here you are.
>
> Antipholus S.: Well, is that surprising?
>
> Dromio E.: Huh?
>
> Antipholus S.: What are you doing back so soon?
>
> Dromio E: Looking for you. Listen, Maestro . . .
>
> Antipholus S.: Maestro? (1.1, p. 13)

Having momentarily questioned the use of the word "maestro," Antipholus S. doesn't persist. But the audience hears it. Earlier, "Boss" had peppered the Syracusan Dromio's speech. Here, with a simple one-word stroke, the Dromios, too, are individualized and identified for the audience even as Antipholus remains confused.

Then follows another exchange derived from Shakespeare's play. American vernacular speech mimics its source. "Where is the money I gave you?" asks Antipholus S. in *The Boys from Syracuse,* resembling Shakespeare's "Tell me and dally not, where is the money?" Repeating himself, as does his Renaissance model, Antipholus rephrases his question: "Where is the gold I gave you?" (1.1, p. 14). Again, this resembles Shakespeare's "Where is the gold I gave in charge to thee?" (1.2.70). While the lines are slightly shorter in the adapted dialogue, their essence remains. "To me, sir? Why you gave no gold to me," asserts Shakespeare's Dromio E. (71), while in *The Boys from Syracuse,* he simply asserts, "No gold" (p. 14). The men speak at cross purposes; whereas Antipholus S. is concerned for his money, Dromio E. is fulfilling his mistress's orders.

In this first phase of the organic American musical Shakespeares, the adaptors stuck closer to Shakespeare's text than would those who followed. Although he retained much of Shakespeare's text, George Abbott expanded not only the tailor character but also those of the Courtesan and Luce, Adriana's servant. Along with Rodgers and Hart, Abbott gives the women an early twentieth-century veneer so as to emphasize their outspokenness. This is particularly apparent in their songs. The musical strives to enhance the original through song and dance rather than by seeking to capture a specific element of Shakespeare's play. The adaptors follow the Renaissance dramatist's lead, confirming the uncanny resemblance between the twins, then build their own comic scene.

When Dromio E. tells his master—that is, the man he believes to be his master—that his wife wants him home and dinner is waiting, Antipholus S., a single unattached man, responds first with astonishment, then with anger. His Dromio knows he is unmarried. As the confusion develops, Antipholus S. becomes more and more angry, hitting his (brother's) servant, who finally escapes. In *The Boys from Syracuse,* Dromio hides in the town square, where his wife, Luce, discovers him. In *The Comedy of Errors,* Antipholus S. responds in bewilderment, believing the town is hexed. Although, in both play and musical, Dromio E. returns to his mistress and reports that her husband is mad, in *The Boys from Syracuse* Dromio E. and Luce sing "What Can You Do with a Man?" a duet occasioned by Antipholus S.'s strange behavior.

Hart's skill shapes our understanding of Luce, developing her role far beyond her appearance in *The Comedy of Errors.* Seen perhaps on the balcony and heard from within, reprimanding the Ephesian Antipholus and Dromio in *The Comedy of Errors,* she plays an important part in *The Boys from Syracuse.* To her belong many of the women's comic songs. In addition, she physically resembles Dromio S.'s description in Shakespeare's play of the woman—a large, greasy kitchen maid who claims him as her husband-to-be:

> She's the kitchen wench, and all grease, and I know not what use to put her to but to make a lamp of her and run from her by her own light.
> (3.2.95–98)

He describes her complexion as "swart," and says that she measures "no longer from head to foot than from hip to hip. She is spherical like a globe" (113–14). He and his master compare parts of her body to different countries, the references becoming increasingly bawdy. Not only have the adaptors built her on Shakespeare's dimensions and created an equally aggressive Luce, but, conforming to twentieth-century mores, they have married her to Dromio E. rather than making her his intended.

Her songs provide an insight into the interaction between husbands and wives in the late 1930s. Whereas the love songs given to the main women characters—Adriana and Luciana—offer a romantic picture of marital relationships, Luce's songs do not. They suggest some of the problems arising in the society of the time, where different sets of mores mark the relationships between husbands and wives. Luce belts out the first of these songs, "What Can You Do with a Man?" shortly after she discovers her Dromio hiding from Antipholus S. in the town square. Triggered by Dromio E.'s description of the strange behavior of his "maestro," the song enumerates the obligations of husbands to their wives. Although it develops into a duet, the major ideas are Luce's. She brings a lower-class perspective to those obligations, offering a bitter commentary on marriage, despite couching her observations in humor. She also lists what is expected of husbands and wives by their mates, highlighting their different perceptions of the ideal marriage. Luce begins with "Listen to your lady who speaks. / This affair has run its course. / I'll reside in Athens six weeks / While I get me a divorce" (1.1, p. 16). This is a thinly disguised contemporary reference, with Athens substituting for Reno; in the 1930s Nevada's divorce law was the most lenient in the country, requiring only six weeks' residency. Hart's skill with language emerges again in the refrain to this song: "He eats me out of house and home" and then later "That's nothing new with a man / What can you do with a man?" (1.1, p. 16).

Exploring the nature of sexual conflict, Dromio E. insists, "Listen to your lover who asks / Why this battle has begun." Quickly she responds, complaining about his lack of attention to certain "tasks a husband should perform." Primary among these is his responsibility to provide sexual satisfaction. "Some men wear half pajamas. / I took a chance. / I bought the guy pajamas— / He wears the pants," she sings. But in case the audience misinterprets this to mean that he is the dominant, bossy member of this duo, Luce becomes more explicit: "By day he's like a five-year-old / At night he's ninety-seven." She then goes into the refrain, "What can you do with a man like that?" He responds by asking for patience: "when you get mad don't count to ten, / go on and count a million." Since the men playing the Dromio roles were short, the lyricist could also refer to their height: "I'm only four foot ten right now— / I once was five foot seven. / That's what you did with a man like that!" But she has the closing lines, where she reiterates her complaint: "I shook the tree of life one day / And got a cold potato." The lyricist extends the potato metaphor into that of a stew, even as he creates an internal rhyme of "stew" and "you" rather than the more usual end-stopped rhyme. "I'm in a stew with a man. / What can you do with a man?" (1.1, pp. 16–17). Luce's song brings the first scene of the musical to a close. Internal rhymes on "he," and "me," and again on "out" and "house" and on "new" and "do," as well as alliteration, characterize these lines, and she concludes with the line "Home's like a zoo with a man," with "zoo" offering a third example of internal rhyme.

Luce next appears rushing into her mistress's home with Dromio E., who fears his master has gone mad. The tight interweaving of various stories emerges here. The love song gives way to what appears to be a strong rejection of Adriana by her husband:

> He says what dinner, where is my gold? I say the missus is waiting. He says, what missus, where is my gold. I says I want to take you home. He says what home, where is my gold. So I thought I'd do a little *what* business myself. So I says, *what* gold . . . and now I'm a fugitive. (1.2, p. 20)

Despite being sent back to the square by the sisters, Dromio ignores their instructions. The scene closes with the sisters arguing about Antipholus E.'s motive. "He's with some woman," Adriana asserts and then determines to go looking for him herself.

Here, the two works overlap for a moment in scene 2 of the musical and act 2, scene 1 of Shakespeare's play. In both, Adriana, Antipholus E.'s wife, along with her unmarried sister, Luciana, awaits his return for dinner. Whereas Luciana preaches patience, Adriana launches into a diatribe on women's rights. "Why should their liberty than ours be more?" she asks (2.1.10), as Shakespeare raises issues of gender. Quickly, Luciana replies, "Why, headstrong liberty is lash'd with woe," then enumerates the animal kingdoms in which "the beasts, the fishes, and the winged fowls / Are their males's subjects and at their controls." And "Man, more divine, the master of all these . . . are masters to their females." Not to be outdone, the married sister then immediately notes, "This servitude makes you to keep unwed." "Not this, but troubles of the marriage-bed," Luciana quickly replies, then superciliously asserts, "Ere I learn love, I'll practice to obey" (2.1.15–29). The sisters, particularly Adriana, are questioning their society's ideas about women's rights.

The complexity and intensity of Shakespeare's debate between the sisters on a wife's role disappears from the adaptation. Unlike Luce's song, which spells out some marital problems (such as the man's wearing the pants of his pajamas and acting ninety-seven at night), Adriana's song offers a romanticized version of what a woman expects from marriage. Her sophisticated speech on the relationship of husband and wife in *The Comedy of Errors* is gone. No longer heard are her lines "For if we two be one, and thou play false, / I do digest the poison of thy flesh, / Being strumpeted by thy contagion," which she says to the wrong Antipholus (2.2.142–44). Infidelity reflects not only on the morals of the unfaithful man but also on those of his wife. She is stained by his infidelity. Gone too is another comment in this speech that also offers insight into her character. It parallels Antipholus S.'s soliloquy on the sea and the mingling of waters that makes them inseparable. Shakespeare uses the metaphor of the sea several times in this play. Here Adriana is speaking about marriage. For a moment, we glimpse the mature Shakespeare, who wrestles with easy concepts surrounding marriage:

> For know, my love, as easy mayst thou fall
> A drop of water in the breaking gulf,
> And take unmingled thence that drop again,
> Without addition or diminishing,
> As take from me thyself and not me too. (2.2.125–29)

No divorce is possible here. The mingling of blood cannot be separated or undone. Shakespeare has created a thoughtful, assertive woman, who is not seen in the musical.

On the Broadway stage, a sewing circle replaces the sisters' debate. Cynically responding to her sister's advice to "have patience," Adriana swiftly replies, "What do you think I'm having. What is this big sewing circle act we're doing, if it isn't patience. Is there anything more pathetic and foolish than to be a neglected wife. I won't stand for it much longer.

I'll tell you that." She then proceeds to refer to accusations of a "sword's point marriage," another concept rooted in the 1930s, rejecting the idea of a shotgun wedding. In defending her decision to marry Antipholus E., she says,

> There're some that say it was a sword's point wedding, but that isn't the fact. He pursued me night and day. . . . He even wrote a poem about my beautiful feet—it used to give him a thrill just to peak [sic] at them. Now—my God . . . Oh well, never mind me. Come, my ladies, smile. It doesn't do any good to sit here and mope. Bring in the tapestry—Let's get on with our work. (1.2, pp. 18–19)

What a resigned attitude, and one we hear again from Adriana when she forgives Antipholus for his many indiscretions. Here the reference to a "sword's point wedding" defines the times.

It's hard for us today to recognize the strength of the taboos on premarital sex that existed in the 1930s. Nor is there today any need for Adriana to defend her decision to marry Antipholus E. The mores have changed. This speech belongs to 1938 and the period preceding it. The reference to his praising her feet adds humor to the image of their chaste relationship prior to marriage.

Returning to their weaving, and accompanied by other women, Adriana and Luciana next sing of the blindness of love, in "Falling in Love with Love." Referring first to weaving "with brightly colored strings," Adriana then moves into the refrain: "Falling in love with love / Is falling for make-believe." Melodious, wistful, lyrical, the music has all the markings of a love song. Only listening closely to its words reveals their irony; they refer to falseness and "juvenile fancy." Ultimately, Adriana states, "I was unwise with eyes / Unable to see" (1.2, p. 19). The reference to love's blindness intrudes on the romantic notion. Once again Hart exhibits his skill with language. The rhyming of "unwise" with "eyes," the trailing "z" sound of "was" and "unwise," the slanted rhyme of "was" and "wise," and finally a linkage of ideas of love to sight and blindness are all packed into this brief refrain. Hart suggests here that love makes us unable to see a lover clearly; we must struggle for hints of his reality.

Bringing Shakespeare's work into the twentieth century, the adaptors also suggest ways in which women are "bridled"—restrained and held back. Adriana in *Boys* declares, "He didn't have to marry me, you know. . . . He pursued me night and day. He told me those dull stories about how wonderful he was." And she fell for them. Now, trapped in a marriage to a man who doesn't seem to care for her, she tries to warn other women against the blindness of falling in love. In the refrain Adriana berates herself for having fallen in love with Antipholus E.:

> Falling in love with love
> Is falling for make-believe.
> Falling in love with love
> Is playing the fool.

Love is an illusion; it's not real, and to believe in it is to be a clown and an innocent. Giving just the right twist to the lyrics, Hart suggests the uselessness and foolishness of falling in love. Picking up the "f" sound from "falling," he moves it into the last line to "fool," just as the repetition of "love" is modified into the end of "believe," with a slant rhyme from love to "believe." Through the specificity of the next two lines, the lyricist emphasizes the childishness of women's expectations.

> Caring too much is such
> A juvenile fancy.
> Learning to trust is just
> For children in school.

Hart then defines "juvenile," emphasizing the importance of growing up and rejecting the childishness of "caring too much." One should be mature, skeptical, and questioning. Finally, Adriana explains herself and the seductions of women:

> I fell in love with love
> One night when the moon was full.

Sex, moonlight, and seduction conspire together as Hart weaves the language of the song. Moonlight can deceive us, giving a new hue to reality. We must beware, letting the light of day illuminate the lover and give meaning to his words. Hart plays with the "n" sound, repeating it in four words in the second line. He also bounces the "w" sound from "one" to "when" to "was" and then into the next line:

> I was unwise with eyes
> Unable to see. (1.2, p. 19)

From the internal rhyme of "wise" with "eyes," Hart again picks up the concepts of sight and blindness. This time he suggests that women are blind to their surroundings and see only the suitor.

At the close of the corresponding scene by Shakespeare, Adriana expresses her despair:

> Since that my beauty cannot please his eye,
> I'll weep what's left away, and weeping die. (2.1.114–15)

In contrast both to Luce's individuality in *The Boys from Syracuse* and to Adriana's outspokenness in *The Comedy of Errors,* Adriana of the musical remains a more stereotypical portrait of a wife, complaining but hardly doing anything about her situation. Hart alters the emphasis of her words. No longer speaking of her possibly lost beauty, he picks up the more ephemeral concept of falling in love with love.

> I fell in love with love,
> With love everlasting,
> But love fell out with me! (1.2, p. 19)

No man is mentioned; rather, the lyrics are concerned with the absence of attention and love. With Rodgers's music capturing the mood of the lyrics, the song became a great hit. Not only does the music relate to the play, but it is later reinforced by the choreographer, as the women of the sewing circle express their feelings for men, or at least Adriana's feelings for her husband—exasperation and annoyance intertwined with love. Adriana's song seems to be a contemporary romantic expression, and it is created specifically for this musical, in a genre that requires several love songs. These songs also fit into the flow of the plot, in the major new development in this musical. But the adaptors have failed to capture Shakespeare's more complex portrait of Adriana. The dialogue in the musical closes with her explaining to her sister,

> I'm not like you. You don't know the meaning of love. I'm just an or-
> dinary female woman . . . I'm jealous, but I won't let him know it. I'll
> roam the streets until I find him and then I'll coo him home as sweetly
> as any dove. (1.2, p. 21)

This unrealistic psychology fails to match Shakespeare's brief but provocative discussion by the sisters. And in a later scene, the dances of the Courtesan and Adriana offer additional insights into these two women.

Before that, however, the adaptors bring the audience back to the town square, where Antipholus S. is still searching for his Dromio. But that servant, who is actually the hometown boy, has long since disappeared with Luce to Adriana and their home. Antipholus S. is being observed by an incredulous Dromio S., who can no longer resist asking what his boss is doing. Delighted that his slave has come to his senses but annoyed by his (actually Dromio E.'s) earlier references to home and wife, Antipholus takes a swat at him, although Dromio has no idea why. Then suddenly he notes two women approaching. Here the musical follows act 2, scene 2 of *The Comedy of Errors,* where Shakespeare offers an extended exchange between the Syracusan pair. Characterized by punning, their banter reveals the closeness of their relationship, much like that between another master and servant, Petruchio and Grumio in *The Taming of the Shrew.*

Meanwhile, believing that a little loving kindness might bring her husband home, Adriana has gone in search of him in town. In *The Comedy of Errors* Adriana and Luciana make the trip together, and thus meet Antipholus S. at the same time, but in the musical Adriana is accompanied by Luce, so that Luciana first meets him only after they return. The texts merge again during the meeting between Adriana and Antipholus S.

In this bold adventure into a new form, *The Boys from Syracuse* illustrates the first steps toward the organic musical by adhering closely to the spirit of Shakespeare's text although translating his words into the modern vernacular. As both works seek to establish Antipholus S.'s strangeness to Ephesus, for instance, the adaptors retain much of Shakespeare's essence while slightly altering the dialogue. "Plead you to me, fair dame?" Shakespeare's Syracusan asks Adriana, then asserts, "I know you not: / In Ephesus I am but two hours old, / As strange unto your town as to your talk" (2.2.147–49). This resembles the musical's "My dear lady, why do you plead with me? I don't know you. I am a stranger. I've been in your city only a day" (1.3, p. 25). In both examples, Adriana is grossly insulted by her husband calling her "dear lady" or "fair dame." How can her husband speak to her this way before the women of the sewing circle? Finally, again demonstrating the similarities between the brothers, Adriana, calling him "husband," invites him to come home. Bewildered, Antipholus S. wonders if he were married to her in a dream. And here, too, Dromio pinches his master and wonders if they are bewitched. Thus the adaptors feel free to move away from Shakespeare's text at times and to closely follow it at others.

Shakespeare's emphasis on bewitchment inspires the adaptors. They invent a sorcerer character, who appears out of smoke and tries to sell fortunes. Later on, he becomes the vehicle for a ballet sequence by the two Dromios. Dromio E., longing to see his brother, turns to the Sorcerer and begs, "Show me Dromi" (2.2, p. 19). The Sorcerer, after protesting and setting a high price, finally complies. Seeing the second Dromio onstage, he instructs Dromio E. to look into a crystal ball.

Balanchine's ballet for the two Dromios again fosters the new idea of the organic musical, where all the elements are integrated. Dance and song support the thrust of plot and character development. The twin Dromios dance with one another as though each were looking into a mirror. This introduces a dream ballet, a feature that became important in the organic musical. The dream ballet expressed the hopes and wishes of the characters, often reviving someone gone or lost, as occurs later in *West Side Story,* and in *Oklahoma!* before that. Sometimes a dream ballet dramatizes a situation, clarifying a new direction for a character's actions, as occurs in *Carousel.* Here, in *The Boys from Syracuse,* the dream ballet briefly suggests the later reunion of the Dromios. Their movements dramatize the mirror quality of the men's actions. When the dance ends with one Dromio leaving the stage, neither is aware that he has actually seen his twin. *The Boys from Syracuse* thus sets the pattern for the dream ballets that follow in such later American musicals as *Oklahoma!* and *Carousel.* Unlike those later ballets, however, this one features two men. Indeed, it hints at homoeroticism, although the fact that the men are brothers masks this aspect.

Larry Hart wrote a particularly moving song for his brother, Teddy, who played Dromio E. It dramatizes the intensity of Dromio's feelings for his "big brother," onto whom he projects his own sense of being alone in the world: "Where will you wander tonight, / Big Brother? / Is the world treating you right, / Big Brother?" The song then considers the places "east or west" where his brother might be, and emphasizes the concept of family: "Come to your twin, / I'll treat you like a mother." This same family feeling pervades Shakespeare's denouement when the Dromio twins finally meet. There, too, the sense of incompleteness that needs to be remedied by a new wholeness seems to overwhelm the Dromios. Once again the song, with its haunting melody, translates the characterization in the source play to the musical.

A scene in the town square follows, rich with incident. Finally the adaptors go off on their own, bringing in the Sorcerer trying to sell his tricks and the Courtesan searching for Antipholus. The Sorcerer points out the way Antipholus S. and Adriana went, but is astonished to see Antipholus E. entering from the opposite direction. It's a wonderful trick, the Sorcerer concedes.

Meanwhile the Courtesan begs Antipholus E. to stay. "I have to go home once in a while, baby. You know that," he explains (1.3, p. 30). Clearly he has two women, as Balanchine demonstrates in the accompanying ballet. In it a single man dances with two women, one on pointe, the other in tap shoes. Often all three bodies interweave, then separate, with the male dancer accompanying first one and then the other. Pictures of this dance show one woman wearing a black bra-style top and a chiffon skirt with black circles, while the other woman wears almost the reverse, a light-colored outfit with a polka-dotted top and a tiara. The male dancer wears a helmet and a toga-like top wrapped around his upper body. The women's costumes are seductive and suggest their different forms of appeal. The dance courageously combined tap, ballet, and adagio. Labeled "sensuous" and "beautiful" by some critics but "controversial" by others, it translates the language of the musical into a visual experience for the audience.[12] It also makes tap equal to ballet, where usually one is high-class and the other low-class. According to Camille Hardy, "What made this one of the most interesting dances in *Boys* is that Balanchine had three very fine dancers and used them to expand the plot situation. A man has relations with two women simultaneously."[13]

The dance is also distinguished by the fact that its choreography not only interweaves these three dancers, their bodies sensuously interacting, but also gives an impressionistic interpretation of what is happening onstage. The dance captures the essence of Antipholus E., who finds both the Courtesan and his wife attractive. As the scene continues, Antipho-

1.2. George Balanchine brings ballet into the American musical, interweaving the bodies of the three dancers to indicate that Antipholus E. (George Church) is torn between two women—or, more specifically, having relations with them both. Heidi Vosseler and Betty Bruce dance the roles of the women, one wearing ballet slippers, the other in tap shoes. This 1938 musical presented an extraordinary meshing of two distinct dance forms. *Billy Rose Theatre Division, New York Public Library for the Performing Arts, Astor, Lenox, and Tilden Foundations.*

lus meets Angelo the jeweler, who wants to show his customer the gold chain he has ordered. But again, Antipholus has no time: "Not tonight. . . . I'll get it later" (1.3, p. 30). This eventually leads to his singing "The Shortest Day of the Year" to the Courtesan, explaining how much his wife loves him. And therefore, indeed, he must go home.

The next scene takes us inside Adriana's house, where she attempts to make the man she believes to be her husband comfortable. When she asks if he's hungry, he admits that he is. "Would you like to have sister read to you?" she offers. "Oh, have you a sister?" he asks, at which she and her women laugh, thinking him amusing (1.4, p. 34). Nevertheless, her sister does appear, and in a change from Shakespeare's comedy, Antipholus S. asks, when they are alone, if she believes in love at first sight. He then describes his background:

> Seven years ago I left my home in search of my mother and my brother.
> I've travelled by land. I've travelled by sea; people of all countries, of
> all climes I've seen, I've talked to. My search is over now. I'm about to
> go home defeated, but my defeat is a victory—because my mother, my
> brother, I've forgotten them—I've found you. (1.4, pp. 34–35)

But she doesn't believe him. Nor does he accept her dismissal of the
concept of "love at first sight." Whereas Shakespeare leaves a lacuna of
time, and a good deal of ambiguity as to what goes on during the night,
before Antipholus S. proposes to Luciana the next morning, the adaptors
have him propose at once with the question "Do you believe in love at
first sight?" And in *The Comedy of Errors,* Luciana questions his sincerity
and criticizes his behavior:

> And may it be that you have quite forgot
> A husband's office? Shall, Antipholus,
> Even in the spring of love thy love-springs rot?
> . . . .
> If you did wed my sister for her wealth,
> Then for her wealth's sake use her with more kindness. (3.2.1–6)

So begins Luciana's speech to Antipholus S., which continues for twenty-
three more lines, suggesting he even lie to her sister, his wife. The adaptors have resolved that difficulty. As their scene develops, Luciana, like
her model in Shakespeare's play, also reprimands him for disloyalty to
his wife. But Antipholus S.'s response differs from that of his Shakespearean model. Turning to Luciana, he asks, "Why did you look at me that
way?" "Because I thought at first you were someone else," she responds,
and continues, "I had a queer thought you were not you" (1.4, p. 35). And
of course, he isn't the man she thinks he is: her brother-in-law.

Outside forces, particularly the social conventions of the late thir-
ties, also had an impact on the adaptors. In an interview shortly after
the musical opened, Rodgers and Hart explained that "they could not
have the two sing, 'I love you.' That would be incest on her part and a
dirty trick on his."[14] They found a solution with "This Can't Be Love."
The song's short lines and ironic twists are reminiscent of the poems of
the Renaissance writer John Skelton. Most importantly, the song opens
with a reference to *Romeo and Juliet,* a major example from Shakespeare
of love at first sight. As another critic observed, we are being confronted
with metatheater here.[15]

> In Verona my late cousin, Romeo,
> Was three times as stupid as my Dromio,
> For he fell in love and then he died of it,
> Poor half-wit!

Rodgers's music captures this syncopation. The famous refrain—"This can't be love because I feel so well, / No sobs, no sorrows, no sighs, / This can't be love, I get no dizzy spell, / My head is not in the skies"—denies that Antipholus could possibly be in love.

> Luciana responds to the *Romeo and Juliet* reference:
> Though your cousin loved my cousin Juliet,
> Loved her with a passion much more truly yet,
> Some poor playwright wrote their drama just for fun.
> It won't run.

Hart was having fun with the lyrics as he emphasized the long-running, famous tragedy. Luciana then repeats the refrain, which closes with "But still I love to look in your eyes" (1.4, p. 36). They dance and sing until suddenly she realizes that she is involved in a taboo situation: this is her sister's husband. She is flirting with incest. She runs out. About to follow her, Antipholus S. meets his man, Dromio. The slave is facing pursuit by a woman, rather than rejection, since Luce blocks every avenue of escape. Both Syracusans want to leave. Meanwhile, Luciana becomes aware of her feelings, later admitting, "This must be love, for I don't feel so well."

The two Antipholuses offer other insights. In them Shakespeare addresses a subject he will return to in *Twelfth Night*—the similarities and differences between twins. In that play the dramatist crosses gender lines. In this one, personality differences immediately distinguish the men. Antipholus of Syracuse never pretends to be anyone other than who he is. His first soliloquy in *The Comedy of Errors* establishes his introspective nature. Antipholus of Ephesus's self-centered nature also emerges in his first speech, when he complains of having no time to see the gold chain, needing to rush home because his wife is "shrewish" when he's late for dinner. Both qualities also characterize the men even when they are transformed in *The Boys from Syracuse*—for they are changed, Antipholus E. by his relationship to the Courtesan, Antipholus S. by his blossoming love affair with Luciana.

Differences between the twin Antipholuses emerge more fully as the musical develops, and they serve to enlarge the portrait of the Courtesan. In *The Comedy of Errors,* she hardly appears, being mentioned merely to provoke Adriana's jealousy. But in the adaptation the Courtesan comes to life as a high-class madame who has a secretary and a string of "girls," or prostitutes, working for her. A member of contemporary urban society, she also has an easy relationship with the Sergeant of Police and his men and is comfortable with Antipholus E. Suggesting the centrality of her house of entertainment, the Sergeant and Corporal next enter, reminding everyone, "Having an execution tomorrow at noon. Hope to see a good turnout" (1.3, p. 30). They are completely oblivious to the implications of their announcement, once more suggesting the Nazi mentality.

Meanwhile Antipholus E. has decided to go home, suddenly extolling the virtues of his wife. "You know what she said to me this morning. She said a single kiss is a thousand dreams come true." Unlike his Shakespearean model, he decides he really misses his wife and continues to describe her charms: "She said, the shortest day of the year has the longest night of the year" (1.3, p. 31). He then begins the song "The Shortest Day of the Year," ending with "And the longest night / Is the shortest night with you." At this point, he is standing outside his own home. Whereas Shakespeare's Antipholus rushes home because of his wife's shrewishness and invites Balthazar to join him for a "tableful of welcome," in the musical the husband drifts homeward singing, "The longest night / Is the shortest night with you," accompanied only by his servant Dromio. The moment is brief and laced with irony, for Antipholus first sings the line to the Courtesan, to impress her with his wife's virtues. Later, the song evolves into a duet between Antipholus E., standing in the street, and Adriana, who is inside singing to the Syracusan Antipholus. As her husband begins the song, ending with "And the longest night / Is the shortest night with you," the shutters on Adriana's apartment close, taking the audience from the street outside to the room inside. Humor, sentiment, and pathos then merge as the husband finds himself locked out of his own home (1.3, p. 32).

Both the musical and Shakespeare's play have a lockout scene, in which Adriana and her entire household deny entry to Antipholus

E. and his Dromio. This again demonstrates the absolute resemblance between the two sets of twins, as Adriana and Luce (who in the musical are their wives) insist that their husbands are at home and dismiss those seeking entry as imposters. Shakespeare's version comes earlier in the plot sequence than does the equivalent scene in the musical. As Shakespeare's Antipholus E. moves from gentleness to cajolery to anger and finally fury, he threatens to use a crowbar to break into his own house. But Balthazar, whom Antipholus has invited home with him, advises against such rash action: "Have patience, sir, O let it not be so! / Herein you war against your reputation, / And draw within the compass of suspect / Th' unviolated honor of your wife" (3.1.85–88). He advises instead that they go to an inn called the Tiger for dinner. Antipholus E., however, has a counterproposal: the Porpentine. There presides a wench "of excellent discourse / Pretty and witty; wild and yet, too, gentle"; a woman whom his wife has often upbraided him about—but, he assures his guests, "without desert" (3.1.109–11). And so they leave.

The lockout scene in the musical appears later, following Antipholus E's tribute to his wife: "And the longest night / Is the shortest night with you." The scene captures in music the great variety of moods Antipholus E. goes through as he pleads for entry to his own house. As the music changes tone, Antipholus only repeats in ever more ardent tones the one line "Let Antipholus in." A tour-de-force on the part of the composer, the scene develops musically into one of the most remarkable songs of the play. It takes Antipholus E.'s frustration, anger, attempt at rationality, and, ultimately, his fury—all found in Shakespeare's *Comedy of Errors*—and translates these into song. This is not done through lyrics, as they consist only of the repeated line "Let Antipholus in," but through the combination of music, dance, and staging. The words are simply repeated, in different keys, with different tones. The song "Let Antipholus In" not only builds to the fury exhibited in Shakespeare's comedy but goes beyond it by drawing on dancers and singers to dramatize the response it provokes. Basically, a riot takes place in front of Antipholus's house, as a mob shows up to bang on the door. Eventually the entire company is singing the song, but first the Tailor's apprentice performs a solo, then Dromio E. sings some sections, and the crowd sings some sections. The Courtesan and her assistant enter and whisk Antipholus

1.3. "Let Antipholus in," the irate husband shouts as townspeople watch him attempting to break down the door of his own house. Jo Mielziner's set, with the small house in the center—more than just a background—picks up some of the satiric ideas in the production. Mielziner uses a revolving stage, allowing the audience to watch all the scene changes. The set illustrates how the musical is totally integrated in all its component parts. *Vandamm Studio, Jerome Robbins Dance Division, New York Public Library for the Performing Arts, Astor, Lenox, and Tilden Foundations.*

E. and Dromio E. home with them while the crowd beats on the gate and circles the house. Brooks Atkinson, of the *New York Times,* wrote, "Particularly at the close of the first act, Mr. Balanchine has found a way of turning the dancing into the theme of the comedy and orchestrating it in the composition of the scene."[16]

The song not only showcases the composer's skill and the choreographer's talent, but also beautifully exemplifies the new organic American musical form as applied to a Shakespeare text. And photographs of the set of the lockout scene reveal the richness of its colors and the intricacy of its design. Against a large orange mock-up of a temple, Antipholus E.'s house, an eight-sided structure, stands in the center of the stage, its shutters closed, creating a background for the dancers and singers as they demand, "Let Antipholus in." Standing center stage, the diminutive house allows plenty of room for the crowd of dancers to move around it. Their vividly colored costumes enhance the spectacle and add to its humor and wildness. Rosamond Gilder wrote,

Jo Mielziner does much with his debonair scenery which trots into place when needed and whisks out of the way as occasion requires. The house of Antipholus of Ephesus not only comes forward but also turns around to order and is in just the mood of playfulness and visual grace that the idea demands.[17]

Following the raucous finale of act 1, in which Antipholus E. seeks entry into his house, act 2 of *The Boys from Syracuse* opens quietly in the early morning, with the ladies of the evening and the policemen singing their song "The Ladies of the Evening in the Morning." The women bemoan their appearance in the morning, while the Sergeant and policemen assert their triumph: "All that we ever aim to catch / Is the ladies of the ev'ning in the morning." Balanchine choreographed a dance to this music, a pas de deux of policeman and prostitute, with Heidi Vosseler (of the American Ballet) and George Church. Although not identified as a ballet in the original *Playbill*,[18] it exemplified just what Balanchine was striving for: to use ballet dancers and to create dances that drew on his ballet background to build a new and diverse audience for this genre.

Hart also created a song for Luce that reflects the lyricist's cynicism. Probably inspired by Antipholus S.'s line in Shakespeare's text "For if that I am I, then well I know / Your weeping sister is no wife of mine" (3.2.41–42), the musical team of Rodgers and Hart developed a song for Luce and Dromio S. in act 2 called "He and She." An extraordinarily original ballad in which he sings responses to her as she paints a picture of marriage, "He and She" is also a strange, off-beat song. Shakespeare's phrase "I am I" reappears in a new form in "He and She":

> I was I
> You were you,
> And now we're only we.

These lines suggest the irreverence of the entire piece, which also includes

> He won renown as the father of a squadron
> She helped the stork make his annual report.

It closes with

> And when they died—
> And when they died and went to heaven
> All the angels moved to hell,
> And that is he and she! (2.1, pp. 5–6)

Angels refuse to remain in a heaven inhabited by this amoral pair. Lifting lines from Shakespeare's play, Hart gives them a new meaning. His cynicism is seen most fully later on in the musical *Pal Joey* (1940), but despite the amazing ways in which most of the lyrics in *The Boys from Syracuse* help develop the plot, from the earliest "Hurrah, hurroo" to the double meanings in many of the more romantic tunes, that same cynicism appears here.

Luce's song and the earlier "What Can You Do with a Man?" dramatize the appeal of divorce. The contrast between this song and Adriana's earlier "Falling in Love" also involves class. Luce can speak of divorce, albeit in a comic context, while Adriana perceives marriage as an unbreakable relationship. In Luce's more ruthless song, Hart further twists conventions and sarcastically, sardonically examines blatant disenchantment with gender relations. His detailed description of marriage—or rather non-marriage, because the song implies that the couple first had children and then married—offers yet another insight into sexual relations and marriage. Although the song is a ballad, the kind of ballad perhaps sung in nightclubs of the time, it also suggests the seamier side of gender relations.

In a play having to do with love, marriage, and extramarital affairs, the song criticizes and pokes fun at any romanticized notion of marriage. A biting commentary, it discusses the choices made by "he" and "she." It contrasts men's and women's expectations in marriage as well as paralleling their lack of respect for one another. Throughout, sex is a constant source of provocation. The song's portrait of the role of women—to be mothers—differs greatly from those presented later on—in the post-war *Kiss Me, Kate,* for example, where women's independence is the major source of conflict.

Examples of mistaken identity then multiply in the musical's second act. First, Angelo the goldsmith gives Antipholus S. the gold chain meant for Antipholus E.; then Luciana keeps resisting the advances of Antipholus S., who still hopes she will change her mind. Convinced that he is her brother-in-law, she questions him about his imminent departure: "You say that as though you were never coming back." He responds, "Well, I'm not. I'm never coming back. But I shall remember" (2.1, p. 9). He then sings "You have Cast Your Shadow on the Sea," a lyrical, wistful song in a minor key. It borrows from Antipholus S.'s early soliloquy and his speech to Dromio in *The Comedy of Errors* where he plans his departure, including lines like "And if the wind blow any way from shore / I will not harbor in this town tonight" (3.2.148–49). The lyricist and composer have captured both his wistfulness and his hope that she will change her mind in

> You have cast your shadow on the sea,
> On both the sea and me.
> Not a shadow dancing in the sun,
> That fades when day is done. (2.1, p. 10)

The lyrics indicate the permanence of Luciana's influence on him, and his poignant hope that she will be with him forever. The shadow she casts is unusual because it will not fade with the fading light, but will persist.

In contrast with this sentimental parting of Luciana and Antipholus S., the next scene swings into multiple complications of mistaken identity. With Antipholus E. facing charges brought by the jeweler for not paying for the gold chain—delivered to his twin—the musical team creates a song that has the robustness and joyousness of Rodgers and Oscar Hammerstein's later "Oklahoma!" the title song of their 1943 musical.[19] Sung by the Sergeant, policemen, Angelo, and Antipholus E., "Come with Me" is an invitation to jail. In a rousing melody with the same swing as "Oklahoma!" the song describes jail's many advantages:

> Come with me where the food is free,
> Where the landlord never comes near you.

Internal rhyme ("me" and "free") and alliteration ("food" and "free"; "never" and "near") catch the reader's eye as well as the listener's ear.

> Be a guest in a house of rest,
> Where the best of fellows can cheer you.

The music changes slightly to accommodate the description:

> There's your own little room
> So cool, not too much light.

Not until the very end of the first stanza is the destination explicitly referred to as jail. Instead, all of its advantages are enumerated—"no wife waits up at night," and "when day ends you have lots of friends / who will guard you well while you slumber" (note the internal rhyme of "ends" and "friends," and the alliteration of "who will," "well," and "while").

No family will barge in on you or press you to do uncomfortable things. Moreover, you can "snore and swear and stretch and yawn" (and here the lyrics feature not only alliteration, but single-syllable verbs in succession, borrowing a technique used with such skill by Shakespeare) in this "strictly male house," the "jail-house" (2.2, p. 16). And so Rodgers and Hart have managed to put a joyous face on Antipholus E.'s fate as he is carted off to jail for disturbing the peace as well as for not paying his debt to the jeweler, all because the chain was delivered to the wrong Antipholus. The lustiness and joyousness contradict the song's ideas.

Whereas most of the material and the overall plot of *The Boys from Syracuse* owe a great deal to Shakespeare's play, the male-female relationships differ greatly and spring from contemporary mores. Adriana is furious at her sister for listening to Antipholus's declaration of love in *The Comedy of Errors,* whereas she appears to be a resigned wife in *The Boys from Syracuse.* In Shakespeare's play, she explodes when Luciana pleads, "have patience, I beseech" as she tries to tell her story. "I cannot, nor I will not hold me still," asserts Adriana. "My tongue, though not my heart, shall have his will. / He is deformed, crooked, old and sere / Ill-fac'd, worse bodied, shapeless every where; / Vicious, ungentle, foolish, blunt, unkind, / Stigmatical in making, worse in mind" (4.2.16–22). Shakespeare's command of language, his string of adjectives, allow her to vilify every aspect of Antipholus's appearance and personality. He is not only a crooked old man, but also cruel and vicious. To this, of course, Luciana responds, "Who would be jealous then of such a one? / No evil lost is wail'd when it is gone" (23–24). She has taken her sister at her word. But Adriana then admits,

> Ah, but I think him better than I say,
> And yet would herein others' eyes were worse:
> Far from her nest the lapwing cries away;
> My heart prays for him, though my tongue do curse. (25–28)

Here Shakespeare's insight into a wife scorned is clear and sensitive.

Compare this with Adriana's instructions to her women in "Sing for Your Supper," a sexist song where she suggests catering to male fancy. "But if you're smart, you'll try to please them," she insists, then discusses the virtues of the canary who "only sings," whereas "hawks and crows do lots of things." But the canary wins the men. She describes the canary as resembling "a courtesan on wings." After Luciana has revealed her experience with Antipholus S. and is drying her eyes, her sister wonders why she was crying. "I don't know," responds Luciana; "he said he didn't belong to you. He said he was a stranger here. He said he loved me. (Cries) And I let him (Cries harder)." Then comes Adriana's response: "You mustn't be so upset. Men are like that" (2.3, p. 20). How different from Shakespeare's character, and how compliant! Moreover, whereas the sixteenth-century dramatist has a real sense of women's intensity and humanity, his adaptors create a woman who may reflect the mores of her time, but lacks dimension.

On the other hand the Courtesan, her women, her secretary, and Luce grow in importance as they are adapted from their counterparts in *The Comedy of Errors*. Their songs reveal their self-confidence and awareness of their roles in society. The composer and lyricist seem to be bowing to the mores of the times with their songs. Luce, who serves in Shakespeare's play as little more than a butt of jokes, has a sizable role and sings some of Rodgers and Hart's more creative songs, including "He and She" and "Show Me an Honest Man—Oh Diogenes." In the first, Luce and Dromio sing a duet, alternating passages describing men's and women's expectations of marriage. In the second, Luce responds to the Courtesan's wish to meet an honest man. Again, Balanchine has choreographed a dance; Diogenes wears a long beard as he sings his words of wisdom to the women.

As the play progresses, the earlier argument between the sisters about a wife's role evaporates when Luciana falls in love, and deeper questions arise. She must confront the challenges of her seeming brother-in-law's ardent declarations of love. The question of the equality of men and women disappears, replaced by questions of adultery. In other words, does a man have the right to pursue an adulterous relationship if he is no longer in love with his wife? But even more challenging is the suggestion of incest. Shakespeare permits himself to raise this question, buried in a seemingly zany comedy, although his resolution remains puzzlingly ambiguous. Interestingly, Luciana provides some of the answer, by suggesting he not tell his wife the truth about his feelings for her.

Like *The Comedy of Errors,* the musical contains a debate between the Courtesan and Antipholus S. about the gold chain, which has been mistakenly delivered to him. Seeing the chain hanging around his neck, she immediately assumes it's the one promised her by Antipholus E. "Is that the chain you promis'd me to-day?" she asks in Shakespeare's play. "Sathan, avoid, I charge thee tempt me not," Antipholus S. exclaims, to her astonishment (4.3.47–48). Then he and his Dromio begin to banter about devils and the devil's dam. Not knowing what has happened to him, the Courtesan finally repairs to Antipholus E.'s house to report that he has gone mad, confirming his wife's conclusion.

Jettisoning the concept of devils, the musical's adaptors allow Antipholus S. and Dromio S. to pursue a conversation with the Courtesan before telling her to leave them. "We're engaged," asserts Dromio S., thinking of Luciana. "I gave you my ring last night at dinner. Either give me the chain you promised, or give me back my ring," she demands of Antipholus (2.4, p. 29). But he has no ring. Finally, cursing him, she decides to report him to a policeman. Before she can do so, however, she meets Luce. The adaptors then introduce another song relevant to the situation. "I'm looking for an honest man," the Courtesan explains to her. Luce replies by singing "Oh Diogenes."

> Oh, Diogenes!
> Find a man who's honest.
> Oh Diogenes!
> Wrap him up for me. (2.4, p. 30)

A dance, with George Church in a Diogenes costume and surrounded by young women to whom he gives advice, accompanies the song. Once again Balanchine's strong dancers Betty Bruce (the Courtesan) and George Church (the dancing policeman), together with the ensemble, accompany and enrich the presentation of the song. In one of the later productions, the direction indicates that the stage

> is cleared of all people by a series of five (5) freezes . . . : The dance ends in a freeze and during a three count black-out the first group leaves the stage. The lights come on for three counts and the process is repeated leaving fewer people on stage after each black-out. Finally, the Courtesan is left alone on stage.[20]

Having consolidated some material from Shakespeare's fourth and fifth acts so as to include song and dance, the adaptors stress those elements that lead to the denouement. Shakespeare imbues his play with worries about witchcraft. The Syracusans are afraid they have been hexed. Combining the scene of the Courtesan and her insistence on receiving the chain with a scene of Antipholus S. getting into a fight in Shakespeare's act 5, the adaptors bring their musical to a close. "There's going to be a riot, Boss. You better beat it," Dromio S. advises, and so, like their models in Shakespeare's play, they head for an abbey and enter, seeking sanctuary (2.4, p. 29). And they receive it.

Meanwhile Egeon, about to be hanged, sees Antipholus E. and happily identifies him as a long-lost son. Neither Antipholus E., his Dromio, nor the Duke, now arrived for the hanging, verify his identity. Rather, just as occurs in Shakespeare's play, the Duke says, "Old man, I see that age and danger make you dote. Antipholus has never been to Syracuse. He has lived his life among us since he was brought here as a babe" (2.5, p. 36). Moments later, the abbey door opens and the abbess appears with the Syracusans close behind her. Addressing the Duke, she asks for his help. Meanwhile the two Syracusans, recognizing their bound father and boss, rush to Egeon. The abbess fills in the remaining story of the twins and how they ended up in Ephesus. Having revealed their identity, she then asks Egeon whether he had a wife named Emilia. He says he did, and she reveals that she is his long-lost wife. The frame has been closed.

The musical ends joyously. Nevertheless, as in Shakespeare's play, the women remain confused about the identities of the men. Adriana asks, "Which one of you dined with me last night?" and the Syracusan answers, "I did, fair lady." She follows up with "Are you my husband?" and is answered immediately by the Ephesian: "No he isn't. I'll promise you that." As for the two Dromios, Antipholus S. directs them to become friends. "The Dromios eye each other. Dromio E stoops, hands on knees. Dromio S. crosses to him, and assumes the same position, eye to eye." Then Dromio E., who had longed to see his brother, observes, "Isn't it wonderful to have you around," noting that "it's just like a mirror." Suddenly the ballet they performed becomes a reality. "And what a very attractive fellow you are," continues Dromio E. as they embrace (2.5, pp. 37–39). The adaptors capture the tone of Shakespeare's closing, where the two Dromios go out hand in hand, not one before the other. These musical artists have also given the two servants another dimension through the "Big Brother" song and ballet.

The adaptors have opened a new area of theater for Shakespeare's plays. When next a Shakespeare work comes on the American musical stage, it too will have a frame, but a more complex one, as its adaptors work with a play-within-a-play and offer *Kiss Me, Kate.* The women will take on a new shape and philosophy, and post-war optimism will dominate. The men who adapted *The Comedy of Errors* into *The Boys from Syracuse* not only translated Shakespeare's story into twentieth-century terms, but simultaneously initiated a new form of musical comedy that was to dominate the American stage for most of the rest of the century. Men and women of talent found a fresh outlet for their strengths in Shakespeare's plays.

As the songs picked up the lyric strength of these talented and creative voices, dances expanded far beyond the range of dance in the theater. Wending their way through this combination of song and story, the dances created by Balanchine capture the characters' varying responses to their problems. Particularly notable are "The Ladies of the Evening," which opens act 2, and the exchange between the two Dromios, who are overwhelmed by their resemblance to one another. Whereas Balanchine could start from ballet and look forward to moving into tap and more popular dance, Hanya Holm, the choreographer of *Kiss Me, Kate,* could find in American dance the freedom of movement to release the body.

In this bold adventure, with Shakespeare as their inspiration, Richard Rodgers, Larry Hart, and George Abbott opened a new era and introduced a new form, the organic musical. Preceding *Oklahoma!, The Boys from Syracuse* demonstrates the possibilities of American musical theater as a fresh artistic form. The richness of the Renaissance dramatist's skills, especially his sensitivity to gender and his insights into human behavior, provide the means for American innovation, crossing the boundaries between high and low culture, serious and comic art.

TWO

Double Vision
Kiss Me, Kate and
The Taming of the Shrew

With great exuberance, *Kiss Me, Kate* opened on Broadway at the end of 1948. Exploring the roles of women in Shakespeare's *Taming of the Shrew,* this musical employed song, dance, and plot to present a woman's dilemma of marriage versus career. Because the creators of *Kiss Me, Kate* framed the Renaissance comedy as a play-within-a-play, they could also immediately leap into the more accessible modern world and offer contemporary parallels.

The lights dim, the theater darkens, and the overture invites the audience into this double-leveled world. When the music ends, the curtain rises on a bare stage where actors and actresses in leotards—probably dancers—seem to be practicing their steps while others, in street clothes, are lounging or moving about. A ladder leans against a brick wall in the background and light bulbs dangle from the rafters. "Is that alright, Mr. Graham?" the conductor calls out from the orchestra pit, and a disembodied voice answers from out of nowhere, "Yes. The cut's good." Then Fred Graham, who plays the role of the director in the backstage play and Petruchio in Shakespeare's *The Taming of the Shrew,* materializes, seeming to come from the front row of seats. "Ok, now let's set the curtain calls," he begins. "First call: all principals." "May I leave now?" asks an older man. "I have to go to the dentist." "In a minute, Harry," the director answers. Meanwhile a pretty young ingenue is coyly asking "Fred, I mean Mr. Graham," details about her role, particularly the "thees, and thous." "In a minute, Lois," he sympathetically assures her, suggesting

2.1. "You bastard," Lilli mutters. She (Patricia Morrison) and Fred (Alfred Drake) are backstage, preparing for a curtain call at the end of their play-within-a-play, *The Taming of the Shrew*. The hostility between them reflects the difficulties women have in choosing between marriage and a career. *Spewack Collection, Rare Book and Manuscript Library, Columbia University, by permission of Lois and Arthur Elias.*

she not leave the theater before the opening. "Whatever thou say," she promises (1.1, pp. 1–3).[1]

We are backstage at what turns out to be the last moments of rehearsal for *The Taming of the Shrew*. We watch the actors preparing. Calling the roll for the last bows, Fred discovers that everyone but Lucentio is present. "Lucentio. Where the hell is Lucentio?" he shouts. Substituting the actor's real name for that of his character, Lois defensively offers, "I think Bill Calhoun went to the chiropodist." Cursing this hoofer, to whom he offered the opportunity to play in a Broadway show, Graham next turns to an elegantly dressed woman. She sits haughtily to one side, scowling. "Care to join us, Miss Vanessi?" he icily queries. She saunters over. Sharing a bow with her, since he is not only the show's director but also a lead, he asks his co-star in the most formal language, "How about a smile, Miss Vanessi?" Did they know one another before, or does he

2.2. Hattie, in the role of the maid, belts out, "Another Op'nin', Another Show," assisted by an all-white chorus, so characteristic of a 1948 American musical. *Spewack Collection, Rare Book and Manuscript Library, Columbia University, by permission of Lois and Arthur Elias.*

just have it in for her? "Let's repeat that bow," he orders. She complies. Smiling sweetly at him and bowing low, she mutters, "You bastard." The stage darkens (1.1, pp. 2–3).

Piercing that darkness, a spotlight focuses on Hattie, Lilli Vanessi's maid, who, with an accompanying chorus, begins belting out the play's first musical number, "Another Op'nin', Another Show." It captures the anxiety and hope of those performers who were lolling about the stage moments earlier. "Another job that you hope at last / Will make your future forget your past," the singer continues, and then moves to the intensity of the moment: "It's curtain time and away we go, / Another op'nin' / Of another show" (1.1, p. 5). The song not only dramatizes what has been happening onstage and defines exactly how performers feel in those nerve-racking moments before a new play begins, but also reveals the art of the collaborators. Bella Spewack, who wrote the book, and

Cole Porter, the composer and lyricist, are working within the new genre of the American stage, the completely organic musical: song, plot, and dance combine to tell a story and define character.

In this instance, the plot revolves around the backstage antics of a group of players who will be performing Shakespeare's *The Taming of the Shrew*. In that comedy a merchant father seeks to marry off his two daughters. However, he refuses to consider the many suitors for his younger daughter, the sweet, agreeable, attractive Bianca, before finding one for his elder daughter, the abrasive, angry, and shrewish Katharine. Bianca's suitors vow to work together to find Katherine a man. And then Petruchio blows into town. A dear friend of Hortensio, one of Bianca's suitors, the newcomer proclaims his mission: "I come to wive it wealthily in Padua" (1.2.75).[2] After some hesitation, Hortensio admits to knowing an appropriately endowed young woman, beautiful and rich, but a shrew. Unfazed, Petruchio not only meets her father but makes a bargain, sets the wedding day, and rides off; eventually he will seem to tame this shrew. Meanwhile, Bianca's three suitors vie for her, one winning her hand by deceiving her father. Although Kate gradually seems to change into a compliant, loving wife, Shakespeare tricks his audience by having the story of Kate and Petruchio performed as a play-within-a-play. A troupe of strolling players act their story in front of a drunken tinker, who dreams of retribution because he has been thrown out of an alehouse by a woman. Shakespeare calls it "the Induction." Borrowing this device from Shakespeare's play but transforming it, the collaborators too rely on the play-within-a-play device. There, characters in a play watch a play being performed for them, much as characters in a television skit may sit and watch television. In *The Taming of the Shrew,* as well as the drunken tinker watching the story of Kate and Petruchio unfold, another character, Lucentio, originally also an observer, steps out of his role as audience and enters the actual play being performed.

Spewack and Porter, while adopting Shakespeare's technique, alter its emphasis. In *The Taming of the Shrew,* the primary story is that of Petruchio and Katharine, and the characters in the framing play merely watch it. But in *Kiss Me, Kate,* the primary story concerns the characters in the frame, who do not merely watch but actually perform the internal play, which consists of episodes from Shakespeare's work. The collaborators select elements of Shakespeare's comedy in order to explore the meaning of marriage and relationships between men and women in the mid-twentieth-century world.

The musical centers on Lilli and Fred. As the opening scene hints, they know one another very well. In fact, they are ex-husband and -wife. Although after they parted she went to Hollywood and became a movie star, while he pursued an artistic life in the theater, they are still emotionally connected. Now temporarily reunited because Lilli's fiancé, Harrison Howell, has invested money in Fred's play, the two co-stars find themselves as torn by their temperaments as they once were. "Strange, dear, but true, dear, / When I'm close to you, dear, / The stars fill the sky, / So in love with you am I," each sings privately in soliloquy at different moments (1.3, p. 20). But, like Katharine and Petruchio (whom they play), each strives for dominance, and each reveals a mode of speaking to counter the other's lines.

Here again Shakespeare sets the pattern. In *The Taming of the Shrew* several major issues arise. For example, the dramatist explores questions about gender. Are men superior to women? What are the expectations of women regarding their roles? Is there a pattern they must follow? And what happens if they don't? This was a time when Queen Elizabeth sat on the English throne, so that any definitive claims that women were subservient or inferior to men had to be tempered. By presenting the contrasting figures of Bianca and Katherine—the one seeming to listen to her father and then follow the conventionally accepted role for women, the other challenging any simplistic ideas—Shakespeare suggests the variety of behavior found in women, especially daughters.

As a part of doing this, Shakespeare also explores the issue of a daughter's economic value. Kate and Bianca, the two daughters of the wealthy Baptista, are in some sense sold to the highest bidder, although their father claims to be trying to bargain for an excellent financial settlement for each girl. Since that settlement also means his own financial gain, he is in fact using the girls for profit. Shakespeare shows us that actually neither daughter is exempt from this treatment, despite the father's favoring the seemingly sweet Bianca over the outspoken, shrewish, but honest Kate. Nor does either daughter have a say in her choice of spouse, although Bianca, through her wiliness, weds the man she herself has chosen whereas her sister must work at getting to know the man chosen for her. Indeed, records exist of fathers during Shakespeare's time insisting that daughters marry those chosen for them. The eminent historian Lawrence Stone documents a case in which a father who hoped to benefit from the political connections of his future in-laws tied his daughter to the bedpost because she refused to marry a mentally retarded man.[3]

Questions about women's economic value and social role also drive *Kiss Me, Kate*. Although a successful film actress, Lilli/Kate feels compelled to show off her large star sapphire engagement ring to Fred—a sign of the wealth she's going to be acquiring by marriage as well as of her success at measuring up to society's expectations for women. Her fiancé, Harrison Howell (a very thinly developed character), represents economic power and political influence. He advises presidents; he can commandeer an ambulance when Lilli complains to him of maltreatment by Fred; even more significantly, he is recognized by Lois. "Why, Harold! Don't you remember? In front of the Harvard Club? I had something in my eye and you took me to Atlantic City to take it out?" Denying the name "Harold" and protesting his innocence, he changes his mind when she mentions the diamond bracelet with rubies in her safe deposit box. "I think of you all the time when I go down to my safe deposit box," Lois assures him (2.4, p. 16).

Thus the issues of a woman's social vulnerability and of her economic insecurity enter the play in two ways: through the legal knot about to be tied by Lilli and Harrison, and through the more mundane selling and buying of sexual favors by Lois and Harrison/Harold. Just as Kate and Bianca deal differently with the role society has thrust them into—being married off to the highest bidder—so Lilli and Lois react differently to societal norms and expectations.

Cole Porter creates several songs for Lois that expand our knowledge of her personality. As Bianca in the play-within-a-play, she reveals her indifference to the particulars of her suitors: "I'm a maid who would marry / ... Any Tom, Dick, or Harry / Any Harry, Dick, or Tom," she sings to a bouncy melody (1.5, pp. 28–29). The composer-lyricist gives her a similar message in two songs he combines in the backstage play. The first follows her discovery that Bill has been gambling. To a blues melody she bewails her lot, reprimanding him for his behavior. "Why can't you behave?" she sings, and goes on to describe the life they might lead together were he only to behave (1.2, p. 9). When, however, he overhears her conversation with Harold, she goes into a long defense of her actions: "But I'm always true to you, darlin', in my fashion / Yes, I'm always true to you, darlin', in my way." In that song, verse after verse lists men around the country to whom she has traded sexual favors for material gain. She enumerates her many lovers: from the boss of Boston, Mass., she goes on to Milwaukee, where Mr. Fritz, "who's full of Schlitz," will move her to the Ritz; to Ohio, where Mr. Thorne, who "once cornered corn," calls her from night to morn; to the oilman known as "Tex" who is "keen to give her checks," proving that sex is here to stay (2.4, pp. 18–21). Like Katherine and Bianca, Lois and Lilli are joined through their shared intimacy with an older man, although for them this man is not their father but rather Harrison/Harold. In this way the collaborators have, like Shakespeare, dramatized the economic power of men as it affects two very different women, even while further developing Lois as a character.

In Shakespeare's time, the public tried to balance two competing ideas of the proper relationship between husbands and wives. While the belief in a father's power over his daughter and a husband's power over his wife was probably the more dominant one, the concept that a good marriage required the "goodly consent of them both" had also taken hold, according to Stone.[4] Religious tracts and marriage pamphlets, particularly Puritan ones, propounded this notion. *The Taming of the Shrew* puts both ideas before us. On the one hand, when Petruchio boasts before his marriage that he will "board her [Kate], though she chide as loud / As thunder when the clouds in autumn crack," he is braggingly illustrating male dominance (1.2.95–96). But on the other hand, when on their wedding night he merely deprives Katherine of dinner and sends her to bed hungry, lecturing her on "continency," he is respecting her person as an individual; he is not at all intent on rape on the wedding night. Here the concept of the "goodly consent of them both" prevails.

Shakespeare creates a frightening portrait of a husband for the new bride. In *The Taming of the Shrew* Petruchio arrives for the wedding dressed as a madcap and insists on marrying without changing his clothes. *Kiss Me, Kate* also presents a frightening portrait of a husband, but a new one. No longer the madcap, he is now depressingly dull, obtuse, and sedentary—not Fred, but Harrison Howell. His ideal of the happily married life consists of retirement to his estate "down in Georgia . . . thirty thousand acres. Ride for days and not see a soul, except my tenant farmers" (2.5, p. 25). To an actress accustomed to crowds and applause, such an existence hardly sounds appealing. The collaborators have joined the issue of the independent woman—the professional woman—with the question of marriage. In one of the earlier typescripts, Lilli actually responds to this idea by saying, "I don't have to marry anyone." The line disappeared from the final text. However, it survives in the script registered with the copyright office two months before opening night.[5]

The creators of *Kiss Me, Kate* adapted Shakespeare's play through a mid-twentieth-century lens of music, song, and dance. In this populist version, the major issues raised in Shakespeare's play still exist. However, they appear in the dual characters of the backstage actors and the roles they have in the play-within-the-play. Thus the contrast between Petruchio's speech about taming his wife and his actions on the wedding night in Shakespeare's comedy emerge in *Kiss Me, Kate* as the contrast between Fred's braggadocio and his eventual coming to terms with Lilli and his feelings for her by the musical's close.

Nor is such reworking unusual in productions of Shakespeare's plays. Taking the major issues that Shakespeare addressed, David Garrick in the eighteenth century reduced the play to *Catharine and Petruchio.* He eliminated the contrasting story of Bianca and her suitor Lucentio, and stressed Kate's shrewishness.[6] Augustin Daly in late nineteenth-century America compressed the original to four acts and created a tremendous hit for his leading lady, Ada Rehan.[7] Spewack and Porter, too, created a populist *Taming of the Shrew* in *Kiss Me, Kate,* where music and dance contributed to the totality of the whole and Kate and Petruchio are a movie star and a stage director. In each case a version was created for its own time.

To present Shakespeare's play for the contemporary stage and cultural climate, actor-managers, producers, and adaptors often relied on specific devices, such as stage sets, costumes, or dialogue. Lines were cut, new ones were added, and sometimes additional characters were introduced. To emphasize Kate's shrewishness, for example, David Garrick added soliloquies for her. "Look to your seat, Petruchio, or I throw you / Cath'rine shall tame this Haggard," she confides to the audience.[8] In other words, "I'll marry him to tame him." No such revelation spills from the lips of Shakespeare's Kate.

In *Kiss Me, Kate*, Lilli reveals her thoughts both in her soliloquizing song "So in Love with You Am I" and in her conversation with her maid, Hattie. In that conversation we discover Lilli's reason for being in this production—it offers her a second chance to be with Fred. Shakespeare's Katherine has no such intimate as Hattie. We see how conflicted Lilli/Kate is, how she wonders about Fred/Petruchio's feelings for her at the same time that she refuses to sacrifice her own sense of self. She is aware of what independence means for a woman. Nevertheless, many dilemmas—such as the difficulty of maintaining simultaneous careers and the question of whose career should take precedence in time of conflict—remain unsolved, opening the text to further interpretation. Shakespeare offers directors and managers many options for ways to present the play and develop the characters for their own time.

Bella Spewack, the woman who wrote the script of *Kiss Me, Kate*, hated the idea of male dominance, the superficial message of Shakespeare's play. Thus, she created two characters for each of the leads: Lilli/Kate and Fred/Petruchio. Significantly, in one of the early scripts, Spewack has Lilli, disguised as a boy, tell Petruchio, "I pity the sex [i.e., women]."[9] While that scene later disappeared, its attitude did not. The Lilli we know wears no disguise. However, her mixed attitudes become apparent in the moments when she confides in her maid. She has become a career woman who seems self-possessed and independent. Porter and Spewack capture the message of Shakespeare's character, an independent spirit who faces complex challenges in a world where men and men's values prevail.

Verbal games dominate both the original comedy and its twentieth-century musical adaptation, distinguishing the characters from one another and defining relationships among them. When first introduced, for example, Kate has enough command of language, despite her anger and hostility, to pun on the worthlessness of her sister's suitors. "I pray you sir, is it your will / To make a stale of me amongst these mates?" she asks her father, who insists on marrying her off before considering Bianca's suitors (1.1.57–58). Here "stale" means whore or prostitute, and "mates" refers to rough or uncouth men, while "stalemate" suggests the position she is in. Petruchio, too, who bounces into town with a servant, immediately indulges in such extensive wordplay that only the appearance of a third party saves the servant from a battering, although he truly understands his master's message. "Here, sirrah Grumio," Petruchio orders, "knock, I say." "Whom should I knock?" the servant replies, although he knows he has been ordered to knock on a door. "Villain, I say, knock me here soundly!" the master persists. Neither man will give way (1.2.5–7). And so Shakespeare introduces us to the attention to verbal details that characterize both Petruchio and Kate.

Although Bella Spewack and Cole Porter jettisoned Grumio, they adopted the linguistic hijinks of the comedy. Like Kate and Petruchio, both Lilli and Fred understand the subtleties of language. When, for example, they look back on experiences they shared and he remarks, "I understudied the lead," she quickly counters, insisting on the specifics: "No, dear, you were in the chorus" (1.3, pp. 13–14). In scene 3, where we finally meet them alone onstage, again language engages them. "Calling me a B— on stage," Fred mutters, standing in his dressing room. "I didn't say it—I just indicated it," Lilli replies, from her adjoining dressing room (1.3, p. 10). These rooms, visible to the audience and alternately illuminated or darkened depending on where the action is, allow them both privacy and shared moments.

One such shared moment occurs when Fred strolls into her room, still in his dressing gown, just in time to hear the telephone ring. "Go on, pick it up—it's probably Harrison," he snickeringly comments, noting her hesitancy. "Hello, hello, Harrison darling," she coos into the phone. "You're still at the White House? . . . What, the President wants to talk to unimportant me?" Fred can stand it no more. "Ask him if they serve borscht at the White House," he shouts loudly into the phone as she seeks to cover the mouthpiece (1.3, pp. 10–11). Indeed, Harry Truman's informality and candor color this exchange. Earlier drafts of this section mention Margaret Truman and her piano playing, but the collaborators must have decided that a reference to a Jewish soup would bring more laughs. The line also reflected Truman's liberalism, as well as his fame as the president of the first country to recognize Israel as a Jewish state at the United Nations.

Later in the scene, Fred and Lilli share recollections of their life together. They recall a little "British makeshift of a Viennese operetta . . . that was laid in Switzerland." "There was a waltz in it—something about a bar," she recollects, and together they exclaim in unison, "Wunderbar."

Here a song as well as a dance—a waltz—help tell the story. The collaboration here includes the choreographer, Hanya Holm, another professional woman associated with this American musical. As the principals dance a waltz, first upstaging one another then eventually dancing in unison and singing, "Wunderbar, wunderbar / There's our favorite star above, / What a bright shining star / Like our love it's wunderbar," they kiss. But the moment passes, interrupted by the announcement "Fifteen minutes to curtain time." Nor does the recollection last long. "Whose fault was it?" she asks. "Could have been your temper," he volunteers. "Could have been your ego," she counters, and they sound very much like Kate and Petruchio (1.3, pp. 13–16).

In exploring the role of an independent professional woman in the twentieth century and including it here, the creators have expanded the range of meaning of the original. Lilli exemplifies the professional: the actress who clearly loves her profession but who, unfortunately, seems also to love her ex-husband, now paying attention to the young ingenue, Lois. He sends her flowers in anticipation of the opening: "Let my lovely Lois shine through Bianca tonight and there'll be a new star in the heavens," says the accompanying note (1.6, p. 45). Unfortunately the flowers are delivered to Lilli instead. "My wedding bouquet," she sentimentally exclaims to Hattie. "He didn't forget!" "Of course not, Honey," her maid replies, searching for the card (1.3, p. 19). Racing into the room, Fred tries to do some damage control. But Lilli is already thanking him. Seemingly lost, the note surfaces after the last "onstage" call. Aghast, Fred ad libs its contents and convinces Lilli to postpone reading it. She says she'll put it next to her heart, tucking it into the bosom of her gown (1.3, p. 23). But when she enters as Kate, exploding with all the fury the role demands— throwing flowers and a flowerpot—it is clear she has read the note. Thus the adaptors interweave the frame with the play-within-a-play. They are all part of the same story.[10] They also illustrate the challenges facing an independent woman.

Emphasizing this interweaving, the closing song of the first act, "Kiss Me, Kate," presents both a duet and a duel. Another very different version of the song closes the play. Here, however, in its first incarnation, Cole Porter has invented a series of rhymes that illustrate the hostility between the principals. "Kiss me (him), Kate, / Thou lovely loon, / Ere we (they) start / On our (their) honeymoon," Petruchio sings, backed by the chorus, but Kate responds, "I'll never be thine." As the duet continues, Porter interweaves her reactions to Fred's deception with the flowers. Following one of his refrains, she calls him "Fred" rather than "Petruchio." To his "Darling, devil, divine," she responds, rhyming with his name, "Drop dead." Maintaining the pace and the rhythm they have established, his next "Darling, devil, divine" is met with "Kindly drop dead." Eventually the duet ends with Petruchio and the male chorus singing "Now I shall ever be," while Kate and the women simultaneously sing "Now I shall never be," all ending with "thine." The characters of Kate and Lilli have merged, as have those of Fred and Petruchio (1.9, pp. 56–59).

The questions of gender roles and power raised by the Renaissance comedy still exist. And parental favoritism often permits one child to get away with murder, or at least with deception, while the other speaks her mind. Spewack and Porter explore these areas as well, by showing a flattering young ingenue play up to the man she hopes will give her the chance she's looking for. "Bill Calhoun," she warns her boyfriend, "if anything happens to Mr. Graham before I'm a star on Broadway, I'll never forgive you." And, explaining Fred Graham's role in her life, Lois says, "He's a scholar and a gentlemen. He's just culturing me . . . but there's nothing wrong between him and I . . . I mean he and I" (1.2, p. 8). In creating Lois, the twentieth-century adaptors follow Shakespeare's lead, bringing up questions of deception and honesty. Although they have eliminated some characters, such as the servants, and introduced others, such as gangsters, the adaptors are still dealing with major issues alive in our own time between men and women—issues of ambition and dominance.

The collaborators have also drawn on the contemporary American scene. In a significant departure from the Lucentio of Shakespeare's play, Bill Calhoun, who plays Lucentio in *Kiss Me, Kate,* turns out to be an inveterate gambler who has signed Fred's name—"Your hero," he calls Fred to Lois—to a ten-thousand-dollar IOU. This is why the gangsters appear: two wonderful underworld characters who wish to ensure that the loan is repaid. They shadow Fred and Lilli, preventing them from making any untoward moves. When caught onstage while guarding their prey and anxious to prove their seriousness, these gangland heroes shoot at a fake flying bird in one of the play's last scenes. The bird falls to the ground.

Despite their modern aspect, the gangsters are derived from a long comedic tradition that goes back at least as far as Shakespeare and surely much further, to classical comedy. Their lines also capture some of the verbal play between Petruchio and his servant, Grumio, in the original *Taming of the Shrew*. However, in this musical incarnation, their combination of dance—a soft-shoe routine—and songs about their years in the penitentiary also illustrate the specific unifying characteristics of the mid twentieth-century American musical, where song and dance are integrated with plot. Their song "Brush Up Your Shakespeare" expounds on the virtues of familiarity with the Bard, so that "the women you will wow!" Once again the musical takes up the subject of women, their role as arbiters of culture, and their importance in the contemporary world. As the men sing stanza after stanza, Cole Porter provides them with extraordinary rhymes. He captures the tone of these American gangsters while revealing his own amazing skill in creating lyrics: "With the wife of the British embessida / Try a crack out of *Troilus and Cressida*." Wending his way through the plays, the lyricist crafts lines particularly relevant to specific works: "Better mention *The Merchant of Venice* / When her sweet pound o' flesh you would menace." He also combines the present and the New York world with the plays: "If your goil is a Washington Heights dream," they sing, referring to a Manhattan neighborhood that the audience of the time would have known and where some may have lived, "treat the kid to *A Midsummer Night's Dream*." And then more specifically, "If she then wants an all-by-herself night / Let her rest every 'leventh or *Twelfth Night*" (2.7, pp. 35–38). Porter's gangsters range far and wide in their song, but always with women and Shakespeare in mind.

When *Kiss Me, Kate* went on tour, it frequently omitted much of the material in this song as well as others. Letters from Bella Spewack to Cole Porter about the show reveal censorship—for the British audience, for the radio audience, and later, when it was adapted for film, for the movie audience. By then the censorship department in Hollywood reigned, and films could not contain corrupting language or explicitly sexual scenes. Here, however, in the musical's New York premiere, the creativity of the adaptors could be exploited and enjoyed.

Moreover, the exuberance and creativity that are visible in the songs reflect in some ways the unabashed freedom of Shakespeare's lines, particularly those in Petruchio's first wooing of Kate. More frequently cut than included, they illustrate the verbal ingenuity of the principals, as she calls him a stool and they banter about wasps: "Who knows not where a wasp does wear his sting? In his tail." "In his tongue." When she tells him to start packing and leave, he asks, "What, with my tongue in your tail?"—lines usually excised (2.1.213–18). In *Kiss Me, Kate,* however, the exchange remains in the play-within-a-play (1.5, p. 42). And its retention may be due to another influence.

Kiss Me, Kate owed its popularity not only to its relationship to Shakespeare's play and to the mood of the post-war era, but also to one of its theatrical predecessors: the 1935 Alfred Lunt–Lynn Fontanne production of *The Taming of the Shrew.*[11] Starring one of the most famous American husband-and-wife acting teams, this production not only opened to rave reviews and toured the country from coast to coast, but it also brought the complete play back to the stage. By then, the "induction," which precedes act 1 and frames the play-within-a-play, had gone so long unperformed that a critic for a San Francisco newspaper thought it was Lunt and Fontanne's invention. The writer calls it "a *Shrew* with flourish" and says that the couple have added a "few flossy touches—a song, an ensemble, and a prologue, which they call 'an induction.'"[12] So much for his knowledge of Shakespeare's play. It is significant, however, that the restoration of the drunk, Christopher Sly, and the induction once more distanced the story of Kate and Petruchio. Once again the possible didactic message of male domination was overshadowed by the questions raised by the induction and by the talents of the performers.

Lunt and Fontanne were outstanding comic actors who worked brilliantly together. Their voices, his flat and quizzical in tone, hers resonant and lyrical, complemented one another. Their ability to capture the subtleties in Shakespeare's text and their skill at comic hijinks conspired to make this play one of their greatest hits. Brooks Atkinson of the *New York Times* wrote,

> All Shakespeare needs at any time is actors. He has them here. . . . For Petruchio and Katherine, well, here are the actors who have more gusto for every sort of stage hocus-pocus than any other performers on the American bulletin board.

Atkinson's column suggests the gaiety of the production and its possible influence on *Kiss Me, Kate*. He calls it a "carnival junket—adding a band with drums, a troupe of tumblers, a cluster of midgets, a pair of comic horses and some fine songs set to good beergarden music."[13]

The illustrations and the script, however, tell us more. See, for example, figure 0.1, with Christopher Sly watching the action from a box in the theater. It shows how Sly was incorporated into the production and yet was kept at a side. Other illustrations of that production help clarify his role. The Lunt-Fontanne production opens with a figure trying to play a flute on the stage. He leaves when Christopher Sly, the tinker, enters. "After several dizzy maneuvers [Sly] falls flat on the floor and remains there." Later, when he becomes an audience for the players, Sly occupies the stage box of the theater. The Lord who has ordered the players to perform joins him there, leaving the stage vacant for the troupe of strolling players.

The 1935 production's colorful troupe of players again set the pattern for *Kiss Me, Kate*. Their costumes, splashed with diamond patterns, resemble those in the later musical. A harpist, in a cart pulled by her comrades, leads them as they enter. Wrapped in capes, the players come next, wearing large black hats and white domino masks. Two of them, Petruchio and his servant, Grumio, stand to one side with a large hamper. As each actor approaches, the pair dig into the hamper and retrieve a bundled costume for that particular player. Meanwhile other members of the troupe rig the set, including the curtain that will soon be raised to reveal "an elaborate baroque picture of Padua." Clearly that production emphasized the concept of a play-within-the-play. Moreover, some lines were added for Sly to comment on the activities and conversation of the performers on stage before him. The illusion was clear.

Carolyn Hancock designed the production's gorgeous sets.[14] Ornate, scalloped flats framed the set both on the sides and above, thus creating the illusion of seeing a play within a play. Within that frame appeared two balconies, one on each side of the stage. The larger, on the right, was Kate's balcony in her father's house. Facing it, the smaller one on the left belonged to the inn where Petruchio and his friends met. Most of the action took place on Kate's balcony and in the piazza below. Large shuttered windows and a fountain with a statue filled the background space. Later, on Kate and Petruchio's wedding day, the background shifted.

Rectangular carved columns of the buildings provided a slightly different view, giving the area a sense of angularity and capturing the feel of an Italian street. At angles off the piazza, partially glimpsed stairs led to the two balconies. After the wedding, for the trip from Padua to Petruchio's house, Hancock retained the scalloped flats and designed a drop depicting green-topped trees against a white background. Equally imaginative were her designs for Petruchio's house and the final scenes.

Since the action of *Kiss Me, Kate* moved back and forth between the backstage space and the stage for *The Taming of the Shrew,* its sets only partially resembled those of the Lunt-Fontanne production. For one thing, when the players enter in *Kiss Me, Kate,* singing "We Open in Venice" and identifying themselves as "a troup of strolling players," they are already wearing their costumes for the play-within-a-play (1.4, pp. 24–25). By that time, the audience has seen the various backstage venues: the bare stage of the opening number; the fourth-wall view of Lilli's and Fred's adjoining dressing rooms; the spiral stairs to the upper dressing rooms, on which are set the dances of Lois and her hoofer boyfriend, Bill; and the shabby spot near the stage door for the working area backstage. Later, they see the outdoor space behind the theater where the players relax in the Baltimore heat between the acts.

The resemblance between the two works is more apparent in the costuming and certain staging techniques. Undoubtedly this was due to the fact that the shows had the same director, John C. Wilson, and the same costume designer, Lemuel Ayers. For instance, the players in *Kiss Me, Kate* enter dancing before a moving backdrop and singing, "A troup of strolling players are we / . . . That never ceases to troop / Around the map of little Italee." They then go into their refrain: "We open in Venice, / We next play Verona, / Then on to Cremona . . . / Then Mantua, then Padua / Then we open again, where?" (1.4, pp. 24–25). As they move through a series of verses, always with the same cities as locations, the players become weary. Instead of rigging the set, as their counterparts did in the 1935 *Taming of the Shrew,* they stop and the "Shrew drop," a background curtain, rises, and we are in Padua's streets, where a pavanne is in progress (p. 26). The play-within-a-play begins. Petruchio will "come to wive it wealthily" (1.2.75), Kate will enter after having thrown a watering can from the balcony, and Bianca's suitors will try to woo her. Spewack and

Porter adopt many of Shakespeare's lines, although they compress the plot and eliminate some characters.

The Lunt-Fontanne production may also have influenced *Kiss Me, Kate* in other ways. Both included a prominent career actress. Although not divorced, like Lilli and Fred, Lynn Fontanne and Alfred Lunt were the famous pair in that earlier production. Moreover, references to similarities between Lilli and Lynn appear in correspondence. From Hollywood, Cole Porter wrote to Bella Spewack about "two girls here working like maniacs for the Kate part." One had the charm for the role, the other, "apart from her voice which is a high mezzo, . . . look[ed] like Lynn Fontanne and Kate."[15] Some people have noted the resemblance of the names, Lilli to Lynn and Fred to Alfred.

But *Kiss Me, Kate* is not merely a backstage musical; it is also a story about relationships between husbands and wives, and between men and professional women. It explores the topic of strong women (such as Lilli and Kate, and even Bella Spewack) who are torn between their roles as wives and as independent professionals who have a clear sense of self. Spewack, for example, was brought up by a single mother, a Jewish immigrant, in great poverty. Determined to be a writer, she got a job with a socialist newspaper after graduating high school and later married another reporter, Sam Spewack. Although they frequently collaborated, *Kiss Me, Kate* was written when the two were estranged. Only later, after the musical had been registered with the copyright office, did Sam officially become involved. Sam was peripherally involved but had his own writing to pursue. His name is inserted by hand on one of the early typescripts of the play. However, he did not initially want to be included. Relations between husband and wife are not easy to decipher. It was a complicated marriage, as Bella, who loved Sam, also insisted on retaining her own individuality. We do know that an introduction to the 1953 publication of the play lists "Samuel and Bella Spewack" as authors.[16]

Hanya Holm, the musical's choreographer, is another example of a strong woman. Trained in Germany in the expressionist school of dance, she came to the United States and modified her style to capture the American ideal of freedom in the movements of her dances. Although she was briefly married in Germany and had a child, she is usually thought of as a single woman pursuing a career.[17] Holm believed one expressed one's soul through dance. This meant that no particular type of dance or dancer had a monopoly on the medium. Rather, it was available to all those who found an outlet in body movement. Her left-wing ideology supported the notion that anyone could dance, whether or not at a professional level. Her theory of dance was not elitist. In addition, she was the first person to copyright a choreography in the United States, and used the technique of Labanotation, invented by Rudolf Von Laban, with whom she had studied before leaving Germany.

Two other career women were also connected with this production. Both had previously been involved with the 1935 *Taming of the Shrew*. The first, the great comic actress Lynn Fontanne, continued to work on the stage after her marriage and starred with her husband throughout most of her career. In contrast, the second woman, Carolyn Hancock, the set designer whose work on *Taming of the Shrew* was so extraordinary, married Lee Simonson, also a set designer, had children, and retired. Her career apparently ended, whereas his soared.

The dilemma faced by women torn between their roles as wives and as independent professionals surfaces more and more in *Kiss Me, Kate* as Lilli, having fought with Fred onstage—she bites him, he paddles her so hard she can't sit down—vows to leave. She calls Harrison and promises to quit the show right in the middle. "I'll marry you tonight," she promises. "You don't know what that villain's done to me" (1.7, p. 48). Hearing her say she'll quit, Fred threatens to bring her before Actors' Equity, the union, for breach of contract. She doesn't care.

This is when the gangsters reappear. Earlier, they invaded Fred's dressing room to collect on the IOU Bill signed with Fred's name, and expressed the hope that he would "jostle his memory" and pay the debt. They obliquely threatened him, remarking to each other that he was a "fine-looking fella" and "clean-cut." "What a figger!" "What a profile!" "If I hadda do something to him, I'd cry like a baby" (1.3, pp. 16–17). They left, promising to return. Now they enter again and comment on the show. "What a performance," exclaims one. "You think the audience is getting it? It's way over their heads," the other responds. "Bunch of lowbrows," his partner notes. Suddenly Fred "jostles his memory" and admits signing the IOU, to their relief. When he assures them he would pay if he could, "if the show could run," they assure him that "it'll run. It's entertaining, vivacious, and calculated to please the discriminating

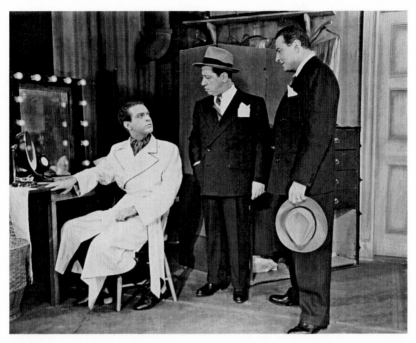

2.3. Gangsters invade Fred's dressing room and threaten him unless he pays the debt incurred by Bill, the hoofer who has won Lois's heart. The gangsters' presence and their later trailing of Lilli suggest the many obstacles women face in pursuing their dreams. *Spewack Collection, Rare Book and Manuscript Library, Columbia University, by permission of Lois and Arthur Elias.*

theatre-goer." These lines are exactly what Spewack and Porter would want to read in a critic's review. But Fred sadly tells them, "Unfortunately, Miss Vanessi, my co-star, is quitting" (1.7, p. 50). Opening the door to the other dressing room, he introduces them to her. Flattering her and moving their guns from one pocket to another, the gangsters tell her how much they are looking forward to seeing the rest of the play. Their shifting of the guns clearly functions as a silent threat.

A woman's freedom of action is again threatened. No longer is this the story of a husband who takes his wife home from the wedding ceremony, proclaiming that he will "protect" her from anyone who gets in his way, as occurs in *The Taming of the Shrew*. In its twentieth-century musical adaptation, the gangsters' "protection" substitutes for Petruchio's rule, which he exercises immediately after the wedding. The result is the same. Lilli is not free to make her own decisions. The gangsters, like Petruchio in the original, deny her the option of choosing her own path.[18] In fact, they shadow her during the entire second act, wearing costumes in an ineffective effort to blend in with the members of the cast.

When the curtain rises on act 2, the stage shows an alley outside the theater. The stage door is visible in the brick wall at the back. Light emanates from windows at the top of the wall. Three large packing cases stand on the left of the stage and a deck of oversize playing cards is visible on the right. Paul, who is Fred's dresser, and two dancers rise for the opening number, "Too Darn Hot." The stage directions for this number read,

> Music underneath "Too Darn Hot." At rear, three Negroes leaning up against wall as if completely overcome by the heat, and humming the tune. Negroes strike up song, 'Too Darn Hot." (2.1, p. 1)

As the music starts and Paul begins to sing "It's too darn hot," the dancers slowly move to accompany the song. "I'd like to sup with my baby tonight / And play the pup with my baby tonight / But I ain't up to my baby tonight / 'Cause it's too darn hot" (2.1, p. 4). As the music gets hotter and the stanzas become more explicit, the dancers increase their rhythm until it sizzles, as does the music. Meanwhile, Bill and dancers from the cast, still in their *Shrew* costumes, pour out of the theater fanning themselves. At the end of the song, Bill "joins the three Negroes in a hot dance specialty" and later is joined by the cast dancers. We are witness to a remarkable mixed-cast number that doesn't rely on racial stereotypes.

The song, like the gangsters' "Brush Up Your Shakespeare," refers constantly to women, but the references are not denigrating. Rather, they reflect on the singer. The dance sequence picks up his topic of male sexual fatigue. In one stanza, we hear, "I'd like to stop for my baby tonight / And blow my top with my baby tonight / But I'd be a flop with my baby tonight / 'Cause it's too darn hot." The second verse mentions the then famous Kinsey report on men's sexual behavior: "According to the Kinsey report, / Ev'ry average man you know / Much prefers to play his favorite sport / When the temperature is low." A list of men follows, reflecting the times and probably the roles they had in service: the G.I., the gob (sailor), and the marine, who "when the thermometer goes way up / And the weather is sizzling hot / Mister Gob [a sailor] / For his

squab, / A marine / For his queen / A G.I. / for his cutie-pie / Is not /
'Cause it's too, too . . . darn hot" (2.1, pp. 3–4).

Just as Porter's lyrics and music emphasize Baltimore's heat and its
effect on these men, Hanya Holm's dances capture that same quality.
Languid, sultry at first, the dancers' movements become more intense
before they suddenly fall back, exhausted. From time to time a dancer
jerks, jumping onto a bench or seeming to walk up a wall, only to fall
back into a slower rhythm. The dance alternates between intense anticipation of a sexual encounter and the realization of possible failure
because "it's too darn hot." In a description of the dance, a critic referred
to "non-intruding but atmospherically effective jitterbug passages for the
ensemble" that act as background for the main dance of the two principals. Holm does not turn to common stereotypes like minstrel show
dances or tap, but rather relies on an expressive dance that captures the
meaning of the song.[19]

The character of the "Too Darn Hot" dance and the fact that its
performers were black and later joined by white dancers suggest that
Kiss Me, Kate was in the vanguard in its treatment not only of women
but also of race. It reflects the optimistic years just after World War II
and is innovative in its mixed casting. *Kiss Me, Kate* is one of the earliest
examples of racial integration on the stage. Not only was Hattie, who
sang the opening song "Another Op'nin', Another Show," black, singing
together with the chorus, but so too were Paul and three original dancers
in the "Too Darn Hot" number.

The mixed cast remained in the stage productions, but not in the
1953 film version. There is no black performer in that movie. Moreover,
the "Too Darn Hot" number is no longer a description of a hot Baltimore summer night; it is a song and dance number at the beginning of
the film where Ann Miller, who plays Bianca, comes in with a band to
audition for a part in the play. She is clearly "out of the front line at the
Copa Cabana," as Lilli says: in other words, a night-club dancer. And her
number hints at strip-tease.[20]

Tremendously successful, the original stage version—with its mixed
cast, its exploration of the role of career women, and its breadth of vision—traveled the globe. A 1952 letter from a theater manager in Europe
discussed its success and its potential:

2.4. Donald Jones, a black dancer, performs in "Too Darn Hot" in the 1964 production of *Kiss Me, Kate* in Rotterdam. When the show first opened in New York City, it was notable for its multiracial casting, which went far beyond the usual practice of having blacks play only servants. However, when Hollywood adapted it, all blacks disappeared from the film and a showgirl auditioning for the role of Lois sang "Too Darn Hot." Gone was Hanya Holm's satiric dance of it being too hot a night for sex, its original meaning. *Vandamm Studio, Billy Rose Theatre Division, New York Public Library for the Performing Arts, Astor, Lenox, and Tilden Foundations.*

I am just shooting off a short note to tell you that we are opening on Friday, August 29th, here in Gothenburg and [from] what I have seen of the rehearsals it looks very promising. I have lined up another production in Stockholm, opening about the 26th of September with an excellent cast and after that will follow another production in Halsingborg, Sweden, and furthermore I have signed a Norwegian production in Oslo and another one in Bergen. I am thrilled with this result and I have not had a play for a long time, receiving such interest from various managements.[21]

Basically, this was only the beginning of *Kiss Me, Kate*'s adventures abroad. Meanwhile, back home, because of a horseback riding accident, Cole Porter no longer was ambulatory. Instead Bella Spewack traveled all over the globe, watching productions, making sure that the play was properly presented, and, most importantly, keeping Porter informed of all the details of its overseas successes.[22] Her voluminous and detailed correspondence suggests the extent of her activity. She mentions contracts in Italy and France, performances in Norway, Denmark, and Sweden, a live TV presentation in Japan, and a production in Israel. In 1961, she delightedly records a moment in Brussels:

EMBRASSEZ MOI, KATERINE opens at le theatre Royal de la Monnaie in Brussels on June 15. Yes, my love, in French with Belgian opera stars, [and] soloist dancers from the Sadler Wells Ballet.

After telling him, "your orchestra numbers 55!" she observes with obvious pride, "Ours will be the first American musical to play the opera house in English or French," concluding that "it will mark KATE'S thirteenth language!"[23]

In 1968, almost twenty years from its opening on Broadway, Bella was writing angrily to the head of the Russian Ministry of Culture at the United Nations Mission in New York. She complained that a Russian troupe was performing *Kiss Me, Kate* without really understanding how to perform an American musical. (The Russians had evidently acquired a bootleg copy of the play, since the printed text was not only out of print but had become a collector's item. At that time Russia was notorious for not respecting copyrights of works from outside the Soviet Union.) She wrote,

> I had the idea of bringing over our own English speaking company to
> show them how they can do their own. In every foreign country that
> we played it has always been in the language of the country. I made it a
> rule. The languages were the following: Norwegian, Swedish, Danish,
> Finnish, Icelandic, German, Turkish, Polish, Spanish, Italian, French,
> Hebrew, Czech, Hungarian, Dutch, Flemish, Ceylonese, Yugoslavian,
> Croatian, Serbian, Japanese.[24]

The range of languages by the year 1968 is extraordinary. The play had touched a human and global nerve. Its three-dimensional portrait of Lilli and the challenges she faces, as well as its integration of music, songs, and dances, all worked together to send a new American form abroad. The obstacles confronting Lilli as a woman had a particular relevance for those audiences. They appreciated the irony of her being "protected" by gangsters as well as the humor in their performance.

When the second act opens with her unwanted escorts trailing her, audiences wonder if she will ever be free. Soon enough, she is. The gangsters pause to telephone their boss, Mr. Hogan. It is the ideal moment to do so. "Hello, hello, Gumpy, I want to talk to Hogan. Mr. Hogan likes me to report in, Gumpy. Why should I call you MISTER Gumpy? Where's Mr. Hogan? Oh, I see . . . yea. Well, certainly, we'll pay you a visit, Mr. Gumpy." With great economy, Bella Spewack tells the story through one end of a telephone conversation. We learn it all. "I guess we got to declare a moratorium," the gangster reports to Fred, tearing up the IOU. "You see, Mr. Gumpy declared a moratorium on Mr. Hogan." Seconds later, Lilli enters in street clothes. She has no more "protection." Instead the gunmen tip their hats; "We want to say au revoir, Miss Vanessi," says one. "It's been a delightful experience," says the other. "Very educational," comments the first (2.6, pp. 32–33).

Lilli, now suddenly given her freedom, must respond to Fred's plea that she stay, but he also must come to terms with his own feelings. The soliloquy that Lilli sang at the opening of the play becomes Fred's acknowledgment of his feelings for her. She leaves the play, as she had sworn she would, and after she leaves he sings "So in love with you am I" (2.6, p. 34). An understudy must play Lilli's role.

Once again the collaborators have captured the quality of Shakespeare's *Taming of the Shrew*. Whereas Petruchio had seemed to bully

Kate, depriving her of food, of sleep, and of new garments, he and Grumio had repeatedly revealed the verbal games they played. In Shakespeare's play, Grumio mentions all the foods she might like, then denies them to her. More significantly, she hears them joshing about the sleeves of the new dress meant for her. "Well, sir," says Petruchio to the tailor, "the gown is not for me," "You are i' th' right, sir," replies Grumio; "'tis for my mistress." When Petruchio then orders, "Go, take it up unto thy master's use," Grumio indignantly responds, "Villain, not for thy life! Take up my mistress' gown for thy master's use!" (4.3.155–59). Only the audience heard their earlier exchange about "knocking at the gate," but this time Kate witnesses their interaction. She is learning, and will eventually outdo Petruchio at wordplay. She has caught on.

The collaborators have also captured the essence of the exchange when Petruchio asks Kate to kiss him on the street upon his return to Padua. "What, in the midst of the street?" she queries. "Art thou ashamed of me?" he responds. "No, sir, God forbid, but ashamed to kiss." When he replies, "then let's home again," her answer indicates a new warmth between them: "Nay, I will give thee a kiss; now pray thee, love, stay." For the first time we hear a term of affection from Kate, and it is returned with equal warmth by Petruchio: "Come, my sweet Kate." Shakespeare has redefined both Kate and her relationship with Petruchio (5.1.144–49). This she will observe at her sister's wedding feast, when everyone continues to be rude to her and only Petruchio champions her. She and he are now in alien territory.

In *Kiss Me, Kate,* Fred concedes that Lilli has won. He must adjust to an understudy. And then the orchestra plays at length, waiting for the understudy to appear. Instead, Lilli returns, having changed into costume. "What is your will, sir?" she queries, back in character as Kate (2.8, p. 39). They pick up from there. Clearly, this is not a one-sided abdication of self. She will remain in the theatrical milieu she loves with the man she loves; but, more than that, he has asked her to stay. "You walked out on me once," she says, referring to his earlier desertion of her before the play began. "But I came back," he replies (2.6, p. 34).

The line gives her strength, just as Petruchio's encouragement enables Kate to stand up for herself against the widow who maligns her at Lucentio and Bianca's wedding banquet. Hortensio, newly married to "the widow," listens as she belittles Kate. "He that is giddy thinks the world turns round," volunteers the widow (5.2.20). "I pray you tell me what you meant by that," Kate challenges (27). The widow replies,

> Your husband, being troubled with a shrew,
> Measures my husband's sorrow by his woe,
> And now you know my meaning. (28–30)

Rather than pulling hair or ranting, Kate merely states, "A very mean meaning." Petruchio quickly enters the fray with his supportive "To her Kate!" (31). When Kate, in her astonishing long closing speech, reprimands the other women for their attitude toward their husbands, she is drawing on this support. The contrast between the hostility Kate faces from others and Petruchio's supportiveness also affects the musical's closing song.[25]

Capitalizing on that shift in perspective, the collaborators revise the lyrics of the song "Kiss Me, Kate" at the play's close. When the song ends the first act, it is full of sly rhymes: "So kiss me, Kate, / Thou lovely loon, / E'er we start / On our honeymoon. / O kiss me, Kate, / Darling, devil, divine / For now thou shall ever be mine" (1.9, pp. 56–59). Her responses there match the hostility of his lines. In contrast, at the end of act 2 the song has a different tenor. Moreover, the collaborators have incorporated Katherine's line from *Taming*, "I am ashamed that women are so simple," as well as ten lines from her long closing speech and Petruchio's response "There's a wench! Come on and kiss me, Kate" into the song. Together, Kate/Lilli and Petruchio/Fred launch into a celebratory duet in counterpoint. Alternating lines call "caro," "carissimo," "bello," "bellissimo," while the chorus sings, "Kiss me, Kate," and Petruchio interjects, "Darling, angel, divine!" (2.8, pp. 40–41).

Criticism of Shakespeare's play often focuses on Kate's last speech. An extraordinarily long monologue addressed to the other women at her sister's wedding banquet, it seems to indicate her complete submission to Petruchio. As I have pointed out elsewhere, there are multiple reasons not to straightforwardly accept its text.[26] For one thing, its great length, forty-four lines, suggests irony. For another, it is difficult to imagine what a performer should do onstage while delivering it. The fact that directors frequently cut the speech rather than recognize the irony in its length suggests a refusal to reconsider its meaning. David Garrick, the great

2.5. "There's a wench! Come on and kiss me, Kate." Kate/Lilli and Petruchio/Fred are reconciled, on a gala set decorated with circles and diamond shapes and enhanced with scalloped streamers. Lilli and Fred have each learned that there must be some give and take in relationships between men and women. *Spewack Collection, Rare Book and Manuscript Library, Columbia University, by permission of Lois and Arthur Elias.*

actor-manager and showman of the eighteenth century, offered another solution. He divided the speech between Kate and Petruchio, giving the husband most of the lines. In this presentation Petruchio was instructing Kate in proper behavior, reflecting the eighteenth-century attitude toward women, one that persisted for a long time. The fact that Shakespeare introduces the tinker creates a distance between the audience and the story of Kate and Petruchio. One cannot read this, therefore, as a moral stance on woman's submissiveness. Rather, Shakespeare asks us to view the story through a double lens.

The Lunt-Fontanne 1935 production provided different responses than Garrick's to those questions. It not only retained the Tinker but, through its stage directions, suggested that Kate was not submissive to Petruchio. Moreover, it recognized the rapport between them. In it, Kate's lengthy speech on a woman's duty to her husband so astonished Petruchio that he crossed the stage, arriving at her side at the line "Then vail your stomachs, for it is no boot." She raised her hands above her head as she said, "And place your hand beneath your husband's foot," and with "my hand is ready," according to the stage directions, she "swings her hand to punctuate her meaning, it strikes Petruchio on the cheek."[27] Although she curtsies as she finishes her speech, the earlier action could not have been lost on the audience. There is no submission here. As for the Tinker, he was an important part of the early action.

Having, like Shakespeare's play, raised questions relevant to women, the musical doesn't try to solve them, but rather illuminates them in twentieth-century terms. The first adaptation of *The Taming of the Shrew* by a woman, *Kiss Me, Kate* expands the roles of the women characters, particularly Kate, and provides insight into the possible motivations for her actions. Although apocryphal stories exist that Bella Spewack did not initially want to write the book for this musical, the fact is that she did write it. Moreover, in the multiple drafts preceding the final version that was performed on Broadway, we hear a woman's voice and observe a woman's experience. They affect the overall story as well as the development of character. Whereas Shakespeare's Kate had no soliloquies, and David Garrick's Kate acted in a stereotypical manner, her soliloquies reflecting the thoughts of a vengeful Catharine, Bella Spewack's Kate/Lilli does have a soliloquy and expresses the thoughts and humanity of a twentieth-century successful career woman. The choices facing her are multiple and challenging. And while creating this character, Spewack, along with Cole Porter, also developed a Petruchio/Fred who must rethink some standard male reactions.

Although this is a musical comedy, the term "comedy" implying "happy ending," *Kiss Me, Kate* is also a representative of a new genre, the American musical, that was evolving at mid-twentieth century. Here was a moment in theatrical history when elements of realism joined with the exuberance and democratization of staging to express themselves in musical form. In *Kiss Me, Kate,* the sixteenth century and the twentieth century interwove and fed one another, and a woman's voice could be clearly heard in Shakespeare's enigmatic play.

THREE

The Challenge of Tragedy
West Side Story and *Romeo and Juliet*

Sharply jarring music plays; the curtain rises on a group of teenagers seen near steps leading up from irregular pavement in the left rear of the stage. Wearing dungarees and black sleeveless tops, they slowly move into a dance, leaping across the space with their arms fully extended. Here come the Jets, a gang from the streets of New York, who declare that they own the territory. As another teenager moves in, the group obstructs him with their bodies. He halts. They continue, at times leaping diagonally, then moving in a circular pattern that covers the stage. They snap their fingers. They own the space. Finally they allow the intruder to pass. He's the leader of the rival gang, the Sharks, and this is the prologue to *West Side Story,* told through dance.

It's 1957, and this musical, based on Shakespeare's *Romeo and Juliet,* has finally reached Broadway. It was a long time coming. Jerome Robbins, the choreographer, had first mentioned it to Leonard Bernstein, the composer and lyricist, eight years before: it seemed a "noble idea" worth pursuing. In Bernstein's "log" of the musical (which was not in fact written during production, but much later), he noted,

> January 6, 1949. Jerry R. [Jerome Robbins] called today with a noble idea. A modern version of *Romeo and Juliet* set in slums at coincidence of Easter-Passover celebration. Feelings run high between Jews and Catholics. . . . Street Brawls, double death—it all fits. But it's all much less important than the bigger idea of making a musical that tells a tragic story in musical-comedy terms, using only musical-comedy techniques, never falling into the "operatic" trap. Can it succeed? It hasn't yet in our country.[1]

Although this account may be fabricated, Bernstein did understand how challenging it would be to tell the "tragic story in musical-comedy terms." Here was a task worthy of his considerable talents: not merely telling a story with musical accompaniment, but dramatizing it in the new form of the organic musical, where all the parts—dancing, song, and plot—belong to an organic whole. Bernstein's language in this diary reveals the challenge.

Both Bernstein and Robbins had worked on musical comedies before. They knew the form of the organic musical from their earliest venture, *On the Town* (1944), a hit musical about sailors on a one-day pass who try to take in all of New York before being deployed overseas. Now they sought to expand the genre to tragedy, although no example of a musical tragedy existed. Unlike musical comedy, the norms of tragedy mean creating a work that will evoke an emotional response of pity and fear. The characters must be worth caring about. Their lives at the moment we meet them must contain the potential for success. And yet, elements of the environment and of the characters themselves must contribute to their ultimate failure. Despite their strengths and intentions, a happy ending eludes them. Always the ending is inevitable, no matter how accidental it may, at first, seem. The tragic hero must have great potential for good, yet be aware of the hazards he or she faces. Shaped by the world and by society, the hero is defined not only by language, but also in this case by song, dance, and setting. All must conspire to dictate the tragic ending.

Only a certain type of artist would want to try something so new and different, something so different there wasn't even any language to describe it. Both Bernstein and Robbins were such artists. Each had already won accolades in his individual field, and both loved pushing the boundaries separating classical expression from popular culture. Robbins had been named associate artistic director of the New York City Ballet in 1949 and had also created the dances for *On the Town*. He had since choreographed dances or directed such Broadway musicals as *High Button Shoes* (1947) and *Look Ma, I'm Dancing* (1948), and in the classical field had choreographed *The Cage* and *Fancy Free* for the City Ballet. Thus he was, at this point in his career, an important young choreographer who moved easily between popular director and classical dances. Favored by Balanchine, who by then was leading the City Ballet,

Robbins had dreams for the future of dance in this country. He believed that classical ballet should be combined "with other theater forms in order to experiment and achieve a wider horizon."[2]

Leonard Bernstein, the composer of the music for Robbins's dances in *On the Town*, was also a young man of much promise, who similarly moved between Broadway and the world of classical music. In August 1943, Artur Rodzinski, the conductor of the New York Philharmonic Orchestra, had offered Bernstein the position of assistant conductor. His job was to sit in on rehearsals and learn the scores so that, at a moment's notice, he could substitute for his boss or for any guest conductor of the Philharmonic. That moment came sooner than Bernstein expected. On November 14, 1943, Bruno Walter, a guest conductor, took ill. At the time, Rodzinski was snowbound in Stockbridge and gave the order to have Bernstein take the podium. He was a tremendous success.[3] Bernstein's career as a conductor blossomed, although he always had his hand in a multitude of endeavors. By 1949, when he received the call from Jerry Robbins proposing a tragedy based on *Romeo and Juliet* using musical comedy techniques, Bernstein was already well known and open to the suggestion of a new project.

The third of the collaborators, Arthur Laurents, had also been successful in his field, which in his case was the legitimate theater. His moving play *Home of the Brave*, produced in 1945, focused on four GIs, one of whom, a Jew, is the victim of his buddies' anti-Semitism even when on a dangerous mission in the Pacific.[4] The drama explores their interaction and illuminates the problems men face in trying circumstances. It suggests that each of us is different in some way. Hailed for its honesty, Laurents's play reflected his own wartime experiences of prejudice, although he did not serve in the Pacific. Like Robbins and Bernstein, Laurents did not restrict himself to the legitimate theater but also worked in Hollywood as a scriptwriter. Robbins suggested that Laurents be brought in to write the musical's book, and Bernstein agreed. "I didn't know Arthur very well," Bernstein observed later, "but I had been terribly moved by his play *Home of the Brave*."[5]

Only the fourth collaborator, Stephen Sondheim, focused his efforts entirely on writing musicals. Not interested in blurring the distinction between classical expression and popular culture, Sondheim sought to work within one field, expanding its possibilities. Eventually he came to dominate it. Not until 1955 did he join the others. In that year Sondheim, who had at one time auditioned for Laurents in another context, met him again at a party. Making small talk, Sondheim asked what Laurents was doing. When told the writer was beginning to start work on a musical, the young composer-lyricist asked, "Who's doing the lyrics?" According to the story, Laurents smote his forehead with his hand and exclaimed, "I never thought of you and I liked your lyrics very much."[6] Laurents then explained that originally Leonard Bernstein had planned to write both music and lyrics, but the music had expanded greatly. As he noted, it included "ballet music, symphonic music and developmental music."[7] In addition, Bernstein was finishing his work on *Candide,* a musical with operatic ambitions. Sondheim played some of his songs for Bernstein, who was impressed and asked Sondheim if he'd be interested in collaborating on the lyrics. Sondheim consulted with his mentor and neighbor, Oscar Hammerstein II, by then a successful composer of Broadway musicals. Sondheim asked his advice and Hammerstein enthusiastically encouraged the young man to grab the opportunity to work with these professionals. It would give him just the experience he needed. It did.

Not dependent on a specific setting of time or place, *Romeo and Juliet* dramatizes the fate of young lovers in rebellion against their parents and the rules of their society. Although the play shows us a young woman coming to maturity and suddenly becoming aware of her marriageability, Shakespeare does not particularly link her story to that of Verona. Rather, we feel that this story might have occurred in the dramatist's own world. The playwright seems to be asking for tolerance for youth even as he develops both characters—Romeo: brash, self-confident, blessed with the tongue of the Petrarchan lover; and Juliet: direct, thoughtful, committed to honesty, and not fully aware of the adult world she is entering.

How to turn this timeless tragedy into an American musical without making it either overly operatic or merely a play with music challenged these twentieth-century adaptors. Should it remain in Verona, with a prince and a friar, or should the adaptors place it in twentieth-century America? Might New York be a suitable environment? And who should make up the musical's cast as they move to the new organic form?

"An out and out plea for racial tolerance," Bernstein had written on his copy of *Romeo and Juliet* some years before.[8] He was marking up his copy of the play to try to transform it into a vehicle for racial tolerance and was referring specifically to the original idea of a Jewish-Catholic conflict. In 1949, when Robbins first relayed his idea to Bernstein, the composer believed racial tolerance to be an important enough theme for an American tragedy, fulfilling his concept of a "noble idea." Bernstein was Jewish, as were the other adaptors, and felt very strongly about bias against Jews as well as other peoples.[9] By this time, the world was becoming aware of the horrors of the Holocaust. Robbins had visited his grandfather in Rozhanka, a Polish shtetl, when he was six years old, and carried that wonderful memory with him, although the place had been leveled and all of its Jews transported to a ghetto and liquidated during the Holocaust.[10] Both men, Robbins and Bernstein, believed in the importance of racial and religious tolerance.

Unlike Shakespeare, the collaborators would tie their play to a specific time and place. They would set it in New York City in the present, with its gang wars and hostility between groups, and they would dramatize a world still marred by intolerance. That marked-up copy of *Romeo and Juliet* offers the first hints of where Bernstein hoped to move this tragedy and reveals some of his earliest thoughts for this adaptation. A short fight should interrupt the prologue as gang violence explodes. The notes also introduce the adaptors' earlier concept of two warring families—Catholic and Jewish—on the Lower East Side of New York at the time of the Mulberry Street festival celebrating Easter, which coincided with the Jewish Passover seder. Many of the names later used in *West Side Story* appear in its predecessor. Bernard, for example, who later became Bernardo, was Juliet's brother, and a character named Tante, meaning "aunt" in Yiddish, replaced Juliet's nurse. In a typescript for one of the early versions, the Romeo and Juliet characters are called Tonio and Dorrie. Tonio was later converted to Tony.

The plot is outlined on the small volume's inside cover, breaking it into scenes and indicating the setting: a street scene with pushcarts, "enter R. or Mulberry St. Festival or Easter=Passover." This reference to Mulberry Street places that first try in the heart of a New York City neighborhood. All four creators were probably familiar with Mulberry Street, since Robbins had an apartment at 24 West Tenth Street and Bernstein at 32 West Tenth Street in Greenwich Village.[11] For young men walking in New York, this was not too far from Mulberry Street and the

Lower East Side. They could easily have visited the Italian festivals on Mulberry Street. However, the creation of a space where both Italians and Jews met was one of the early fictions in this first version, which imagined that the two neighborhoods were one. The Jewish neighborhood was a distance from the Italian. Although these men were not originally New Yorkers, with the exception of Sondheim (who grew up in Westchester), they quickly made New York their home. Bernstein hailed from Boston; Robbins migrated from New Jersey; Laurents, although born in Brooklyn, moved to New York; and Sondheim, actually a New Yorker, grew up in Westchester. In fact, in the famous chapter on Sondheim and *West Side Story*, "I've Never Even Known a Puerto Rican," in Zadan's book on the lyricist, he protested that he was unfit to write about Puerto Ricans. He contrasted his wealthy background with their underprivileged one. But he was told that the musical is about star-crossed lovers and economics is not relevant here. And then, according to the story, the writer emphasized that "the have's and have-nots have more to do with their psyches than their economics."[12]

The adaptors knew that Italian Catholics lived on Mulberry Street. Jews lived nearby in another neighborhood. By placing Jews and Catholics in the same neighborhood, the adaptors were creating the first of many fictions that would later also pervade *West Side Story*. In this early version, Bernstein lists proposed scenes in a general outline, then jots down in Hebrew letters "Motzay Shabbas," which means "the end of the Sabbath" or "Saturday night," when the enforced leisure of the Sabbath ends.[13] Bernstein's Hebrew note reflects an unintentional response imagined through the lens of his Jewish upbringing and sensibility. He sought to capture this moment of intensity between quiet and the beginning of a new week—in this case, a new, unexpected relationship—in the scene. His outline then continues with the rest of act 1. It includes scene 3, the balcony; scene 4, a drugstore (with the comment "Rendezvous, Tante"); scene 5, a bridal scene; and the closing scene 6, "a street fight," which ends the act. Act 2 includes five scenes: "Chase (Roofs?)"; "Sex," including a plan to escape to Mexico; "Scene chez Capulet"; and two death scenes, the first "Romeo's death with Tante," and the second "Juliet's death."

Markings in this text also indicate characters. The adaptors interweave Shakespeare's names for characters with some of their newly invented names. For some time they retain R. for Romeo, even after he has a tentative new name. Next to the Prince's speech beginning "Rebellious subjects," where he addresses the Montagues and Capulets, Bernstein writes, "Priest? cop—? (kindly) Druggist? (Song on Racism)" and at the bottom of the page, enclosed in parentheses: ("It's the Jews"?) as a possible title for a song. The Nurse in *Romeo and Juliet* is a garrulous woman, Juliet's confidante early in the play; beside her long speech in act 1, scene 3, Bernstein jots the note "Talk, talk, number for Tante (used as running gag)."

In addition, in one of the scripts in the Bernstein Collection at the Library of Congress, the writer wonders about a possible shift of character: "Can Tybalt be Juliet's brother?" an idea further developed in *West Side Story*. There the Tybalt character has been transformed into Maria's brother, Bernardo. In that script, the adaptor or adaptors consider character motivation. Although only Bernstein's name is certain, because they were in his possession, the scripts did circulate among him, Robbins, and Laurents. In that particular script, the writer considers character motivation: "Perhaps R[omeo] has no one girl, but boasts of his promiscuity: defeated in this at dance (musically) when he meets J[uliet]."[14]

To understand *West Side Story,* one must go through *East Side Story.* The adaptors are particularly intent on creating a story that is set in a particular place and time. Moreover, the first attempts at *East Side Story,* which was known for a while as *Tonio and Dorrie,* show a partially conceptualized musical. In it, many of the initial issues of plot, setting, and characters confront Bernstein, Robbins, and Laurents, who by then had joined the other two. In a section of a very early draft still entitled *Romeo and Juliet,* but with the working title "Tonio and Dorrie" handwritten on it, they develop the Jewish—Catholic theme. The setting of scene 2 gives a flavor of the neighborhood. It also reveals elements that will continue to exist, although in a Puerto Rican setting, in *West Side Story:*

> We can see part of a candy-drugstore and/or its sign: Doc's; possibly something of Stronsky's Bridal Shoppe; a sign with the symbol for ko-sher; Pizzeria, etc. One or two floats with the Virgin; a couple of push-carts or stalls selling religious figures, souvenirs, penny candy, etc.[15]

A song is to be sung, followed by a dance. The next description introduces the Juliet character, here known as Dorie or Dorrie:

> Through the crowd come a lovely young girl, Dorie, her old Aunt, Tante (Both wear hats, traveling clothes) and, in a bright blue silk shirt, carrying two valises, Joshua. Dorrie runs forward to better see the dancers. . . . Dorrie finds herself thrown in Tonio's arms. Immediately the rest of the stage goes into half light, the music goes into half time, the dancers, watching Tina and Ricca again upstage, into half-tempo.

This captures the later meeting of *West Side Story*'s Tony (Romeo) and Maria (Juliet), who also meet accidentally at a dance. But they have not yet evolved as characters. Here we are still in the Jewish—Catholic tragedy; Joshua suddenly appears and jerks Dorrie away from Tonio. "Stick to our side of the street," he commands. Tante asks, "What's such a rumpus," then notes that Tonio is "a shane boychick," meaning a nice or good-looking boy. Joshua, on the other hand, sees only "a wop," a derogatory term for an Italian. In a more fleshed-out version of this scene, Dorrie identifies Joshua as her cousin.[16] The lines of prejudice have been drawn and the potential for tragedy already exists.

This small excerpt contains elements that will later be developed in *West Side Story*. Doc's drugstore, where Tony works and the Jets hang out, becomes an important location in the play. Stronsky's Bridal Shoppe is converted to the bridal shop where the Puerto Rican women work and where Tony and Maria take vows of marriage, with dressmakers' mannequins as witnesses. The line "Stick to our side of the street" also appears in a new form in the musical. Near its end Anita, who has evolved from Tante, who in turn derives from the Nurse, reminds Maria that Tony (derived from Tonio, the Romeo character) is "not one of ours" and sings, "Stick to your own kind." Even the stage's going dark and the other characters' moving into the background as the Romeo and Juliet characters discover one another appears here.

Four years after the end of World War II, racial tolerance was a significant enough theme to drive a tragedy. Returning troops could verbalize the horrors of racial intolerance. The idea that the Other, while different, need not be threatening deserved a chance. Bernstein's draft of a script, as well as Robbins's efforts with other scripts, seemed to be promoting the concept that people with different backgrounds could, nevertheless, get along. It demanded that they suppress learned prejudices, not allowing them to spring up again to inflame hatred and bias. People needed to recognize the innate goodness of others, despite the shape of their eyes, the color of their skin, or the accent of their English—which they might have only recently learned.

This was not the first post-war Broadway musical to explore the subject of racial prejudice. Richard Rodgers and Oscar Hammerstein II, the composing team that supplanted Rodgers and Hart when that earlier partnership dissolved, delved into the theme in their 1949 musical *South Pacific*.[17] Set on a South Pacific island where sailors long for a taste of home, the musical depicts two brief romances between Americans—a nurse and a lieutenant—and islanders. The nurse falls for a widowed planter, the lieutenant for a Polynesian woman. When the nurse discovers that the planter has two children who are natives, she rejects him, and similarly the lieutenant decides he cannot take the woman he loves home with him to his family's mainline Philadelphia society. Lyricist and composer create a song that explains what haunts these two Americans—"you've got to be taught" to hate, the lieutenant explains. The lessons must be ingrained "before it's too late," when you're very young. Since the romances are not the overriding story of the musical, which is celebrating the troops' victory in the South Pacific, they do not have primacy of place. Nevertheless, audiences are relieved when the nurse realizes her error near the musical's close, although the lieutenant has been killed in battle.

One is not born with prejudice. One learns it, just the way, perhaps, one learns table manners. The musical divides the tragic and happy endings. The nurse's change of heart closes the musical on a happy note. Not a completely honest response to the problems of racism, it allows the audience to avoid fully confronting the prejudice that still pervaded American society.

West Side Story, on the other hand, was based on a tragedy and developed its tragic dimensions from the start. Animosity existed among peoples of different racial backgrounds; skin color was not even introduced into the equation. Nor did the musical suggest that racism was a learned trait. It seemed to have been bred by the living conditions of the two groups who fought for space on the sidewalks of New York. But it had been learned in disadvantaged homes. In fact, the ballet near the musical's close, "There's a Place for Us," seems to temporarily suspend hatred. But the hatred is too deeply ingrained and overwhelms the two gangs. And although the Puerto Rican Maria can turn to Tony, who belongs to an "American" gang, and comment, "Imagine being afraid of you" (1.5, p. 28), different groups were indeed afraid of one another.[18] People with different accents and traditions aroused suspicion and hatred. When Leonard Bernstein wrote that his adaptation should be "an out and out plea for racial tolerance," he saw that it could be a tragedy rooted in a specific time and place and yet match the empty hostility of Shakespeare's Renaissance families.

This transformation of Shakespeare's tragedy also borrowed from the newly developing sphere of dance. Here Jerome Robbins brought new expansion and expression to the form. The New York City Ballet and the Ballet Theatre were beginning to vie for prominence. The School of American Ballet became the New York City Ballet in 1948, with Lincoln Kirstein as its first director.[19] Dance critics were exploring the meaning of modern dance, a style that many American dancers were pursuing. Deborah Jowitt writes that "allowing subject matter to determine form and movement choices" was a particularly "American" technique.[20] Much of this choreographic criticism was also related to the leftist direction of some of the modern dancers, such as Helen Tamiris and Anna Sokolow.[21] Then there was the direction Hanya Holm took. Her concept of the universality of dance and the ability of everyone to participate grew out of her reaction to her German training. Robbins's special gift was to join dance as an expression in the theater with the formal technique developed in ballet. All of these streams contributed to the explosion of dance numbers in *West Side Story*, where they expressed the emotions and even the thoughts of the characters.

In 1949, however, all of this was yet to come, and the three collaborators struggled to bring the Romeo and Juliet story to the stage as a musical tragedy. Arthur Laurents wrote of his attempt in January 1949 to take a crack at an outline for the Jewish-Italian story, "East Side Story." But he found the idea too familiar, resembling an earlier comedy entitled *Abie's Irish Rose*.[22] He also didn't see the possibility for tragedy. Rather, he found the idea stale. However he did send it to Bernstein, who by then agreed with Laurents.[23] The language between the gangs had become ugly—much worse than appears in *West Side Story*. "I didn't like the too-angry, too bitchy, too-vulgar tone of it," recalled Bernstein of that earlier try.[24] Eventually the collaborators discarded the project.

In that outline synopsis, however, the author introduces the basis for conflict that will set off the tragedy:

> Act One, scene one is an alley and has a stylized prologue showing
> the restlessness of the youth and indicating the various areas in which
> they let off steam, including gang wars, including with the Jewish gang.
> (These are Italians) Seeking trouble, they go to the street scene, where a
> festival is in progress.[25]

As the story progresses, Romeo is introduced with Mercutio, who in this version is his brother. (In *West Side Story,* they became best friends who live together, Tony having invited Riff to live with him and his family. "Four and a half years I live with a buddy and his family. Four and a half years I think I know a man's character," says Riff. He admits that he stays "'cause I hate livin' with my buggin' uncle, uncle, UNCLE!" [1.2, pp. 10–11]. The brief exchange establishes that Riff had no true home before moving in with Tony.) Later in *East Side Story* came "disclosure to R's gang that Juliet is a Jew." By scene 7, there is a "possible scene between the two brothers—Romeo and Mercutio." At another point, there is a reference to a moment when "Bernard, as gang chieftan [*sic*], meets Mercutio as gang chieftan [*sic*]." Like many other episodes, the scene of the main characters' make-believe wedding, with the mannequins as witnesses, occurs here much as it does in the eventual *West Side Story.* The use of the mannequins emphasizes the absence of family in the modern version. The young people have taken on themselves the responsibility for their future.

Not until August 25, 1955, when Laurents and Bernstein happened to meet in Los Angeles, did they once more think of *Romeo and Juliet.* According to a story that may be apocryphal, the two collaborators were sitting around the pool at the Beverly Hills Hotel and saw an article in the *Los Angeles Times* about gang warfare.[26] The article triggered an idea. They moved the story from the Lower East Side to the Upper West Side of New York and they altered the tension between groups from religious to ethnic. In Los Angeles, Mexican, Black, and Japanese gangs fought one another; there were no Jewish gangs (although there were

Jewish gangsters). Jews, who had migrated from the East and Midwest after the Second World War, had disappeared from the gang category and been assimilated as "Anglos" because of their skin color and, more importantly, because they could speak and write in English.[27] Laurents and Bernstein's meeting in Los Angeles led them to rethink their gangs and create a Puerto Rican gang and an "American" gang. The tragedy now turned on ethnic bias and conflict rather than religious differences and prejudices.

Once again the names changed: Dorrie, based on Juliet, became Maria; Tonio, based on Romeo, was shortened to Tony; and Juliet's nurse, at first known as Tante, became Anita. From Shakespeare's Benvolio and Mercutio, Romeo's cousin and buddy, the adaptors created a single character, Riff. A close friend of Tony's, Riff is the impulsive and hostile leader of the Jets, a position he inherited when Tony left the gang. Shakespeare's highly antagonistic Tybalt, Juliet's cousin, becomes her protective brother, named Bernard in *East Side Story* and Bernardo in *West Side Story*. However, Bernardo is not a loner, as Tybalt is, but social and Anita's boyfriend. Nevertheless, the structure of the musical follows Shakespeare's play very closely.

The language, however, does not. Instead, a new dimension enters this adaptation: the expansion of dance replaces the expressiveness of language. Shakespeare's Romeo, for example, uses an extended metaphor to describe Juliet in his speech below her balcony. He compares her beauty to the sun:

> But soft, what light through yonder window breaks?
> It is the east, and Juliet is the sun.

Extending the metaphor, he continues:

> Arise, fair sun, and kill the envious moon
> Who is already sick and pale with grief
> That thou, her maid, art far more fair than she. (2.2.2–6)[28]

Hyperbole characterizes Romeo's language, especially when it is compared with Juliet's far more direct vocabulary. "By whose direction foundst thou out this place?" she plainly asks. "By love," he replies, and then extravagantly expands, "He lent me counsel, and I lent him eyes. . . . Yet wert thou as far / As that vast shore [wash'd] with the farthest sea /

I should adventure for such merchandise" (2.2.79–84). Both the repetition and expansion of "far" to "farthest" and the imagery of a vast shore washed by oceans of water exemplify hyperbole.

In *West Side Story,* hyperbole characterizes dance rather than language. Extravagance of movement provides insights into character as Robbins borrows techniques from his ballet experience. Walter Kerr, in his New York review of the musical, described the rumble, the fight between the gangs in which individual gang members face off, and the ways Robbins used hyperbole of movement to capture and captivate his audience. The critic noted that Robbins exposed the deep hostility and youthful self-confidence of the gang members through dance. To Kerr, dance epitomized their passions:

> Mr. Robbins' conquest of space is absolute, and it is achieved by the apparently simple device of letting a dungareed dancer stand poised at the edge of the stage, his fingers flexing and his blood coming to a boil, until that secret spring of demonic violence that lurks in all of us is explosively touched and a pulsing, writhing figure is catapulted high in air. Venom becomes visible, splatters with the mindless fury of a thousand Roman candles.[29]

Hyperbole of motion expresses the characters' thoughts in extravagant ways. Whereas Shakespeare had offered language that boiled and exploded, Robbins was presenting moving bodies that seemed to do the same thing. The dancing exploded far beyond the usual limits of the Broadway stage. It was emotional and angry. Kerr's understanding of the ways dance could interpret ideas and characters testifies to Robbins's amazing skill. Peter Brinson, critic for the *London Times,* also wrote of Robbins's particular strengths, emphasizing the choreographer's ability to cross over from classic to popular. He saw Robbins as combining the dancers' backgrounds. "Robbins demands in his dancing the discipline of the ballet, but he takes his choreographic ideas from the streets."[30]

In his response to the idea of moving the play to the West Side of New York and dramatizing gang hostility based on ethnic and economic differences rather than religious ones, Robbins suggested the collaborators develop the musical's general structure. They did, and in a letter dated October 18, 1955, he responded at length to their outline. Politically astute, he started with a hearty endorsement of their plan, but then detailed particular areas needing changes. He insisted that some of the main characters had to be dancers, and disagreed about the development of Anita.[31]

Robbins's perceptive letter indicates his vision and experience. First he discusses the dancing, which, he argued, "will never be well incorporated into the show unless some of the principals are dancers." He conceded the importance of the Romeo and Juliet characters being singers, but insisted that Mercutio and Anita, as well as some of the gang members, be dancers. "It's a sorry sight and a back-breaking effort, and usually an unsuccessful one," Robbins wrote, "to build the numbers around some half-assed movements of a principal who can't move." Robbins didn't want to push the principals to the sidelines each time there was a dance. More than forty years later, in his 1998 tribute to Robbins, Harold Prince, co-producer of West Side Story, noted that this insistence distinguished Robbins's choreography. Agnes de Mille had brought story-telling to dance, but she had separated the dancers from the principal actor-singers in musicals. "Jerry took the process a giant step further," Prince said. He "required his actors to dance as well as sing. In West Side Story, the entire company filled all three assignments."[32] They would dance, sing, and act, reinforcing the qualities of the organic musical. This was a revolutionary idea at the time. Never before in a Broadway musical had dancers also sung and acted.

Robbins's second comment in that 1955 letter also greatly affected the final form of the material. Anita had replaced Tante and morphed into Bernardo's girlfriend, yet she still remained a good deal older than he. Revealing his sense of theater, Robbins noted that an older Anita would resemble "the typical downbeat blues torch-bearing 2nd character (Julie of SHOWBOAT, etc) and falls into a terrible cliche." Moreover, he warned that audiences might expect "my man done left me" blues. Overall, he vehemently objected to the age gap between Anita and Bernardo. Citing Laurents's description of her as an older girl "kicked by love," Robbins considered her "much too experienced for the gang or else [she] is sick, sick, sick to be so attached emotionally and sexually to a younger boy." The choreographer then advised his friend to rewrite Anita so that she was "either older, (like Tante) or younger with the same emotional timber of the rest of the gang."[33] Taking his advice, Laurents jettisoned all remnants of Tante and created a much younger woman, who is not only Bernardo's girlfriend but also Maria's confidant.

As *West Side Story* finally evolved, it dramatized the story of two teenage gangs: the Jets and the Sharks. American-born and living in the slums, the Jets call themselves Americans in contrast to the Sharks, who are Puerto Rican immigrants. When the play opens with the Jets lolling on their territory and asserting their rights to it, snapping their fingers, leaping across the stage, and preventing Bernardo, the leader of the Sharks, from moving through the space they control, they resemble Shakespeare's Montagues, who similarly vie with the Capulets. Although Shakespeare's two families do not control separate turfs, intense hatred between them causes conflict.

While the parallels between the works are not exact, particularly as the musical progresses and dance moves to the forefront, replacing language, the adaptors capture the intent of Shakespeare's text. As the four collaborators explained years later in an interview, they (especially Laurents, who wrote the book) followed the general pattern of Shakespeare's play, except in the closing scene. Robbins praised Laurents's skill in the adaptation, noting that "Arthur manage[d] to follow that story as outlined in the Shakespeare play without the audience or critics realizing it. . . . These scenes follow each other in a certain way in the long arc of the Shakespearean pattern, but everyone gets so caught up in our story that they don't refer back for similarities."[34] Actually, audiences seldom overlook the closeness of *West Side Story* to *Romeo and Juliet,* but they tend to focus on the similar passions of the lovers and their dedication to one another. The settings of the two works are so different that they often don't realize the other similarities between the shows. Probably much of *West Side Story's* setting is due to the skills of Robbins and Bernstein, whose dance and music help create a fictional world, one which is of its time—the mid-1950s—and its place—New York City.

Shakespeare's play opens with a sonnet prologue delivered by a chorus—a single character—who describes the tragedy that will befall a pair of "star-crossed lovers":

Two households, both alike in dignity,
In fair Verona, where we lay our scene,
From ancient grudge break to new mutiny,
Where civil blood makes civil hands unclean. (prologue, 1–4)

In contrast, a musical prologue opens *West Side Story.* Music and choreography replace language. The music itself draws on flute, clarinet, alto saxophone, and bassoon. Then horns, trumpets, and trombones play. Finally an electric guitar and pitched drums close the introduction as the cops blow their whistles.[35] Although the prologue in the musical originally included words, the adaptors felt that it might work better without them. Robbins proved this was the right approach by converting the prologue to a dance. According to Laurents, at Bernstein's request, Laurents wrote a scenario that suggested what the gangs were dancing about: "a line of action, incidents revealing character." The scenario would make "a seamless transition into dialogue" without any pause, or applause.[36] This is just what happens.

Onstage, as we have seen, the prologue introduces the two warring gangs by having them compete for space. After the Sharks are completely outnumbered, Bernardo leaves, only to return later on with his gang mates. By then, the triumphant Jets have temporarily left. Only A-rab, one of their younger members, remains. Whistling to himself, he zooms into a power dive pretending to be an airplane. "On this, TWO BOYS plummet down from the alley wall crashing him to the ground. His cries are smothered in harsh, sudden percussive music."[37] One critic compared the opening notes to the sound of the shofar, a ram's horn that is blown on the Jewish holiday of Yom Kippur; others have compared it to the opening of a Wagner opera.[38] When the Jets return and pick up A-rab, an all-out brawl ensues until a cop's whistle halts the fighting gangs.

Lieutenant Schrank and Officer Krupke confront them. "Well, if it isn't Lieutenant Schrank!" sardonically observes Riff/Mercutio, the leader of the Jets. "And Officer Krupke," notes Bernardo, the leader of the Sharks. But the cops will have no part of the gang wars. Moreover, they reveal their racial intolerance: "Boy, what you Puerto Ricans have done to this neighborhood. Which one of 'em clobbered ya, A-rab?" solicitously asks Schrank. The boys refuse to fall for the officer's apparent friendliness. "As a matter of factuality," volunteers Riff, "we suspicion the job was done by a cop" (1.1, p. 2). Clearly, cops and gangs have a long record of hostility, even longer than that of immigrants and Jets.

The scene also had a contemporary specificity. "Didn't nobody tell ya there's a difference between bein' a stool pigeon and cooperating with the law?" asks Shrank, to which Riff politely answers, "You told us the difference, sir. And we all chipped in for a prize for the first guy who can figure it out" (1.1, p. 3). According to Laurents, who wrote the script for *West*

Side Story, this conversation was a veiled reference to Robbins's appearance before the House Un-American Affairs Committee in 1955, when the choreographer named names, as he testified to his short-term membership in the American Communist Party and identified fellow Party members.[39] HUAC saw its mission as the investigation of those possibly affiliated with communists. People, particularly in the theater and film industries, lost their jobs and were banned from working in their fields. Some committed suicide, some fled to Europe, some attempted to work under pseudonyms. The virulence of the times destroyed many lives, as some of the people who named names ruined the lives and careers of former friends. Thus, woven into the musical are comments on the political atmosphere of the times, while the opening dance prologue speaks to the growing importance of dance in the development of musical theater. Shakespeare's timeless play allows the creators of *West Side Story* to yoke together two of the most contradictory developments of the era: the devastations of ethnic tension and political strife and the openness and creativity of dance.

In Shakespeare's Verona, the Prince interrupts the fighting: "Rebellious subjects, enemies to peace, / Profaners of this neighbour-stained steel," he exclaims. Then, as if to himself, "Will they not hear?" And he announces his edict:

> On pain of torture, from those bloody hands
> Throw your mistempered weapons to the ground,
> And hear the sentence of your moved Prince. (1.1.81–82, 87–88)

Noting how the brawls of the two houses are often prompted by an "airy word," he promises that the next time this happens, their "lives shall pay the forfeit of the peace" (97). Although Lieutenant Schrank and Officer Krupke lack the style of Shakespeare's Prince, nevertheless they too are responsible for keeping the peace among teenage gangs.

After the cops leave, Baby John, another Jet, observes his friend's pierced ear. "Them PRs, they branded you!" he exclaims in shock, while Riff asks, "Which one of the Sharks did it?" A-rab, imitating the Puerto Rican accent, replies, "Bernardo. Cause I heard him say: thees ees for stink bombin' my old man's store." Another Jet, Action, swiftly interjects, "You shoulda done worse. Them PRs're the reason my old man's gone bust." But Riff wonders, "Who says?" Action responds, "My old man says." Another less formidable Jet interrupts, "My old man says his old man woulda gone bust anyway." "Your old man says what?" challenges Action. The gang members lack cohesiveness until they face an "other." Suddenly they are all blaming the Puerto Ricans. The use of the epithet "PRs" reflects their bias. They want revenge (1.1, pp. 4–5).

These scenes are an adaptation of the opening action of *Romeo and Juliet,* in which a quarrel breaks out between servants of the Capulets and of the Montagues. "Do you bite your thumb at us, sir?" asks Abraham, a Capulet servant; biting the thumb was a rude gesture. "Is the law of our side if I say ay?" asks Sampson of his fellow Montague servant. "No," Gregory replies, so Sampson equivocates: "No, sir, I do not bite my thumb at you, sir, but I bite my thumb, sir" (1.1.44–51). And the quarrel escalates until one of the principals of the House of Montague, Romeo's cousin Benvolio, enters.

Following these exchanges, Tony/Romeo then Maria/ Juliet appear in their respective plays. First the men enter, each in conversation with a friend. Tony is arguing with Riff about going to a dance at the gym of the local social hall that night. Romeo is arguing with his cousin, Benvolio, about finding another girl instead of pining after Rosaline, who is not interested in him.

That first introduction of Tony indicates he has jettisoned his gang affiliation—or at least he thinks he has—and has gone straight. When the musical opens, he works as a delivery boy for Doc, the druggist. As far as Tony is concerned, he has outgrown gang membership. But loyalty and affection still tie him to Riff, and ultimately entrap him. This inevitably leads to tragedy.

Since Riff grows out of two of Shakespeare's characters, Mercutio and Romeo's cousin Benvolio, here the adaptors rely on Benvolio for source material. Benvolio pleads with Romeo to look at other women. Only that way will he get over his crush on Rosaline, who will have nothing to do with him. But Romeo objects. He will wait for her despite rebuffs. When he discovers she will be at a ball the Capulets are planning, he decides to crash the party, along with his two friends. The three young men will go masked, in order to get in without being recognized as Montagues. In the musical, Tony is not hoping to see a specific woman at the dance at the gym, and he is not interested in challenging the Sharks. But he finally agrees to join his friend Riff in attending. The adaptors have strengthened his ties to Riff beyond Romeo's to his friends, in order to set the tragedy in motion.

To develop this portrait of Tony further, the adaptors give Riff a song boasting of the Jets' superiority. This is childishness to Tony. "The Jets are the greatest," Riff asserts, trying to win his friend. "Were," responds Tony. "Are. You found somethin better?" challenges Riff. "No, but—" Tony then describes a feeling of "something coming": 'round the corner, down the street (1.2, p. 11). He resembles Romeo, who also feels that something is about to happen just before he and his friends go to the ball. But Tony is indulging in wishful thinking, while Romeo's premonition is ominous:

> . . . my mind misgives
> Some consequence yet hanging in the stars. (1.5.106–107)

And yet he goes to the ball, because he hopes to see Rosaline. Tony, on the other hand, goes only as a favor to Riff. Tony is more open, and in many ways more naive, than Romeo. Riff's departing lines "Who knows? Maybe what you're waitin' for'll be twitchin' at the dance" (1.2, p. 12) sound like Benvolio's invitation to Romeo to meet someone new and compare his former love's "face with some that I shall show / And I will make thee think thy swan a crow" (1.2.86–87).

Through Tony's song "Something's Coming," the adaptors give a sense of his mixed emotions before he meets Maria. In the organic musical, song moves the plot along. Actually "Something's Coming" grew out of Laurents's script. According to his collaborators, he was most generous in permitting them to cannibalize his writing for lyrics if it would help the musical. Tony's song indicates his character even before he meets Maria:

> Could be! . . .
> Who knows?
> . . . .
> It's only just out of reach,
> Down the block,
> On a beach. . . .
> Something's coming, don't know when, but it's soon—
> Catch the moon,
> One-handed catch! (1.2, p. 13)

The references shift from immediate, nearby things to the moon and its evanescence. This is abstract language, a stream of consciousness, as he jumps from "Catch the moon" to "One-handed catch!" But it is also American in its reference to baseball. "Something's Coming" captures Tony's and Romeo's sense of anticipation, hope, and uncertainty.

In both *Romeo and Juliet* and *West Side Story*, the Maria/Juliet character appears shy and protected, reflecting the mores of her society. But the plays also stress the young women's sudden growth to adulthood, as each of them faces the issue of marriageability. Whereas Juliet, a member of a prominent family, is introduced in a scene with her nurse, Maria first appears as a seamstress in a bridal shop. Juliet listens to her mother's admonition to consider Count Paris as a suitor, and responds, "I'll look to like, if looking liking move; / But no more deep will I endart mine eye / Than your consent gives strength to make it fly" (1.3.97–99). Maria, brought from Puerto Rico by her brother as a possible bride for his friend Chino, is about to attend her first dance. Anita converts a communion dress to a dance dress for her, and Maria begs to have the neckline lowered. "One month have I been in this country—do I ever even touch excitement?" she complains, noting that Chino doesn't stir any feelings in her. "When I look at Chino, nothing happens." Nevertheless, the dress excites her. Once she tries it on, she asserts, "Tonight is the real beginning of my life as a young lady of America!" (1.3, pp. 14–16). It is the immigrant's dream.

Once again the adaptors make their musical place-specific. Maria, now a "young lady of America," will make new choices. She will not hold on to, or retreat into, her Puerto Rican background. Unlike Juliet, who must choose a suitor from her own class who is approved by her family, Maria has been freed—or at least she thinks she has—to choose from outside her group of acquaintances. And indeed, she meets Tony in the next scene, at the gym.

To move to that scene, Oliver Smith, the designer of the musical, created one of his most successful scene changes. The set spins—a technique Smith used with such skill in this production—and slides out of view as gaily colored streamers pour down, and the dance in the gym of the social hall comes alive. Smith, already well known as a set designer, artist, and producer, was inspired, creating contrasting worlds in *West*

3.1. The Sharks and the Jets, two rival teenage gangs, meet on the neutral territory of the social hall's gym for a dance. Riff, the leader of the "American" Jets, a cigarette dangling from his mouth, is facing off against Bernardo, wearing a dark suit, the leader of the Sharks, a Puerto Rican gang. Members of their respective gangs watch, some beginning to dance, aware of the cop (on the far right) supporting the social worker who organized the dance.   *Photo by Fred Fehl, courtesy of Gabriel Pinski.*

Side Story and juggling them through the use of lights as well as the mechanics of movement. The whirling set with its streamers contributes to the shift of action as first the Shark girls, then the Jet girls, enter, followed by the men of both groups. Inside the gym, Glad Hand, a social worker, attempts to ease the hostility between the gangs by organizing dances so that their members will mix, but to no avail.

The dance at the gym begins with instrumental and blues music.[40] According to one source, Robbins went to a high school dance in Spanish Harlem to see how the kids danced and discovered that their movements didn't resemble anything he had ever seen. The couples danced together for a few bars, then separated, the two dancers seemingly in their own intense worlds. "When you look at the floor, each person seems to be having a ball on their own, but I'm told that the partners know damn well who they're dancing with," Robbins wrote to Tanaquil Le Clercq, a friend and fellow dancer.[41] He sought to capture this quality in his choreography of the dance at the gym.

The energetic dancing suddenly ends when Bernardo, Chino, Maria, and Anita arrive. One by one, members of the two gangs withdraw to opposite sides of the hall. Then, under the direction of Glad Hand, with Officer Krupke standing quietly but firmly on the side, they give the idea of dancing together a chance—except that they are competing rather than dancing cooperatively. First comes a promenade, followed by a fast mambo. In the mambo, the lead couples of each gang—Bernardo and his girl, Anita; and Riff and his girl, Velma—dance to the cheers of their supporters.

Although the text indicates that the meeting between Tony and Maria occurs pretty quickly, it actually takes some time to happen onstage.[42] Here Robbins's choreography heightens the tension between the groups, a feeling that spills over onto the audience. Even before Tony and Maria see one another, the lights dim and the crowd seems to disappear. From opposite sides of the hall, Tony and Maria approach each other.

Both dance scenes—the ball in *Romeo and Juliet* and the dance at the gym in *West Side Story*—mark the meeting and the moment the young couple feel instant love for one another. Juliet appears smitten by the handsome young Romeo, who has some ideas of how to win a woman:

> If I profane with my unworthiest hand
> This holy shrine, the gentle sin is this,
> My lips, two blushing pilgrims, ready stand
> To smooth that rough touch with a tender kiss. (1.5.93–96)

he begins, offering the first quatrain of what will be a sonnet. Although overwhelmed by him, the young Juliet knows how to answer, matching his quatrain with another:

> Good pilgrim, you do wrong your hand too much,
> Which mannerly devotion shows in this:
> For saints have hands that pilgrims' hands do touch
> And palm to palm is holy palmer's kiss. (97–100)

Shakespeare exhibits his skill as a poet as he develops the last quatrain in the conversation between them. Juliet may be young, but she has already learned to respond to flirting. As the sonnet ends, they exchange

3.2. Anita and Bernardo exhibit their skills to a crowd of cheering Sharks. Dance functions as structure, motion, and expression as well as tragedy in *West Side Story*. Jerome Robbins was not just the musical's choreographer, but actually conceived the play. He captures in his dances and the dancers' movements the emotions, nuances of meaning, and tragic tone of Shakespeare's *Romeo and Juliet*. Extending Shakespeare's hostilities of families to rival ethnic gangs, the collaborators explore the tragic consequences of bias and unwarranted hatred, showing how they maim the lives of young men and women.   *Photo by Fred Fehl, courtesy of Gabriel Pinski.*

kisses before the nurse interrupts them: "Madam, your mother craves a word with you" (111). And who is her mother, asks Romeo? Why, the lady of the house.

Maria is similarly overwhelmed by Tony. "You're not thinking I'm someone else?" he asks, and the young Puerto Rican girl responds, "I know you are not." A quiet cha-cha plays in the background while the two briefly converse and Tony "impulsively stops to kiss her hands; then tenderly, innocently, her lips." At that "Bernardo is upon them in an icy rage," commanding, "Stay away from my sister!" Like Romeo hearing the news that Juliet's mother is the lady of the house, Tony is taken aback by Bernardo's fury. Abruptly, he orders Chino to take Maria home (1.4, pp. 20–21). As the scene comes to a close, Tony hears Chino say, "Come, Maria" and thus learns her name (p. 23), which will inspire his song "Maria" as he goes searching the neighborhood for her. The song illustrates the lyricist's and composer's skills.

The dance scenes in both play and musical eventually lead to their respective balcony scenes: Romeo overhears Juliet's confession of love while she is standing above him on a balcony; and Tony, having found where Maria lives, serenades her as she stands on her fire escape. Both men also realize they are on alien territory. Juliet warns Romeo during the balcony scene, "The orchard walls are high and hard to climb, / And the place death, considering who thou art" (2.2.63–64). Nevertheless, he seems brashly unafraid, just as Tony disregards Bernardo's warning, "Stay away from my sister." Interestingly enough, Romeo calls Juliet "bright angel" (26) and Tony's line "I'll never stop praying, I'll never stop saying 'Maria'" (1.4, p. 25) implies religious devotion.

Moreover, in this famous balcony scene, Shakespeare draws a picture of the young Romeo through language. His praise of Juliet, his vows of love all exhibit the language of the Petrarchan lover. His comparisons of Juliet to the elements frighten her, since hers is a language of moderation and direct address. When he says, "Lady, by yonder blessed moon I vow, / That tips with silver all these fruit-tree tops" (2.2.107–108) he is expanding into hyperbole. She stops him, charging him, "O, swear not by the moon, th' inconstant moon, / That monthly changes in her circled orb, / Lest that thy love prove likewise variable" (109–11).

In *West Side Story*, hyperbole becomes the bodily language of the dancers. Jerry Robbins always wanted to know what a dance was about, to understand where it was coming from and where it was going. Sondheim told of an experience with Robbins during rehearsal. Having finished writing "Maria," which he was delighted with, he wanted to play it for Bernstein. But he wasn't around, so Sondheim played it for Robbins instead, who immediately asked,

> "Well, what do you see happening on the stage?" I said, "Well, Tony is singing this love song. . . ." Jerry said: "Well, what's he doing?" I said, "He's singing. . . . He's full of emotion." He said: "You stage it!"[43]

Sondheim explained that Jerry taught him the importance of staging any song he wrote, even if the director discarded his suggestions. In "Maria," staging becomes of particular importance as Tony moves from one area of the stage to another in his search before finally finding her on the fire escape of her tenement. Their brief conversation continues as they sing, "Everywhere I go, you'll be." The stage directions indicate, "And now the buildings, the world fade away, leaving them suspended in space" (1.5, p. 28). What has happened here is that song and staging have taken the place of Shakespeare's dialogue.

Arthur Laurents's brilliance emerges here as he interweaves elements from Shakespeare's play into this scene of the lovers on the landing of the fire escape. Shakespeare's scene ends with Juliet arranging with Romeo how they will plan their next meeting. Like Juliet, Maria calls her lover back several times to give him further instructions as to how and where to meet her the next day. He is to come to the back door of the bridal shop. The scene in the musical ends with a joyous "Tonight," a duet sung by the lovers. The tenement walls temporarily disappear, returning when Maria finally exits. The romance will not end happily, but at this moment hope and optimism prevail as the lovers sing to each other, "Good night, and when you dream, dream of me" (1.5, p. 31).

When the world Tony and Maria live in seems to vanish, Smith's sets become a metaphor for the distance between dream and reality. This contrast forms another motif throughout the musical. The sets complement the duet between the lovers. When Maria's father calls her, interrupting the lovers' conversation, and she retreats into the apartment, the stage direction reads, "She goes inside" as the buildings begin to come back into place. This manipulation of scenery occurs again during the dream ballet "Somewhere, There's a Place for Us." In that song, however, Maria and Tony dream of a world where they might live together, whereas at the end of the scene on the fire escape they make concrete plans for the next day.

The next major meeting of the lovers occurs after three scenes that heighten the drama, propel it forward, and introduce the forces arrayed against them, that will inevitably lead to tragedy. In the musical, the scenes concern preparation for the rumble. The first is indirect, because Bernardo and Anita first discuss Maria and their parents' ignorance of the ways in America. It culminates in the song "America." The second more directly expresses the Jets' fear and anticipation in "Cool" while they await the arrival of the Sharks. The third shows how people in the outside world magnify the hostility and intolerance between the gangs, personified by Lieutenant Schrank. Laurents seems to be asking, "If the police exhibit such intolerance, how can society ever achieve tolerance?"

The first of these scenes brings Bernardo and his friends home from the dance to prepare for the rumble. But first he must check up on his sister. He calls her and is reprimanded by Anita, who tells him, "She has a mother, also a father." "They do not know this country any better than she does," he replies. To that Anita asserts, "You do not know it at all" and expands on the virtues of America in the song "America" (1.5, p. 31).

This emphasis on place in *West Side Story,* specifically on America, reiterates the importance not only of America, but also of New York. It is far greater than we find in Shakespeare's *Romeo and Juliet.* The only time we become aware of the importance of Verona is when Romeo mourns his banishment, not because he must leave his hometown, but because he must leave Juliet. In *West Side Story,* awareness of the city and its forms, its cage of buildings all pressed together, its young people with no place to spread their wings and breathe, pervades the musical. The concept of America will echo through the rest of the musical, stressing the fight against bias. In the song, Anita and her friends compare the island of Puerto Rico with America, their adopted homeland. Although it starts with

> Puerto Rico, . . .
> You lovely island . . .
> Island of tropical breezes.

Anita quickly interrupts with

Puerto Rico . . .
You ugly island, . . .
Island of tropic diseases. (1.5, p. 35)

This is a wonderful shift from the usual praise of that "island of tropi-
cal breezes." Sondheim's lyrics reveal his originality and his skill with
language as he offers off-beat rhymes and interesting ideas in the debate
he creates between Anita and the new immigrant, Rosalia. Most of the
women side with Anita, as she counters many of Rosalia's romanticized
images with a strong dose of reality. The song expresses the range of
opinion among the women. In both song and speech, it counterbalances
the hostility to the Puerto Rican immigrants. (In the film version, the
song lost its kick; no longer a debate among women, it became a contest
between the women and the men. The film eradicated the differences
among the women and based the debate on gender.)

Dance complements the song. Robbins's long training in ballet here
integrates with his own more recent development as a choreographer.
He had learned techniques from Balanchine, who had already brought
ballet to Broadway in the 1930s. Robbins knew how to tell a story through
dance. He was aware of how movement could influence audience response and how dance could translate and intensify ideas. Working with
Bernstein's music, with its quick rhythm, its castanets, tambourines,
and Spanish guitar, Robbins created dance that subtly interweaves ballet movements and a version of island dancing. The music stresses the
character of the immigrant, in all its brashness and vivacity, while the
choreography illuminates the women's dual allegiance. "I like the island
Manhattan. / Smoke on your pipe and put that in!" sings Anita, evoking the image of Indians and white men smoking a peace pipe. Anita,
dressed in lavender and wearing orange shoes, and the other women, in
pinks and purples, swirl about the stage as they sing the chorus:

I like to be in America!
OK by me in America!
Everything free in America!
For a small fee in America![44]

The lilt in Anita's voice captures the quality of the music. She picks up the
internal rhyme of "be," "we," "free," then "fee," while Sondheim's lyrics
emphasize "America" and Robbins's choreography links their old and

new homes. The song provides a momentary pause—a comic interlude—in the hostile relations between the gangs before they meet at Doc's.

In the second scene the Jets, too, are preparing for the showdown. Nervously awaiting the arrival of the Sharks, they listen to their leader, Riff, who tells them to "cool it." Bernstein and Sondheim composed the song "Cool," while Robbins created a dance that shows just how "uncool" they are. Their jerky movements indicate a lack of control, suggesting that they may be on drugs. First they display a lassitude, as if overcome by fear; then a dancer suddenly thrusts out a limb in a manner that reveals the presence of drugs in his blood. Then there is a slump into near sleep, then again a brief, awkward, angular dance. This has nothing of the gliding movement, nonchalance, and large, open, circular pattern of the opening "prologue." Riff instructs them,

> Turn off the juice, boy!
>> Go man, go
>> But not like a yo
>> Yo school boy—
>> Just play it cool, boy,
> Real cool!
> Easy, Action.
> Easy.

Again, the dance reflects what Riff is describing. Three girls dance with the guys. They are near the ground, moving at a crawl. Discussing Robbins's technique, Jennifer Tipton—the lighting designer who had worked on most of Robbins's ballets since the 1970s—noted how important telling a story was to him. "I think he made ballet American. In working with Jerry, whatever he did, he managed to tell the story through movement. . . . In theater, he began the whole idea of telling serious stories through movement. And I don't think there is anyone else doing that."[45] "Cool" continues until the Sharks arrive and the negotiation to determine the terms of the rumble begins. The guys separate, and the dance is punctuated with the word "Go," which they call out as they snap their fingers to indicate they are ready.

The third scene shows the gangs at Doc's. All of their hostility to one another spills over as they set up the specifics of the rumble, discuss weapons, and decide on place and time. Suddenly Tony enters and alters the dynamics. Hearing them argue about weapons, he scornfully says,

"Bottles, knives, guns!" accusing them of being chicken, and convinces them to fight with no weapons—merely fists. He challenges them to jettison their weapons and make it a fight between two principals, "each gang choosing its best man."

During this preparation, the subject of bias emerges in all its venom in the withering character sketch of Lieutenant Schrank, who comes into the store at this moment. Suspicious that a rumble is in the offing, he is condescending in his attitude toward both the immigrants and the Jets, the "hoodlums" of the street. Lifting a pack of cigarettes from Doc's counter, Schrank explains his need to "smoke in the can," and then lets off a series of invectives addressed particularly to the Puerto Ricans. In a further effort to ingratiate himself with the Jets, Schrank talks of his power to call on the law to assault the Puerto Ricans. In this extensive monologue, he insults both Jets and Puerto Ricans in his effort to discover the rumble's locale. At the close of his rant, only Tony and Doc remain, the others having silently left. "Well, you try keepin' hoodlums in line and see what it does to you," Schrank mutters, then walks out the door. "It wouldn't give me a mouth like this," observes Doc.

Whereas *West Side Story* is firmly embedded in a cultural context, *Romeo and Juliet* is much more self-contained. The three scenes that follow the balcony scene in the Renaissance play revolve around the forthcoming marriage of the two principals rather than immigrants, drugs, or anticipation of a rumble. The first scene is set in Friar Lawrence's garden, where he is working among the herbs. He is astonished when Romeo arrives, speaking passionately of Juliet. Ultimately the Friar agrees to marry the two young people, hoping their marriage will reconcile their families. Once again the focus of the action is on the relationship between the principals rather than on the specificity of place.

Romeo next rushes off to get the news to Juliet, only to run into his friends. Protesting that he gave them the slip the night before, they banter with him until the Nurse and her man appear on the horizon. Shakespeare's preoccupation with language again dominates. "A sail, a sail," declares Romeo, observing her sail-like shape and size (2.4.102). Although insulted by him and his friends, she forgives him, determined to deliver a message from Juliet. A bit frightened by the assertiveness of the men, she nevertheless pursues her mission, querying Romeo about his intentions toward her young charge. The scene further rounds out the portrait of Romeo's world and further delineates his friends, particularly Mercutio, offering more evidence of his attractiveness, quick wit, punning, and complexity. We will miss Mercutio when he dies.

Still another comic scene, again steeped in language, follows. This time it revolves around the Nurse's delivery of Romeo's message to Juliet. Delighted with her role, the Nurse teases Juliet, constantly interrupting herself with irrelevancies as she is about to get to the point. "Your love says like an honest gentleman, and a courteous and a kind, and a handsome, and I warrant a virtuous—where is your mother?" Exasperated, and aware of the nurse's technique, Juliet explodes, "Where is my mother? why, she is within, / Where should she be?" (2.5.55–59). Finally, the nurse delivers the message. They will be secretly married that day in Friar Lawrence's cell.

When next the lovers meet, they exchange vows. Before marrying them, Friar Lawrence reminds Romeo of the hazards of a hasty marriage. But Romeo, deaf to the Friar's words, simply asserts,

> Do thou but close our hands with holy words,
> Then love-devouring death do what he dare,
> It is enough I may but call her mine. (2.6.6–8)

In these three lines, Shakespeare offers a portrait of the intense young man, while also foreshadowing the unhappy future. The Friar, frightened by Romeo's anxiousness, attempts to warn him: "These violent delights have violent ends. . . . Therefore love moderately: long love doth so" (9, 14). But impetuosity marks Romeo. It heralds his leap into marriage; it will also soon mark his response to Mercutio's death at Tybalt's hands, prompting him to duel with Tybalt and kill him.

Tony and Maria, caught in the cultural contexts of their time, realize, like Romeo and Juliet, that they cannot inform their parents of their relationship. Tony promises to pick Maria up after the rumble, but she reminds him, "My mama"; her mother's hostility means they cannot go to her home. "Then I will take you to my house," he counters. "Your mama," she asserts. Attempting to find neutral ground on which to meet, they pledge themselves to one another in the bridal shop, using the mannequins to fill out the wedding party. Tony picks a female dummy and holds it, trying to bring his mama to life by describing her size. Maria follows suit. Both hope that their mutual pursuit of one another, of love,

THE CHALLENGE OF TRAGEDY · 107

and of a normal relationship between them, of suitor and pursued, will erase the hostility between their families, just as Friar Lawrence hopes that Romeo and Juliet's love will reconcile their families.

But in both *Romeo and Juliet* and *West Side Story,* happiness is found not within the family but with the lovers themselves. Parents are absent. The lovers are the agents for change, because the parents have basically abdicated their responsibility. In *Romeo and Juliet,* the parents are present but foster hostility between the families; *West Side Story* never includes the lovers' parents. The shop mannequins are wonderful surrogates; they can't talk—or fight. As Tony and Maria move from one to the next, the mannequins create a sense of harmony, of parents and families at their wedding.

Song cements their union as they sing alternate lines from the marriage ceremony. During this mock wedding, the participants become serious, singing "Make of our hands one hand. Make of our hearts one heart." The stage direction then reads, "Slowly, seriously, they turn front and together kneel as before an altar." Tony begins, "I, Anton, take thee Maria," followed by her "I, Maria, take thee, Anton . . ." They proceed to the marriage vows: "For richer, for poorer," says Tony. "In sickness and health," responds Maria, "from tomorrow to tomorrow." Tony interrupts with "From now to forever," and Maria concludes, "'Til death do us part." The exchange of vows includes an exchange of rings, leading back into the song: "Make of our hands one hand, / Make of our hearts one heart / Make of our vows one last vow; / Only death will part us now." As they conclude this ritual, they look at one another, smiling, aware that they have enacted only a make-believe ceremony, but also conscious of their own seriousness (1.7, pp. 54–55).

This momentary lapse into timelessness is quickly broken by Maria's request to Tony: "No rumble." "You don't even want a fist fight?" he queries (1.7, p. 52). That was what he had argued for at Doc's. Now he must go and alter the terms again. He agrees to stop the rumble, but stopping it is not that easy. Here the musical differs greatly from Shakespeare's play, where Juliet is unaware, except in a general sense, of the possibility of friction between Tybalt and Romeo. In *West Side Story* the women's backgrounds affect the progress of the story, although they cannot change its outcome. Maria's outlook is shaped by her more independent societal role, even with an overbearing brother who attempts

3.3. On their knees, Tony and Maria pledge their love to one another in the dress shop where she works. The hostility between their families means that only dress-store dummies, not parents, can witness this ceremony. Their faith in one another leads them to imagine a world without fear or hatred. *Photo by Fred Fehl, courtesy of Gabriel Pinski.*

to protect her from the outside world. Juliet's role, on the other hand, has grown out of a religious commitment. Her marriage to Romeo has been sealed by the church—to defy it, as her nurse urges her to do when Romeo is banished, would be to become a bigamist. When later Maria defiantly announces her love for Tony, she brings her character into a world unknown to Juliet, who, waiting for Romeo to appear on their wedding night, dreams of losing her virginity to him:

> Gallop apace, you fiery-footed steeds,
> Towards Phoebus' lodging . . .
> And bring in cloudy night immediately.
> Spread thy close curtain, love-performing night,
> That [th'] runaway's eyes may wink, and Romeo
> Leap to these arms untalk'd of and unseen! (3.2.1–7)

Juliet hasn't the slightest inkling that a fatal combat has just taken place. Maria, on the other hand, idealistically believes that logic and reason can prevail, and trusts in Tony's power to effect change.

A dramatic scene of cross-purposes then erupts, where music dominates. In a five-part rendition of "Tonight," which probably comes as close to opera as any section of *West Side Story,* hatred and passion supplement the pure love and innocence of the earlier duet between Tony and Maria. Gone is the dream of an ideal world. "The Sharks are gonna have their way tonight," Bernardo and his men sing. "The Puerto Ricans grumble, / 'Fair fight.' / But if they start a rumble, / We'll rumble 'em right," sing the Jets. In counterpoint, the Sharks respond, "We're gonna hand 'em a surprise, / Tonight," cut off by the Jets' "We're gonna cut 'em down to size, / Tonight" (1.8, p. 56). Song and dance contribute to the progress of the story, and the choreography and lighting enhance the effect:

> Spotlights pick out Riff and the Jets, Bernardo and the Sharks, Anita, Maria, and Tony against small sets representing different places in the neighborhood. All are waiting expectantly for the coming of night, but for very different reasons.

While Bernardo and Riff are deeply entrapped in their own hatreds, anticipating unfair play, Anita is looking forward to intense sex after the rumble and Tony and Maria are hoping for the impossible—a joyous reunion and love-making. Their idealistic duet closes the song but suggests the impossibility of their dreams: "Today, the minutes seem like hours. / The hours go so slowly / And still the sky is light. / Oh, moon, grow bright / And make this endless day endless night, / Tonight" (1.8, p. 59). Here Sondheim and Bernstein use the internal rhyme of "go," "so," and "slow," alliteration of the "s" sound, and end-line rhyme in "light," "bright," and "night" to emphasize the endlessness of night.

The rumble is the contemporary equivalent of the Renaissance duel. Although Tybalt and Mercutio die in daylight in the town square and the deaths in *West Side Story* occur at night on a dead-end street under the highway, they both grow out of the deep hostility and youthful self-confidence of the young men involved.

The hostility and bias dramatized in *West Side Story* seemed to pervade American society in 1957. Although Senator Joseph McCarthy's anti-Communist crusade had been condemned by the Senate in 1954, the impact of his investigation lasted well beyond that date, affecting people's lives and relationships, as Laurents points out of the HUAC investigation of Robbins. And on a global scale, in May of 1951, the U.S. had tested the first H-bomb, claiming that the Russians had begun to test atomic weapons in 1949. The arms race between the U.S. and the Soviet Union resulted in an era of suspicion that colored American dealings with other countries. The distress of the Cold War replaced the hope and energy of *Kiss Me, Kate.* Juvenile delinquency was spreading despite the experts who thought they knew how to handle it.[46] On the one hand, this was an era of affluence. People moved to cozy homes in the suburbs. On the other hand, they were fleeing the cities. It was a time when the old patterns were being challenged.

In the courts, in 1954 in *Brown v. Board of Education,* the concept of equal but separate education was overthrown. The courts found that it wasn't enough to claim that separate education for Blacks and Whites could possibly be equal. Following this up, in 1955, Rosa Parks, a Black woman, refused to move to the back of a bus in Montgomery, Alabama, when a white man entered. This developed into a boycott of the bus system and eventually led to the Supreme Court ruling in November 1956 that struck down Alabama's laws requiring segregated buses. In September 1957, violence over integration of the schools brought Federal troops to Little Rock, Arkansas.[47]

This culture of fear, distrust, bias, and conflict was the world in which the creators of *West Side Story* rooted their musical. When Doc, disgusted with the gang members' behavior, says to them, "You make this world lousy!" Action answers, "That's the way we found it, Doc" (2.4, p. 28). And to some extent he is right.

Before that, however, the two gangs are prepping for the rumble without quite realizing what they are taking on. As the men of both sides watch intently, Bernardo and Riff get set to fight. Always prepared, as we later discover, to correct any misstep by the "Other," each man watches his enemy for a moment's break, for an opportunity to take the offensive. There in the dark, under the bridge, they express their hatred, their bodies silhouetted against the massive structure of the bridge. Then Tony enters and attempts to stop the fight, just as Romeo attempts to break up the fight between Mercutio and Tybalt, and his effort, like Romeo's, leads to tragedy. In a quick moment someone pulls a knife, and Riff is killed. We watch in horror. Suddenly the gangs are fighting, in a superbly orchestrated dance through which they express their hatred and

3.4. In a dark alley beneath the highway, the two gangs meet. What was to have been a fistfight with bare knuckles develops into a fatal encounter with knives. Bernardo stabs Riff, and Tony retaliates; both Riff and Bernardo are killed. All are trapped in the city's oppressive vise. Although the adaptors attempted to explain that this was not reality, critics at first misunderstood the poetic analysis of these youths caught in the grip of prejudice. Maria's closing statement, "We're all responsible," sums up the senselessness of bias as the adaptors transform Shakespeare's tragedy of warring families into a musical relevant to the twentieth century. *Photo by Fred Fehl, courtesy of Gabriel Pinski.*

contempt for one another. The plunging movements relay what cannot be expressed in words. Robbins "would find movements in the tempo of the times," wrote one critic, commenting on the 1961 film, for which Robbins did most of the staging.[48]

Despite the characters' intentions, they are caught up in tragedy. Borrowing from Shakespeare's Romeo, the adaptors create Tony as flawed by impetuosity. Although he is worth caring about, and his nobility and stature shine through the play, Tony's weakness and unrealistic sense of power lead to tragedy. Attempting to head off the rumble to please Maria, he is, instead, responsible for his best friend's death. Reacting to that death, Tony impetuously picks up the knife that has just killed his pal and goes for Bernardo, killing him, the gleaming knife shining in the darkness beneath the bridge. Suddenly the cops' sirens scream, and the youths disperse. Only Tony remains. Stunned, he wails out "Maria," aware of what he has done, and runs from the scene.

Retribution comes swiftly. In *Romeo and Juliet,* it lies with the forces of law. Romeo will be banished. In *West Side Story* Tony, living in a world of gang warfare, must face not only the law but also the other gang. Both men are devastated by what they have done and the consequences of their actions. Romeo retreats to Friar Lawrence's cell and weeps at his dilemma, the Friar admonishing him to "be a man." Tony, too, retreats, seeking Maria's help before he confesses his role in the deaths to the police.

Both sets of lovers have a brief moment of respite. Helped by the Friar and the Nurse, Juliet and Romeo spend their wedding night together before he must leave at dawn. "It was the nightingale, and not the lark," she insists when the bird of morning wakes them (3.5.2). But they both know better, and wonder if they will ever meet again.

In *West Side Story,* Tony, dirty and disheveled from his part in the rumble, appears at Maria's window, planning to turn himself in to the police after bidding her goodbye. Maria at first responds in anger, resembling Juliet when first given news of Tybalt's death. "O serpent heart, hid with a flowering face! / Did ever dragon keep so fair a face!" exclaims Juliet (3.2.73–74). "Killer, killer, killer, killer," accuses Maria, then, crying, embraces him and tells him not to turn himself in.

Maria and Tony dream of a place where they can safely love. The adaptors of *West Side Story* created a dream ballet to dramatize that wish. Tony expresses it: "We'll find some place where nothing can get to us; not one of them, not anything. And—" He then sings, "I'll take you away, take you far far away out of here / Far away till the walls and the streets disappear" (2.1, p. 7). The words actually tell the story, holding the clue to action. Again we are dealing with a specific location. It's not just anywhere. It's a world that contrasts with the pressures of the city, where youth have no place to grow except on crowded streets. Suddenly Robbins is opening a green world, a space totally unfamiliar to the gangs. Oliver Smith, the set designer, not only created scenery that captured the bleakness of the tenements where the gangs lived but also opened these areas, as if by magic, to dreams. In this dream ballet, Smith makes the walls of the city fall away to reveal an open field. Tony and Maria find themselves in this open space, and dance in it with abandon, singing "a place for us." Members of the rival gangs enter, note the openness of the space, and tentatively reach out to one another in what appears to be a reconciliation. Their feet touch the ground as if it were grass. There is a softness to it and to them. Maria and Tony, on their knees, face one another as if saying wedding vows. Even the costumes of the gang members have changed to light colors and swirling fabric; the women resemble ballet dancers in their soft pouffant skirts. The Jet women wear light greens and yellows, the men wear white shirts. The Shark women wear purple, violet, orange, and pink, the men wear red. All the women of both groups are on pointe. When the music starts, the first young man who comes in feels the grass beneath his feet, and snaps his fingers. He can't believe what he's feeling and seeing. The music is playing in the background. The dancing is programmatic, expressing the joy and relaxed feelings of the dancers as they find an open space, no longer confined by the pressures of the city. They can breathe easily. Their movements are light as they twirl and enjoy themselves. The scene conveys in dance and music what Shakespeare's scene conveys in language.

But then the walls of the buildings begin to rise again; the cage of the city begins to squeeze the performers, who face the realities of the murders of Riff and Bernardo. Aware of their limited living space and the confrontation that engulfs them, the opposing gangs resume their hostility. Desperately, Tony and Maria sing of a place where they can be together. He offers her his hand: "Hold my hand and we're halfway there" (2.1, p. 8). But the buildings continue to rise, enclosing them. Hostility and hatred take over. The importance of place reasserts itself as Tony and Maria realize that only if they flee the city can their love survive.

The music for this ballet captures first the lovers' fear, and then their astonishment. The music also has a dance in it—a speedy dance, enlivened by the click of maracas. It seems to combine Latin elements with American, thus suggesting the reconciliation of the two gangs. Then comes the song—"There's a place for us," "We'll find a new way of thinking." In the background, eventually, the sound of church bells tolling is followed by group singing. But then there is further modulation and the music becomes harsh—the walls are beginning to close.

Robbins's notes for the dance indicate a progression from turbulence to calm as the dancers reach out to one another. When Riff and Bernardo, the two dead men, silently walk on, the mood turns to nightmare as the deadly knife fight is reenacted. The cage of the city reappears. The scene closes in darkness, in Maria's bedroom with the lovers clinging to one another. The dance is an illusion—or a dream—or a wish—an interruption of the movement toward doom and tragedy.

Arthur Laurents wrote later that he loved Smith's backdrops, but hated the "blue box" of a set. Robbins's dance demanded open space after Maria and Tony met in her bedroom. According to Laurents,

> For his second-act ballet, Jerry wanted the entire stage cleared, losing the claustrophobic threat of the city, bringing air, space and light for the first time. But the ballet was led into by Tony and Maria singing on a bed and the bed couldn't be cleared. Why not? Jerry asked angrily. Because there was no opening in the wall of the blue box. Make one, he demanded. The crew carpenter said he couldn't. But Jerry could.
>
> "Get me a saw," he said.
>
> They got him a saw, he sawed through Oliver's set with Oliver standing there.[49]

The bed slid through the opening, and light and air bathed the dancers.

After the dance, the gang swiftly brings the audience back to reality, as the Jets, now leaderless, present a picture of juvenile delinquency. One by one, they reappear, whistling to identify themselves to one another and discussing their experiences after the rumble. It's nighttime. "They get you yet?" asks A-rab. "No, you?" responds Baby John. "Hell no," A-rab assures him. They then discuss Tony, wondering where he is. Finally, they mention the dead men. "Did you get a look at 'em?" They pause, and A-rab states, "I wish it was yesterday." Noting the attitude of his pal, Baby John ventures, "Whadda ya say we run away?" Clearly, they're scared. And then Officer Krupke calls them. "Hey you two." "Who, me?" Their fear gives way to their wiliness. They manage to trip him up and escape (2.2, pp. 10–11). Slowly the rest of the Jet gang members show up. Two of them have already been to the station house. "What happened?" asks A-rab. "A big fat nuthin'!" Snowboy replies. "How come?" A-rab wonders. Snowboy explains, "Cops believe everything they read in the papers." Action elaborates: "To them, we ain't human. We're cruddy juvenile delinquents. So that's what we give 'em" (p. 13).

The Jets sing, "Officer Krupke," a humorous, ironic song, as they try to think their way out of this terrible dilemma—the two dead young men, Bernardo and Riff, and the inevitable presence of the law. The notation beside the music in Bernstein's score is "fast, vaudeville style." As they did over so much of the show, here too the adaptors argued, with some wanting to exchange this song and "Cool." And again Robbins persisted. He found the song absolutely relevant to the Jets' desperation. Sondheim said later, "We didn't exchange them, and of course 'Krupke' works wonderfully in the second act, on the old Shakespearean drunken-porter principle. In the middle of a melodrama, you cut in with comedy."[50] (In the movie version it was moved to earlier in the story, and it just stood as a comic piece, without being integral to the work as it is in the play.)

While the Jets are struggling to find their humanity, they begin their song. In its original form, the gang members take a variety of roles, including Officer Krupke: Snowboy, imitating Krupke, starts with, "Hey, you." Action responds, "Me, Officer Krupke?" "Yeah, you, gimme one good reason for not draggin ya down the station house, ya punk!" Action responds in song, rhyming "Krupke" with the evils of "our bringin' upke" and the fact that their mothers are all "junkies," concluding, "nacherly we're punks" (2.2, p. 13).

The song's introduction at this moment breaks the intensity of the failed "Somewhere" and seals the finality of the murders. There's no going back. And yet the gang members have learned no lesson. They remain as intolerant as they ever were, as we see later when they taunt and nearly rape Anita. The song mocks the idea that, since the boys are not born delinquents but made so by the pressures of society, it must therefore be easy to redeem them, while also highlighting the way that theories of delinquency contradict one another. These are frightened teen-agers who know they are in great trouble. The song, outlining multiple societal analyses of teenage gangs, also comments on the social world of the time.

The collaborators succeeded beyond their wildest dreams in creating this organic musical with a tragic theme. By reworking Shakespeare's play into a musical tragedy that spoke to bias in contemporary culture—ethnic bias, racial bias, and perhaps economic bias—they found an appreciative and responsive audience. The gang members are not, as Krupke claims, hoodlums, but rather inarticulate young people who find family, friends, and support in their gang—things absent from their world. Resembling the gangsters who do a soft-shoe routine in *Kiss Me,*

Kate, but lacking their humor, these juveniles represent a particular American phenomenon of the time: cynical teenage gangs, with ties to the tenements that bred them as well as to the gangster world they will grow into. Like those earlier gangsters in *Kate,* these juveniles, too, have lost all sense of moral purpose. However, they have a deeper and more disturbing world view than do Cole Porter's hoofers, one revealing the scars on their lives.

Shakespeare offers important precedents for the adaptors. He uses language to take us to the heart of his characters as he has them argue, clown, pun, and offer advice. In Mercutio, for example, Shakespeare develops a character endowed with a vivid imagination. He creates, simply through the winding of images, a fairy queen, Queen Mab, no bigger than an agate stone, who spreads her largesse on anyone who thinks of dreaming. Tybalt, too, is defined by language. In him, Shakespeare creates a swaggering, angry youth who would like nothing better than to kill his neighbor. This is obvious from his first entrance in scene 1. There, observing Benvolio attempting to halt the fighting, Tybalt challenges him: "What, drawn and talk of peace? I hate the word / As I hate hell, all Montagues, and thee" (1.1.70–71). The dramatist then creates all these characters to support his story of a pair of star-crossed lovers, and lends them to the adaptors. They refashion that seventeenth-century gallery into the characters of *West Side Story,* whose animosity explodes in dance, song, and language in the world of 1957 New York theater.

Like their model, the adaptors, too, individualize the teenagers and reveal their imagination. While waiting for the Sharks to arrive at Doc's to plan the rumble, Baby John pores over a comic book and suddenly blurts out, "He don't use knives. He don't even use an atomic ray gun." "Who don't?" asks Action. "Superman," Baby John answers. "Gee, I love him" (1.6, p. 37). Meanwhile, in Washington, the Senate Subcommittee on Comic Books and Juvenile Delinquency has been meeting to determine their ill effects on the young.[51] Obviously Baby John knows nothing about any such effects. For him, comic books create a hero. Nevertheless, despite the adaptors' efforts to humanize these kids, Krupke's label "hoodlum" sticks. Doc, too, calls them "hoodlums," disgusted at their lack of judgment. "Don't you call me 'hoodlum,'" says Action, lunging for him. "I wear a jacket like my buddies," claims Baby John, "so my teacher calls me 'hoodlum'" (1.6, p. 41).

While Doc's simple suggestion, "Why don't you play, like other kids?" provides no answer at all, the musical's early scene where A-rab pretends to be an airplane offers a momentary escape into childhood, just as the line about Superman not needing guns shows the teenagers' attempts to understand. In this organic musical the adaptors not only offer a range of scenes, but a world of ideas drawn from the contexts of the teenagers' lives: from the competitive dancing in the gym, to the merging of Anita's and Rosalia's ideas about America, to the rumble where dance absorbs and dramatizes all the action, to the meadow where Tony dreams of taking Maria: somewhere where they can live. Do these characters really exist? Or aren't they the poetry of their creators?

According to Laurents, the adaptors sought "to create a lyrically and theatrically sharpened illusion of reality."[52] But audiences and critics often mistook the illusion of reality for reality itself. Because the characters seemed so realistic, critics had a difficult time separating them from reality. Brooks Atkinson, the theater critic for the *New York Times,* found beauty only in Tony and Maria, seeing the rest of the Jets and Sharks as "the crafty gangs . . . youths of the streets." He heard their language as "acrid and ugly" and saw their conduct as "neurotic and savage." In fact, he bought into Krupke's perception of these kids as hoodlums, deciding that they were "part of the hideousness that lies under the scabby surface of the city."[53] He failed to distinguish the fiction of the play from the world outside the theater. Jay Carmody, reviewing the musical's pre-Broadway opening in the *Evening Star,* wrote of the play's timeliness that seemed almost to rip out tomorrow's front page to paste it into *West Side Story,* comparing its tensions to the front page of a newspaper "on a tense and tormented day."[54] He had missed the point. He didn't quite get it, because illusion is what the adaptors are creating, as they seek to evoke our empathy for these kids.

In explaining this aim, Laurents said, "We didn't want newsreel acting, blue jean costumes, or garbage can scenery any more than we wanted soap box pounding for our theme of young love destroyed by a violent world."[55] And here is where *Romeo and Juliet* and *West Side Story* meet. Both present "young love destroyed by a violent world," although one was written in the Renaissance and the other in the twentieth century. The love takes very different forms in these two works, since their worlds differ so greatly. In the earlier instance, the lovers are defined by family bonds; in the later, families are excluded completely and the world itself is hostile. And yet it does finally move beyond the "bias" Bernstein noted in his copy of *Romeo and Juliet* and expand to a search for understanding. After Tony's death, Maria attempts to feel anger as the gang members do, but ultimately rejects their methods. She expects more of these young men. Juliet, too, rejects her parents and Friar Lawrence and asks for more and better understanding. Perhaps the adaptors, too, as they struggled for an ending, realized that the play demanded that extra dimension to define the lovers' dedication to one another.

Unaware of the aims of the adaptors, the critics were misled by the outward appearance of the characters. For example, Atkinson recognized that the adaptors created an organic work of art but he mistook what Laurents called the "sharpened illusion of reality" for reality itself. But how realistic are these two gangs and how mythical is the environment? The city is mythical in its oppressiveness. Certainly neither the dancing nor the songs that permeate this work and give it shape are realistic. Nor is the ballet that takes the teenagers somewhere where there's a place for them. It suggests the breadth that dreams can bring.

When the show returned to Broadway three years later, Atkinson had second thoughts. He now perceived *West Side Story* through new senses and noted its great success: "The audience saluted the most memorable ballet numbers and songs as if they had never been performed before." In attempting to analyze what captivated him this time, the critic first attributed it to taste: "By comparison with the flaring originality of Jerome Robbins' choreography and staging, taste may seem like a petty thing. . . . But it is the impeccable taste of the music, the lyrics, and the story that seems so astonishing." His earlier reaction to the hoodlums and their grittiness had also disappeared, and now he praised the insights of the authors, who "endowed these characters with humanity" and raised "their hopes and troubles to the level of literature."[56] In 1985, Sondheim answered the critic's question, asserting, "We were writing a poetic interpretation of these kids."[57]

After the Jets sing "Officer Krupke," the adaptors shift the action away from the gang and back to Maria and Tony asleep on her bed, alternating scenes of hope with those of reality. An insistent knocking on the door not only awakens them, but alerts them to the troubles ahead. Once again the adaptors are following the arc of Shakespeare's play, where the Nurse informs Juliet on the morning after her wedding night, "Your lady mother is coming to your chamber. / The day is broke, be wary, look about" (3.5.39–40). Maria and Tony must also look about in response to Anita's knocking. Kissing Maria and arranging to meet her at Doc's, Tony leaves through the window before Maria opens the bedroom door. But Anita takes one look at the bed and realizes what has happened. Maria explains, "I love him." In the duet that follows, "A Boy like That" and "I Have a Love," Sondheim once again propels the plot forward with the lyrics as Anita and Maria argue. The duet presents their two different points of view, with Maria singing, "I have a love and it's all that I have, / Right or wrong, what else can I do?" while Anita exhorts her, "A boy like that, who'd kill your brother. . . . Stick to your own kind." Finally, they sing together, "When love comes so strong / There is no right or wrong / Your love is your life" (2.3, pp. 20–21). At the song's conclusion, Anita quietly informs Maria that Chino has a gun and is sending the boys out to look for Tony.

Attempts to adopt Shakespeare's ending stymied the adaptors, just as they had adaptors of earlier centuries. In Shakespeare's play, Romeo never again meets Juliet, even for a moment. Blocked by Paris from opening the tomb, Romeo then fights him. Paris falls. Continuing on to Juliet's tomb, Romeo notes how lifelike she appears. "Ah dear Juliet / Why art thou yet so fair?" he wonders (5.3.101–102), then takes poison, which works so swiftly that he dies moments before she awakens. Nor is the Friar much help. After suggesting she join a nunnery, he flees, frightened over his role in this tragedy. Meanwhile, Juliet, seeking a drop of the poison that killed Romeo, exclaims, "O churl, drunk all, and left no friendly drop / To help me after?" (163–64). Hearing the sound of approaching voices, she kills herself with Romeo's dagger.

The early derivation of Anita from the nurse may also have fed into the new ending. Both women lose their moral compass as they attempt to save Juliet/Maria. After Romeo is banished, the Nurse begins recommending that Juliet accept Paris. Despairing, Juliet turns to her guide and mentor, asking for an honest response rather than one endorsed by her parents: "O God! O Nurse, how shall this be prevented?" (3.5.204). Reminding the Nurse that Romeo, her husband, lives, Juliet despairingly wonders what to do. The Nurse's answer seals her place as Juliet's confidant.

> Faith, here it is. Romeo
> Is banished. . . .
> I think it best you married with the County.
> O he's a lovely gentleman!
> Romeo's a dishclout to him. (217–19)

Incredulous at this response, Juliet asks, "Speaks't thou from thy heart?" "And from my soul too," is the reply (226–27). The young woman can't believe that her beloved nurse could lose her moral compass to such a degree as to suggest bigamy. Juliet is now alone.

Anita, however, becomes the linchpin of the tragedy in the musical. Determined to help Maria, she goes to the drugstore, intending to tell Tony that the police are interviewing Maria. But the Jets confront her, taunt her, and finally nearly rape her; she is saved only by the appearance of Doc. Infuriated by their treatment of her, Anita says, "I'll give you a message for your American buddy! Tell the murderer Maria's never going to meet him! Tell him Chino found out and—and shot her!" And she rushes out the door as Doc shouts to the Jets, "What does it take to get through to you? When do you stop? *You make this world lousy.*" And then, "Get out of here!" (2.4, p. 20).

Doc brings her message to Tony. "That was no customer upstairs, just now. That was Anita. Maria is dead. Chino found out about you and her—and shot her." As Tony runs out the door, the set flies away, the stage goes dark, and Tony shouts, "Chino, Chino, come and get me too, Chino" (2.5, p. 30). Only after Chino shoots Tony does Maria appear. The two lovers run toward each other, but he has been mortally wounded. Looking for an ending that would retain Shakespeare's romanticism, the adaptors give Tony and Maria a final moment of reunion. She stands over him, then, taking Chino's gun, she first threatens everyone, and then accuses all of them of murder. When Lieutenant Schrank comes along and heads towards Tony, she runs forward, intercepting him. Then, embracing her lover, she warns Schrank, "Don't you touch him" (2.6, p. 33).

Bernstein's music now provides the emotional resolution to the stage action. All of the young men—of both gangs—pick up Tony's body and form a funeral cortege as Maria slowly follows. A Jet, Baby John, then comes forward, pulling her shawl gently over her head (2.6, p. 34). "She is dead already," Rodgers had said, "after this all happens to her."[58] She follows the procession of youths—now united—offstage as the curtain falls.

West Side Story astonished audiences. What can one make of this type of musical, where song and dance push the limits of theater even as the book seems to belong to its time? Does one applaud, or is one paralyzed by the experience? Are these really kids of the streets? Then why is one so completely moved? The adaptors have achieved their aim: to create an American tragedy with the tools formerly reserved for comedy. Dance, music, language, and body movement combine to propel the story forward. Here is a work that evokes not only pity and fear, but also empathy and admiration.

Although critics often didn't see the imaginative framework beneath the superficial ugliness of gangs and prejudice, the adaptors had created a new view of an old work. This new view meant taking a Shakespeare play and exploring it for its nuances, converting its form into something never yet explored. Banding together, a group of artists with backgrounds in music, dance, and theater worked to make all of these parts function as an organic whole: dance and song melding into drama, staging and sets contributing to this transformation. If the aim of the adaptors fooled the critics, who failed to recognize the imagination at work, the adaptors themselves knew what they were seeking. Having started with the intent to plead for racial tolerance, they recognized the breadth of Shakespeare's play, with its families, its group of friends, its strong antagonisms, and its dramatization of the strength of love to overcome adversity. They enlarged their original aim—"an out and out plea for racial tolerance"—into a general plea for tolerance of all those who differ from us. Robbins, Bernstein, Laurents, and Sondheim expanded the boundaries of musical theater and brought Shakespeare's message of the tragedy of young lovers thwarted by the surrounding world to twentieth-century audiences with new vigor and contemporary understanding. In doing so, they gave a new dimension to our knowledge of the dramatist even as they created a new world for his famous love story.

FOUR

Out of the Closet
Your Own Thing and
Twelfth Night

On a cold, windy Saturday night, the thirteenth of January, 1968, bundled-up New Yorkers braved the threat of snow to attend the opening of *Your Own Thing,* a new kind of off-Broadway rock musical. As they took off their coats, they faced an all-white setting, a tiny stage divided by platform ramps crossing at two levels from wing to wing. Music played. Lights flashed on and off and a film of a sinking ship dramatically added to the wonder. People scattered to and fro on the platform ramps while two characters—twins, a brother and sister—argued, their voices barely audible over the mayhem. The curtains that normally frame a stage were gone, replaced by doors, entryways, and openings in the set. Most astonishing, the pair were silhouetted against a cyclorama, or rear-projection screen, while tape-recorded voices added to the confusion.

In these years, the Vietnam conflict was spurring massive and frequent protests. Men were dying for a cause that many Americans could not accept. Lyndon Baines Johnson was president, having inherited the role from the assassinated John F. Kennedy. The Beatles had won success, and the rock musicals, borrowing the methods of the rock stars, were replacing the large Broadway genre. At a time when many Americans were flirting with the idea of people "doing their own thing," but before such behavior was acceptable, the adaptors saw a Shakespeare work that, as Donald Driver said, offered a theme worth fighting for.[1] In 1968 homosexual unions remained hidden in the closet.

As the critic for *Dance Magazine,* Doris Hering, observed, Robert Guerra's white setting of this new rock musical formed the background for slides that were projected on it as well as for a film that emitted sparks of light. The horizontal flat surfaces held the slides and the motion picture sequences, an extraordinary new theatrical development at the time. The film, with its brilliant flashes of light, eventually burst into an explosion that signaled the ship's careening and going down.[2] Suddenly the voice of Everett Dirksen, a reactionary American senator, broke through the sounds. "If music be the food of love," he spouted from his place on a screen, "play on!" Shakespeare's opening lines from *Twelfth Night* greeted the audience. But then he faltered: "I can't remember if that's Marlowe or Bacon" (p. 297).[3]

Through the use of lighting the adaptors had created a world where live characters, illuminated by spotlights, vied with projections for the focus of the audience's attention. At times the stage went black as the adaptors shifted the center of attention from the play itself to the back-lit projections. Sometimes the projections were of speaking heads. At other times, the characters' fears, dreams, or ideas appeared in thought balloons attached to their images. At still other times, the projections depicted the environment—the streets of New York, the gardens around a hospital, or the office of a discotheque owner.

After the floundering ship in the film explodes, the audience's attention returns to the onstage characters, who are rushing toward lifeboats. Sebastian and Viola, the brother and sister, are still arguing. Should they take to the lifeboats or return to the cabin for their orchestration? They break into song, dramatizing their relationship: "Why can't you ever be nice?" he sings, "be nice once or twice?" "Look who's talkin' / Look who's squawkin' / Look who's callin' the pot black," she counters in song. As they continue arguing, she observes, "Some brother you are. You don't give a damn if we end up back in Akron, Ohio." "You want a singing job in the bottom of the ocean?" he quickly responds. Finally the sister sings, "Get off my back. / No one's perfect." She has captured one of the themes of this adaptation. "No one's perfect," they repeat together, just before the ship's purser explodes at them: "For Christ's sake! Don't just stand there, fella, get your sister to the lifeboat!" Although Sebastian tries to follow the purser, Viola insists that he get the orchestration. He heads for the cabin. The stage darkens. Only the film continues. The storm rages as the ship sinks into the sea. So opens *Your Own Thing,* the 1968 musical adaptation of Shakespeare's *Twelfth Night* (pp. 297–300).

Unlike the musical, however, Shakespeare's comedy doesn't bring brother and sister together until its closing moments. Although earlier adaptors often started with Viola's landing in Illyria, a distant magical land, the Renaissance dramatist opens his play with a love-sick Duke Orsino, ruler of that land, bemoaning his fate—rejection by the beauteous Countess Olivia. In stilted, romantic language, known as Petrarchan poetic form, Orsino begins his first speech, addressing the musicians of his court. "If music be the food of love, play on," he instructs them (1.1.1), using the same lines spoken by Senator Dirksen in the twentieth-century musical adaptation. Mocking Orsino's seriousness, the bard is also ridiculing his contemporaries, who were still writing Petrarchan sonnets. "Give me excess of it," the Duke continues, extending the metaphor between love and food, "that, surfeiting, / The appetite may sicken and so die" (2–3). Suddenly, the Duke changes his mind. He's tired of the music. "Enough, no more," he commands, dismissing the musicians (7). He then learns from Valentine, his most recent emissary sent to woo the Countess for him, that she has vowed to spend the next seven years in mourning for her recently deceased brother. The intensity of her feeling for that brother leads Orsino to comment on what to expect when the Countess falls in love:

> O, she that hath a heart of that fine frame
> To pay this debt of love but to a brother,
> How will she love when the rich golden shaft
> Hath kill'd the flock of all affections else
> That live in her. (31–36)

Using metaphors of Cupid and his shafts of love, the Duke guesses at the passion she will then exhibit. Soon enough, she does—not for a man, but for a woman disguised as a man.

In this last of his happy comedies, the dramatist explores the confusion that results when Viola, a shipwrecked young woman, having been separated from her twin brother in a recent storm at sea, decides to adopt his physical demeanor. "Conceal me what I am," she asks the captain who has rescued her, promising him, "It may be worth thy pains" (1.2.53, 57). Certain that her brother has been drowned in the storm, she decides to dress like him and wear her hair in the same fashion. She soon meets Orsino and Olivia.

Not only dressed like her brother, Sebastian, but also disguised as a youth, Viola then introduces herself to the Duke as Cesario, offering her services. She quickly wins his confidence. As a result, he sends her to woo Olivia for him, noting the youth's absence of facial hair and high voice—qualities that should recommend him to the Countess. They do. And here Viola's problems begin. Formerly aloof to all suitors, Olivia is smitten by what she believes is a young man. Her vow of seven years' mourning for a dead brother quickly evaporates. She wishes to marry the youth Cesario, who, meanwhile, has herself become enamored of the Duke. Shakespeare thus shows that people can be attracted to members of the same sex, but he uses disguise and tricks to dramatize this.

All the secondary characters in Shakespeare's play disappear from the adaptation. Only Viola, her twin Sebastian, and the Illyrians Olivia and Orsino remain. Instead, the adaptors boldly depart from Shakespeare's *Twelfth Night,* creating a show innovative both in its theatrics and in its social and political ideology, but more pedestrian in its development of its women characters. Slide and film projections provide a new element, giving this production its liveliness, variety, and depth. Characters on screen frequently comment on the action onstage. The adaptors used songs deriving from *Twelfth Night* but not necessarily addressing the same concerns as the Renaissance play. For instance, the Clown, a character absent from the twentieth-century version, offers a song, "Come Away, Come Away, Death," a song that merely consoles the Duke after Olivia rejects him (2.4.51). The adaptors convert it to a song about Sebastian's close call with death after the ship goes down. But they also invent other songs, such as "I'm Me (I'm Not Afraid)," expressing one of the themes of the musical: the right of people to be different, to be homosexual, or what they will.

The adaptors also created a totally new milieu for their work. Having discarded Shakespeare's subplot, they introduced a new story, setting *Your Own Thing* in a mid-twentieth-century environment of rock bands, concerts, nightclubs, and intimate restaurant clubs. The plot of this updated version involves a four-member rock band called the Apocalypse Quartet, whose agent, Orson (a modernization of Orsino), is distraught because the U.S. Army has drafted one of their number—Disease—for service in Vietnam. The quartet needs a replacement, but although Orson has earnestly tried to find one, he has thus far failed. Meanwhile, his client Olivia, who operates a discotheque, keeps pressuring him. She has already scheduled the band to appear and adamantly refuses to settle for a trio when she was promised a quartet.

The musical's composer and lyricist, Hal Hester and Danny Apolinar, actually first met at a bar in Greenwich Village. Although they had very different backgrounds, the former "a Jewish Filipino from Brooklyn with a long black silky Eskimo bob," the latter "a renegade Southern Baptist from Paducah, Kentucky,"[4] they shared the same dream: to create a multimedia rock musical. They chose a story to adapt in a musical format, but were refused the rights to it.[5] Chagrined, they then turned to the public domain. There they found Shakespeare and his *Twelfth Night*. It was just right. It offered a topic relevant to the times—homosexuality—but with a light touch. They would create a musical based on this comedy.

Hester had studied at the Cincinnati Conservatory of Music. After graduation, he began writing songs and joined the American Society of Composers, Authors and Publishers (ASCAP); more than thirty of his songs were soon recorded.[6] Apolinar sang in a trio, but his background originally was in art. Born in Brooklyn and educated at the High School of Industrial Arts and Pratt Institute, he was on his way to a career in art. However, a stint as an entertainer in the Catskills had lured him to consider the possibility of moving into music and song. Nevertheless, his interest in art also persisted until he was drafted into the army in the late 1950s. Unfortunately, at the time, he and his partner, Hal Hester, were about to go on tour in an act called the Madhattans. He was one of the singers with the group. In the Army, being a resourceful guy, he put together a group called the Madcaps. It was with them that he entered an All-Army Entertainment Contest in May 1959, and won. Reflecting his double interest in art and entertainment, *Stars and Stripes* ran a picture of him looking at prints, hanging on the wall of the Fort Meade Service Club, that he had designed as a commercial artist before his induction into the service.[7] His posting to a place where they were on display was a coincidence, but one that Apolinar treasured. His double interest persisted, although he concentrated primarily on music for the rest of his life. He created the logo for *Your Own Thing,* and his notes for the musical contain numerous costume sketches, suggesting some of his ideas for the play.

The third collaborator, Donald Driver, joined the team when Hester and Apolinar were told that the plot needed strengthening. He came with a background in theater and dance, and was highly recommended by mutual friends. Driver wanted to write a work with a message, and *Your Own Thing*'s stand on the Vietnam War, its open discussion of homosexuality, and its examination of Hollywood stars and people of the cloth in the slide projections offered this opportunity. For Driver, the musical's message was that the brutally masculine world "has got to go." He noted the fluid sexuality of modern youth and observed, "We use the fact that boys look like girls and girls look like boys and who cares?"[8] And he believed in the importance of everyone doing his or her own thing, as the Apocalypse points out in their song "I'm Me (I'm Not Afraid)." A native of Portland, Oregon, Driver went to Pomona College in California and became interested in theater, later becoming artistic director of the Shakespeare Festival in Washington, D.C. He was also a dancer, and was responsible for some of the choreography of *Your Own Thing*, which had a zany and almost impromptu feel to it, unlike the work of such earlier choreographers as Balanchine, Holm, and Robbins.

What is a rock musical and how did *Your Own Thing* differ from the previous Shakespeare musicals on Broadway? One critic described *Hair*, another rock musical, as having "an unmistakable, amplified rock style, with prominent bass lines and strong backbeats. At the same time, nearly every song used the verse-chorus format long favoured on Broadway and eschewed the blues and other simple circular progressions from early rock 'n' roll." Its arrangements were written for "small guitar-and-drum ensembles playing contemporary musical styles."[9] In fact, rock music demands a type of training that many Broadway professionals lacked in the 1960s. Untrained in rock 'n' roll, these musicians were frequently unqualified to play in *Your Own Thing*, despite union pressure to include them.

Hester and Apolinar recognized the need to create songs relevant to the story they wanted to tell. To do this, they relied in part on Shakespeare's poetry and songs, in part on their own inventiveness. Thus, for example, Olivia's "Let It Be" is related to her awareness that she has fallen in love. She is overwhelmed at herself and takes the words from Shakespeare's play: "Let it be." The words derive from a speech of Olivia's in Shakespeare's play after the first meeting of the two women. Orson

4.1. The features of rock concerts replace the full orchestras of the earlier period. Danny Apolinar and the three remaining members of Apocalypse wear white outfits and Mexican embroidered jackets as they play their electric guitars and sing of doing their own thing.   *Photo by Frank Derbas, courtesy of Professor Robert Hapgood, retired, University of New Hampshire.*

OUT OF THE CLOSET · 129

and the Apocalypse, too, draw on their own experience for their song "Do Your Own Thing." In it, the characters are trying to figure out their place in society, particularly Orson, who has fallen for Viola/Charlie and is experiencing, for the first time, what it means to love a man.

Hester and Apolinar may have initially considered adapting *Twelfth Night* as a tribute to Twiggy and the Beatles, both very popular at the time. The earliest version of what became *Your Own Thing* was a script called *The London Look, or What You Wear* (playing on Shakespeare's title and subtitle: *Twelfth Night, or What You Will*). In it, the Apocalypse quartet is called the Bees. Several of the songs in *Your Own Thing* appear in a script identified as a film treatment, which only vaguely resembles the final musical.[10]

Basking on the sunny sands of Puerto Rico, where Hester and Apolinar had a nightclub, the two men composed songs for the project. Their notes and song drafts, scribbled on the backs of flyers for their nightclub, show the progression of their ideas and the changing forms of the songs. (They are reminiscent of the work of another composer who experimented with his material: Cole Porter, whose notes for *Kiss Me, Kate,* on Waldorf-Astoria note pads, also reveal his brainstorming of song ideas and rhymes.) Among the early drafts are such songs as "I'm Me (I'm Not Afraid)" and "This Is a Man." The former, which in its final version was sung by the Apocalypse, reads,

> I'm not afraid to die or live
> I'm not afraid to take or give
> I'm not afraid of anything or anybody
> Most of all, I'm not afraid of me.[11]

The repetition of this last line in several of the stanzas helps emphasize Orson's dilemma as well as that of the Apocalypse—no longer a quartet—as they attempt to work out their own questions of identity. Some of the songs stress the impact of cross-dressing on the relationship between men and women in the context of 1968.

After the first scene, where brother and sister argue and Sebastian goes back to the cabin for the orchestration, the film shows us the ship sinking. The stage darkens as slides of waterfront buildings in semiabstract design appear. The Manhattan skyline slowly emerges. The tumult of the shipwreck gives way to the breathtaking sight of New York from the harbor. Then, suddenly, Shakespeare's *Twelfth Night* is heard as Viola asks the Purser, "What country, friend, is this?" repeating Viola's line to the Captain in Shakespeare's comedy. "This is Illyria, lady," the Purser replies (1.2.1–2). But it's a different Illyria from Shakespeare's; specifically, it is "Manhattan Island, Illyria." She then asks, "Who governs here?" A slide projection of New York's then-mayor, John Lindsay, appears. "Illyria is a fun city. Cough, cough," a voice-over huskily says, an early commentary on smoking and smog (p. 302).

Viola gets the message. Her song, "The Flowers," questions how flowers can grow in this land of steel and glass. The lyricist and composer show this newcomer to the city reacting wistfully to its attractive and unattractive features. The script's stage directions illuminate the handling of the song:

> During this song the motion-picture film shows varying shots of New York City skyline and skyscrapers. This film is at the same time beautiful and impersonal; and in a nutshell, capsulizes the exterior shapes of twentieth-century urban life. The slide projections which accompany this film are stills of steel and glass structures and change constantly during the song. (p. 302)

"So much glass, so much steel, / What's there to care? What's there to feel? / All that glass, all that chrome, / Can I ever call this place home?" Viola wonders (p. 302).[12]

Writing of the songs in this production, Richard P. Cooke of the *Wall Street Journal* observed that although some of the songs were by Shakespeare, most "express[ed] popular present-day themes such as the search for personal identity . . . and they [did] it without being phony or lugubrious." He then mentioned the actress playing Olivia, Marion Mercer (elegantly sophisticated in a sequined miniskirt), who sang "a song about 'The Middle Years' although she's turned only 30. That gives you an idea that things are indeed youth-oriented, as they say these days."[13]

Your Own Thing, for the first time, brings rock music and multimedia projections to an American Shakespeare musical adaptation. Here "film and slide projections, [and] taped and live sound effects accompany the written word to form a mixed media collage which is the final effect of the script," wrote Stuart H. Benedict.[14] The slide projections include not only contemporary political figures such as Mayor Lindsay and the reactionary Senator Dirksen but also movie stars such as John Wayne, Shirley Temple, and Humphrey Bogart and religious figures such as Buddha, the pope, Jesus Christ, and the Sistine Chapel's image of God. Queen Elizabeth and Shakespeare also appear.

Although presented on screen, these projections are not static. They interact, arguing with one another without being constrained by their original context or era. In addition, thought balloons like those in comic strips appear above their heads when they are thinking, connecting the projections with the onstage characters and integrating the multiple dimensions of the presentations. For example, when Viola is worrying about whether or not her brother has drowned in the storm, a balloon appears over her head: "Oh dear God," it says, "I fear Sebastian lost in the shipwreck." The Sistine God announces, "She's talking to me. Shipwrecks, you know, are my specialty." Then another balloon opens over Viola's head: "I've never been without him. How will I ever get a singing job?" A slide of Buddha appears: "Disaster may be your specialty; but next to harmony, mine is rock," he says, addressing the Sistine God. Rock and its opposite, harmony; elements in music—all enhance Buddha's response, suggesting the brilliance of the adaptors and their use of puns. Appearing as a statue with many arms, Buddha holds a card in one hand.[15] "Boy wanted," the stage direction reads. "Viola collapses her chest," then dances off with a job card (p. 304).

With that card in hand, she searches for Orson's address, guided, of course, by Buddha. When Orson and the three remaining members of the Apocalypse see her, he takes the card and looks at it. "Buddha. That your agent?" he asks. "I'm a boy," she blurts out. "Can you sing?" he continues, then, addressing her in her new role, insists, "Disease, let's see your work." Joining the Apocalypse group and tripping over the material, she nevertheless manages. Orson asks her name. "Charlie," she mumbles, a modern equivalent of Cesario. As they watch her, she shifts from following along with the group to just going it on her own. She tries to sing, dance, and even play the tambourine, little realizing how much they need her for the quartet. They attempt to follow her. Loose and relaxed, she resembles a rag doll that has somehow come to life. Their song is "Baby, Baby," mambo rock with a simple stanza: "Somethin's happenin' makes me want to fly / . . . Somethin's happenin', some new kind of high," and then the words "over and over" are repeated

4.2. *Your Own Thing* employed not only popular music but also slide projections; characters shown in them sometimes had dialogue balloons like those in comic strips. Here the Sistine Chapel's image of God, his arm extended, calls to his son, "Hey boy!" In the following balloon, he asks, "When are you going to get a haircut?" *Slide by photographer Frank Derbas, courtesy of Professor Robert Hapgood, retired, University of New Hampshire.*

many times. Viola has no trouble learning the song. "You're real groovy," Orson assures her, while Danny, one of the members of the Apocalypse, notes, "Solid." Later, she and Orson converse. Just as Duke Orsino in *Twelfth Night* chooses Cesario as his emissary, Orson decides Charlie is the perfect messenger to woo Olivia for him (pp. 314–15).

Meanwhile, the screen projections are conversing. "Why do they need a fourth musician?" Queen Elizabeth asks. "In my day troubadours sang alone." Bogart replies, "We call that folk singing. The government frowns on it." The Sistine God flashes, "The old queen's right. Four's not a biblical number." The queen takes exception; "Did I hear that Vatican manifestation on the ceiling refer to me as 'the old queen'?" Then John Wayne, hoping to prevent an argument, contributes, "It don't matter who they put in the group. I can't tell the boys from the girls anyway." But Bogart won't let that go: "You do have a problem," he insists (p. 310).

Lights go on. The projections disappear. Orson complains to the band but they won't listen, teasing him about his frustrating love life with Olivia. Finally they begin the song that defines the play, "This Is a Man," which Hester and Apolinar had worked on in Puerto Rico. It describes all the offbeat ways that a man (perhaps a homosexual) can behave and dress in "doing his own thing." The singers present it in a round. First Michael:

> This is a man, look at his hair,
> Not your idea of a he-man.

Then Danny:

> Think what you will, what do I care?
> I just want to be a free man,
> To be me, man.

John sings the next solo:

> This is a man, look at his clothes,
> Not your idea of a tough man.

Then Danny again:

> Think what you will, this is no pose.
> Don't have to pretend I'm a rough man,
> I'm enough, man. (p. 311)

That's a great line, defying the conventional expectations of a man. Here the adaptors are emphasizing the superficiality of the many areas where gay men are attacked for being different. The song is also thematically linked with Shakespeare's play, where Antonio, the captain who rescued Sebastian from the shipwreck, admits, "But come what may, I do adore thee so," and says that despite the dangers he faces at Orsino's court he will accompany the young man there (2.1.47–48).

In the script labeled "Screen Treatment of *Your Own Thing*," Sebastian is washed up onto the beach at Fire Island, where a group of guys are playing volleyball.[16] They stop to look expressionlessly at the apparent corpse. Then a woman approaches, turns the body over, shakes her head, and signals to the players to come over. They begin to smile, and the camera moves from face to face until focusing on Sebastian, who gains consciousness as "Come Away, Death" begins.

In this treatment, a series of brief sketches dramatize an unfeeling New York. Most of this material has disappeared from *Your Own*

Thing, except for Sebastian's being washed up on the beach. However, a few did have an influence on the musical. Among these were a scene of a "love-in" in Central Park and two scenes in the New York Public Library.

In the Central Park scene, the members of the Apocalypse walk through the park. They see hippies; they pass a demonstration; they argue about their aims; and suddenly they are singing "I'm Not Afraid to Be Me." One of them is wearing a kerchief or ruffles. A hippie carrying a sign saying "Love" pushes him. Nevertheless, the singer continues, affirming his "right to be me." When another hippie questions his manliness with, "This is a man? Look at his clothes. / Not our idea of a tough man," we are one step away from John Wayne and his suggestion, "Why don't they call themselves 'The He-Men' or something?" He has heard the Apocalypse sing this song.

One of the library scenes in the treatment shows a harried Orson attempting to find a book on homosexuality without mentioning the word. He waits patiently for the line in front of the librarian to diminish, then attempts to communicate with her. "Orson clears his throat and tries to speak. He stammers and his voice catches. The inside of the library is kind of grim, and the sound is like a din." The librarian demands, almost shouting, "Yeah? Speak up." Orson looks at the signs requesting silence and "quiet, please." People are starting to line up behind him. "Whaddaya want?" she asks. Uneasy, he attempts to say, "I . . . I'd like . . . I'd like a couple of books . . ." The man behind him then taps him on the shoulder: "Very good! Very articulate." Orson tries to explain: "I have a problem and I can't solve it." "Mathematics is on the — floor." She calls on "Next." "The problem isn't mathematical. It's physical." "Physics is in the science department." As she seeks to direct him, a man in line suggests, "I think he's looking for the gym." When he manages to say, "I think it has more to do with chemistry," another patron volunteers, "Maybe he's looking for drugs." "Maybe he's a junkie," volunteers another person in line. He twirls around. In utter frustration, and almost arrested because he challenges the drug accusation, he is helped by someone who has checked out books by the Marquis de Sade and others with titles like *Whips through the Ages* and *Medieval Torture Instruments.* Apolinar, who wrote this scene, is showing how difficult it is to try to find out about homosexuality and what a loaded subject it is, or at least was, in 1968.

He set the other library scene in the reading room. There, his camera focuses on hands holding open books—Freud, Jung, *Sexual Behavior of Males*. Alone in the reading room, Orson "is interested, nervous, and suspicious." The author then switches to the projections, and notes that "music for this should be a combination of old player-piano and very hard-driving rock."

That early screen treatment for *Your Own Thing* moves back and forth in time and space. Although still committed to the stories of Olivia and Sebastian, Viola and Orson, the adaptors are filling in the framework that will allow freedom later on with the screen projections and film when they finally get to the musical.

The adaptors' concentration on men in *Your Own Thing* differs from Shakespeare's focus on women in *Twelfth Night*. There Olivia and Viola verbally spar from the moment they meet, when Viola, facing two veiled women, asks, "The honorable lady of the house, which is she?" and receives the ambiguous response, "Speak to me. I shall answer for her." Viola begins but quickly decides, "I would be loath to cast away my speech" on the wrong person (1.5.168–69, 72–73). They quibble further. Olivia admits that she is the lady of the house. Eventually challenged by Olivia's maid, Maria, to "hoist sail" (202), Viola decides her words are for Olivia's ears only and wins a private audience. Being a woman herself, Viola is able to anticipate everything Olivia says, and ultimately her words overwhelm the other woman. Viola/Cesario speaks of what she would do were she Orson: she would "make me a willow cabin at your gate / And call upon my soul within the house. . . . Hallo your name to the reverberate hills / And make the babbling gossip of the air / Cry out 'Olivia'" (260–74). Olivia is smitten.

Although these lines are retained in the musical, the earlier banter between the women is not. Nevertheless, *Twelfth Night* seems to explain why Viola understands the wishes of the Countess as if she inhabited Olivia's skin. The disguised woman knows the words that will appeal to another woman; she understands just how such flattery works.

In the parallel scene in *Your Own Thing* Olivia can only comment on Charlie/Viola's age. Nevertheless the musical also presents a distraught

Olivia frustrated by the youth. Drawn right out of Shakespeare's play, the song develops from Olivia's speech after Viola leaves. Olivia responds to that proposal by losing her heart to the disguised youth. "Not too fast; soft, soft, / Unless the master were the man." And then comes the most telling line: "How now? / Even so quickly may one catch the plague?" She then admits that "this youth's perfections" have stealthily overcome her, and sighs in acceptance, "Well, let it be." This line becomes the basis of one of Olivia's most moving songs in the musical: Adopting her line about Viola's perfection—"Even so quickly may one catch the plague? / Well, let it be"—the adaptors create a song, "Well, Let It Be." In it the older woman repeats the phrase in stanza after stanza, as she contemplates this youth's perfection. "Have I really found my groove?" and again "Or is this a stupid move?" each line concluding with "Well, let it be."

> You can catch a cold very fast, well, let it be.
> It can take hold very fast, well, let it be.
> If this happens to me, well, let it be.
> Well, let it be. (p. 327)

As they often did, Apolinar and Hester have adopted Shakespeare's lines and altered them slightly to create a lyrical and moving song. Shakespeare's lines are spoken as a soliloquy moments after Viola's departure, and reveal Olivia's passion for the youth. The musical achieves the same intimacy between speaker and audience by having Viola and the Apocalypse members freeze in position while Olivia is singing. Only after she finishes do they move.

Both Shakespeare and the adaptors then decide this is the moment either to introduce or reintroduce Sebastian, who did not appear at the opening of *Twelfth Night* but did appear, with Viola, at the opening of *Your Own Thing*. The adaptors work at creating a new plot line that differs from Shakespeare's, where Sebastian just seems to walk in on the action and never really establishes a persona. This they do by developing his personality: first creating an age difference between him and Olivia, a subject each of them later worries about. Next the adaptors introduce a plot parallel to Viola's, dramatizing his search for a job. Third, since they have eliminated all of Shakespeare's minor characters, they must now offer a substitute for the duel in Shakespeare's play that first brings Sebastian to Illyria.

They do, by introducing a new milieu, a hospital scene. And it is on the hospital grounds that we first meet him. He appears in a wheelchair, alone on the stage in front of a projection of the outdoors, recovering from a bump on the head suffered when the ship went down. There he soliloquizes of his brush with death, then sings "Come Away, Come Away, Death," the same song that his sister sang earlier, thinking he was dead. The adaptors combine Shakespeare's lines from two different sections of *Twelfth Night* in the song:

> My stars shine darkly over me; my sister
> Vi, though it was said she much resembled me,
> Was yet of many accounted beautiful;
> She bore a mind that envy could not but call fair. (p. 318)

After observing that he will "drown her remembrance / In more stinging brine of despair," he follows with a revised version of the Clown's song, "Come Away, Come Away, Death."

As the lights go up, the projected outdoor environment disappears and a nurse enters with a basin to wash him. Seeing him from the back, she mistakes him for a young woman. "Good morning, Miss," she says. Viola passes herself off as a boy, and Sebastian is at first mistaken for a girl. "You got quite a little crack on the head there, didn't you? What happened?" Beginning to wash him, she comments, "Do we always wear our armpits Italian style?" He can only gurgle in response, since he has a thermometer in his mouth, and she continues, "Oh well, chacun a son goo, as they say." Only when she gets to his crotch does she scream, "You ought to be ashamed of yourself." She faults his long hair, which deceived her into believing him a woman, then tells him he should be in the army and get a haircut. "You're not afraid of going to war, are you?" "No, just of being shot," he replies. The exchange is a comment on the unpopular Vietnam War (pp. 320–21).

With that they exit, and the projections once more take over. "That sort of thing gives aid and comfort to the enemy," observes Dirksen. "My country, right or wrong," John Wayne chimes in. "I think Hitler said the same thing," observes Bogart, while the pope asserts, "But God is on our side," and Buddha quickly interjects, "Which one?" (p. 321). The projections interweave a number of conflicting viewpoints and move the audience to the next scene. In the hospital garden, a recovered Sebastian and the nurse, now on her way to Vietnam, bid one another farewell.

Hostility has turned to friendship. She asks him to write to her, and he kisses her on the cheek. She speaks Antonio's line, "The gentleness of all the gods go with thee," and leaves (p. 322).

With his health returned, Sebastian overcomes his pessimism and looks forward to the future. The setting changes to New York. Like his sister, he receives a "boy wanted" card from Buddha. But unlike Viola, he's a confident young man and bursts into song:

> I'm a guy going places, and I'm leaving today
> I've got plenty to do and I'd do it with you,
> But I've no time to stop. (p. 322)

The lines begin with alliteration and progress to rhyme—"to," "do," "do," "you"—and conclude with a brief line of six single-syllable words. As he sings "I'm on my way to the top," he exudes self-confidence. Like Viola, he goes in search of Orson. But since Viola/Charlie got there first, Sebastian finds an Orson who says, "This Buddha must be a poor loser. *I'm* your new agent," he insists. "You've got to learn to . . . trust me" (p. 323).

The confusion between brother and sister begins with Buddha's duplicate letters of introduction of each of them to Orson. He starts talking about the letter he has already given Charlie—but that was Viola/Charlie—which he now wants to revise. Sebastian's first brush with reality occurs moments later when Orson tries engaging him in conversation about the letter. Sebastian is dumbfounded. He never received a letter from Orson to give to Olivia. As the audience knows, the messenger was Viola, dressed like her brother. But Orson is adamant. He pushes Sebastian on his way. "He's freaked out!" the young man concludes. But he doesn't care, and he joyously begins singing, "This is the life I was made for." Nothing will stop him; he's "on the way to the top" (p. 324).

In Shakespeare's *Twelfth Night*, Sebastian has a comparatively minor role. After his parting from Antonio, Sebastian wanders out to view the town's sights, and while Antonio will not risk accompanying him, he gives his purse to the youth to spend at will. But, being apprehended by Orsino's men after defending Viola in a confrontation with Sir Toby, Antonio apologetically requests the return of his purse. She, of course, doesn't know him. Nor does she have much money. Antonio then bursts out at her, calling her Sebastian whom he snatched out of the jaws of death. Without acknowledging that she might be Sebastian's sister, she does hope that Antonio is referring to her brother.

Your Own Thing, on the other hand, isn't interested in duels, just in pairing the couples and suggesting the variety of choices open to men if they do "their own thing." While rejecting Shakespeare's creative approach to women, the musical opens a new path toward acceptance of homosexuality as a legitimate choice. Orson becomes enamored of Charlie/Viola and must reexamine some of his long-held ideas, just as the audience must confront theirs. The musical creatively misreads Shakespeare, emphasizing the positive possibilities of homosexual unions. As Clive Barnes noted in his review, "Where else, for example, in *Twelfth Night,* would you find Orson so disturbed by his feelings for Viola, . . . that he starts searching in psychology books on latent homosexuality?" The critic also mentions Olivia's falling for a man ten years younger than herself, another unconventional choice explored in the musical.[17]

In the Renaissance text, Orsino makes a last-minute decision to settle for Viola/Cesario, but Orson in *Your Own Thing* clearly falls for Charlie and must face the fact that he loves a boy. This is a major change. The crucial scene comes late in the play, and begins with Orson reading aloud from books of psychology. "It is not uncommon that these latent desires appear, previously suppressed by fear of society's hostility," he reads, and goes on from this to classical and biblical references. When he finally gets to David and Jonathan, he bursts into one of the best and most enthusiastic songs in the show, declaring, "When you're young and in love, / It's a beautiful thing" (p. 361). And so he, too, will do his own thing. But Viola, shocked by his choice, tries to reveal her true identity. Each time he calls her "Charlie," she tells him, "I'm Viola." Thinking she's merely creating a fiction, he repeats what he thinks is her real name, "Charlie," to her disgust. Finally, thinking that he wants a male rather than a female lover, she decides to leave him.

Olivia, too, embraces an unconventional union. Nowhere in Shakespeare's play is there an indication that Olivia is older than Viola and therefore Sebastian. But the age difference is implied in *Your Own Thing.* Olivia is introduced as someone who prefers young people, therefore her preference for Viola naturally follows. This becomes apparent when Viola, accompanied by the Apocalypse, enters her office. Multiple colored lights—constituting the wallpaper of Olivia's office—and brightly colored flowers establish the environment. "I'm the new Disease," Viola announces. Adopting Shakespeare's lines but, like Sebastian, taking them out of context, Olivia observes, "You're kind of young, aren't you?"

She then turns to the other members of the quartet to say, "He doesn't even have a beard." Converting Shakespeare's line from *Julius Caesar,* one of the Apocalypse, John, notes, "The fault is not in his stars, dear Olivia, but in his genes." With that the lights go out and a balloon slides over Viola's head, displaying her thought: "My God, do you think they've guessed?" (p. 325). A slide of Shakespeare's Globe Theater appears in the background and the men exchange the lines of his clowns. Spots pin Olivia and Viola, who has a tambourine hanging from one arm. When they come out of the freeze, Olivia again delivers Shakespeare's words: "Now Jove in his next commodity of hair / Send thee a beard" (3.1.45; p. 327).

An ambitious collage, *Your Own Thing* permits swift scene changes as a projection or a voice moves the audience from one place to another. Background dreaming, projected visually, accompanies some of the songs. Through this multimedia device, the gods—particularly Buddha—are able to effect many happy coincidences.

Shakespeare not only presents Olivia as a self-possessed young woman but also gives us a sense of Viola's feeling for Duke Orsino when he sends her on the mission to woo Olivia. "I'll do my best / To woo your lady," Viola asserts, then adds in soliloquy, "Yet a barful strife! / Whoe'er I woo, myself would be his wife" (1.4.41–42). She has declared herself early in the play, and Shakespeare depicts her as self-sufficient. In addition, he creates an Olivia who is self-possessed and reasonable, and who refuses to be bullied into accepting any of her several suitors (many of whom are involved in the play's subplot, absent from the musical). Of Orsino she says to Cesario/Viola, "Your lord does know my mind; I cannot love him. / Yet I suppose him virtuous, know him noble, / Of great estate, of fresh and stainless youth. . . . But yet I cannot love him. / He might have took his answer long ago" (1.5.257–63). A clear statement, and a rejection. She knows her mind, and has neither brother nor father to dictate any other answer for her. She remains independent. And then she meets Cesario/Viola, who seems to know all the answers to Olivia's refusals. Olivia is enchanted.

In contrast, the adaptors create an aggressive Olivia who likes to be surrounded by young people and dotes on younger men. She dismisses Orson's suits, finding him square, but is very much attracted to the young Charlie/Viola, who is frightened of her. The stage is set for the appearance of Sebastian.

Then follows a scene illustrating Olivia's aggressiveness while also differentiating brother and sister. The two wear identical outfits—a pair of pants and a light-colored jacket with a dark zipper up the left side. Olivia tries to undress Charlie/Viola, unzipping her jacket, but Viola quickly zips it up again. Sebastian, on the other hand, helps Olivia out. Viola skittishly backs away from the discotheque owner; Sebastian accepts her advances with alacrity.

This dual attraction, Viola's to Orson and Olivia's to Sebastian, shifts the weight of the plot from Olivia's affection for Viola to Orson's affection for Charlie. In *Twelfth Night*, Duke Orsino's weak acceptance of Viola follows his rejection by Olivia. "Boy, thou hast said to me a thousand times / Thou never shouldst love woman like to me," he says, and she answers, "And all those sayings will I overswear" (5.1.267–69). Orson in *Your Own Thing* is more insightful, since he goes to psychology books for answers. Moreover, he has no doubt of his affection for Viola/Charlie, only of its social acceptability.

In Shakespeare's play, the discouraged Duke Orsino, once again rejected by Olivia, confides in the disguised Viola. She asks, "But if she cannot love you, sir?" Unwilling to accept this, the Duke maintains, "I cannot be so answered" (2.4.87–88). As Viola attempts to fill in the gap for him, she creates a transparent story, telling him, "My father had a daughter loved a man / As it might be, perhaps, were I a woman / I should your lordship" (107–108). Although Duke Orsino asks the history of that sister, he never really seems to figure out what she's telling him. A similar conversation occurs in *Your Own Thing*, but Orson pursues it. "And what's her history?" he asks, and then again, "What happened to your sister?" And finally, "Is she anything like you?" And here the musical's Viola deviates from her original. "Spittin' image," she asserts. Orson concludes, "She must be very attractive." Viola and Orson exchange glances. The conversation continues with Orson admitting, "There's a lot of things about girls I don't understand." This prompts her to sing, "When you love a girl, be very gentle," concluding with them both singing, "And all through life, she'll be my/your gentle wife" (pp. 336–38). When the song is over Orson leaves, and the stage goes dark.

John Wayne exclaims, "That man's falling for that boy!" "That's your old problem. It's a girl," responds Bogart. Then they argue. "Yeah, but he don't know that." "Would it change anything if he did?" "Sure, it'd be decent," says Wayne. "No, just legal," Bogart replies. And here the adaptors are probing to the heart of the musical. Queen Elizabeth introduces yet another perspective: "I say, 'Pair anybody off with anything.' The only crime I know is loneliness." A moving observation, it prompts Shakespeare's recitation of another of the Clown's songs, "What is love? 'Tis not hereafter; / Present mirth hath present laughter," a song that concludes with the statement, "Youth's a stuff will not endure" (p. 339).

The adaptors use this verse to lead into Viola's song "What Do I Know": "What do I know of me? / What do I know of you?" The song considers the many unknown areas she will encounter. "What do I know of rainbows after rain? / Where does the wind go after the storm?" Her questions reveal her imagination. The listener can visualize possible answers to her questions. In this ballad, she is wistfully thinking of all the mysteries that confront her. Its music is lyrical and crying for understanding as she progresses to "Where does the sky meet the sea?" In Puerto Rico, perhaps, when one is looking toward the ocean? She moves from questions about locations to one about emotion: "Where is that feeling friendly and warm?" And then the Apocalypse choral background offstage offers other insights, closing with "And when will it happen to me?" The song raises a series of questions suggesting her affection not only for Orson but also for the Apocalypse. It closes with "What's to become of me?" (pp. 339–40).

Viola encounters another problem in her disguise as Charlie. Her appeal to Orson has him agonizing over his choice as he attempts to work out this side of his character. Do men really appeal to him, he wonders? The Apocalypse's song "I'm Me (I'm Not Afraid)" helps him expand his frame of reference:

> Why does everybody have to be afraid to be a human being?
> Why does everybody have to be afraid of other people seeing?
> . . . .
> Me—I'm not afraid to cry
> Me—I'm not afraid to die
> . . . .
> I'm not the starry-eyed boy next door,
> I'm not the life of the party,
> I've got to be what I've got to be.
> I'm me! (pp. 311–13)

4.3. Shakespeare's *Twelfth Night*, with its pair of brother and sister twins who so resemble one another that "an apple cleft in two, is not more twin / Than these two creatures," offered the perfect foil for the twentieth-century *Your Own Thing*. At that time long hair and interchangeable clothing characterized the generation of the 1960s. The adaptors also capitalized on Shakespeare's suggestions of homosexuality, although they shifted the show's emphasis from attraction between women to that between men. In this scene, Orson imagines himself being hanged by cowboys for falling in love with Charlie/Viola, who appears to be a young man. The illustration gives an idea of the complexity of the setting as the production team uses white screens, projections, and backlighting to dramatize his dilemma. *Time & Life Pictures; photographer: Ralph Morse. Appeared in* Life, *March 22, 1968, pp. 84–85.*

And so he decides to try to find out more about himself. Where the early draft of the show offered a scene in a library, in the final version he appears onstage with a stack of books, including the classics as well as the Bible. The adaptors then create a mythic dream sequence that lands Orson on the floor after an encounter with Goliath, who is projected onto the screen. Using a slingshot, Orson knocks the giant out with a button pulled from his shirt. He is imagining himself as David, from the biblical story of David and Jonathan, whose relationship may be homosexual.

Like the brother in Shakespeare's play, the musical's Sebastian, although amazed at what's happening to him, is ready to go along with it.

Members of the Apocalypse see him accompanying Olivia into her room, but then, moments later, Viola enters from another part of the stage. The band members do a double-take, amazed at how quickly "Charlie" seems to have gotten from one place to another. When Viola asks them about Orson, they assure her, "You got no problem, You can move in on Orson whenever you like." Astonished, she asks, "Have you finks known about me all the time?" (p. 344). She thinks they've known she's a woman. But she has made a mistake. They've known she's attracted to Orson, and assume she's a man. Gender doesn't matter.

With brother and sister now within shouting distance of one another, the adaptors interrupt the progress of the plot by introducing the hunca munca, a complicated dance for the whole cast.[18] They wear "freak suits" for the dance. According to the stage directions, "the number is staged and choreographed in the style of modern rock dances." Each of them has a brief stanza in the accompanying song. Viola begins, singing, "We're revolting from the age when lines were drawn / To separate the sexes" (p. 346). And yet, when the guys begin to strip to get into their costumes, Viola disappears and in walks Sebastian, carrying his pants, indicating he's had a rendezvous with Olivia. The lights go down. Queen Elizabeth notes, "Will, they're taking their clothes off on stage." Shakespeare responds, "So it would seem, madam." Others remark on the new development, including Shirley Temple, John Wayne, and Humphrey Bogart (p. 350). When the lights are restored, Sebastian is speaking his lines from *Twelfth Night*: "What relish is in this? How runs the stream? / Or am I mad, or else this is a dream" (4.1.60–61, p. 351). Then Olivia enters. "Did you like my audition?" he asks, then corrects himself: "I meant my singing." She reassures him that he's got the job.

Bringing the script into the present, Sebastian confesses that his name isn't Charlie but Sebastian, and he really wants to be a geologist. Olivia says she wanted to be an archeologist, and the parallel is a little too neat, even corny. She tells him that she went to Sarah Lawrence and that her father is an account executive at BBD&O, a famous advertising agency of the time. Fortunately the subject is dropped as they begin to consider their relationship and their age difference.

Interested in breaking the rules that prohibit male-male and older female–younger male partnerings, the adaptors find a new outlet for their creativity. Rejecting Shakespeare's concern with twins and doubling, the adaptors bring a late twentieth-century perspective to their musical. Using the newest technologies of the time, they open the Renaissance dramatist's ideas to further exploration. Olivia's concern that she is in her "middle years" doesn't trouble Shakespeare. Rather, he has a perplexed Sebastian wondering in soliloquy whether Olivia is sane or not. "This Pearl she gave me, I do feel it and see it; / And though 'tis wonder that enwraps me thus / Yet 'tis not madness." The adaptors create an interesting "conversation" between the two through the use of alternate spots on Sebastian and Olivia and the use of balloons. The audience hears each of them wondering about the age difference between them. First she sings,

> He's twenty, I'm thirty. Does it matter?
> When I'm forty, he'll be thirty. Does it matter?
> Rules, labels, slots, categories
> Lead the way to lonely purgatories.
> What does it matter?

She then moves from a mournful tune to one of exuberance as she decides,

> I finally made it! I shook myself free!
> No more wondering what became of me.

And then the resolution:

> I know where I'm going, no crocodile tears
> Solved the riddle, I'm in my middle years.

The internal rhyme on "riddle" and "middle" emphasizes her age and her adjustment to it, and the song continues to develop a long series of rhymes.

> Tune my fiddle, I'm in my middle years. (pp. 357–58)

Olivia has solved the problem that her strong feelings for Sebastian pose.

The lights go down. The technique of handling soliloquies and dreaming takes over. That is done sometimes through the darkening of the stage and focusing on a balloon over the speaker's head, sometimes through the use of a freeze of all others on stage. In the case of each of them thinking about the age difference between them, the technique is slightly more complicated. "Lights down. Both follow spots on Sebastian, Olivia miming conversation, sits and she continues silent monologue" (p. 254). During this interval first he speaks, then the spots move to her. Olivia sings, "I finally made it! I shook myself free. . . . I'm in my middle years!" Each seems to be in his or her own world. When the stage manager appears with the W4 forms required for "Charlie"'s employment with the Apocalypse quartet and asks his age, a balloon appears above Olivia's head repeating, "I asked you how old you were?" (p. 357). The adaptors are engaging with the rule that says the male should be older than the female. Sebastian hands his form to Olivia and leaves. We are reminded of Queen Elizabeth's remark: "The only crime I know is loneliness" (p. 339).

During the course of the musical, Orson sends a series of letters to Olivia, and Olivia always insists that the letter's bearer read it aloud. She then chooses a line or sentence that can implicate the reader in the letter's sentiments. For instance, the first time Viola (as Charlie) brings her a letter, the older woman catches her off guard. Only when Olivia refuses to read the letter herself does Viola agree to read it aloud. "Anyone can see you prefer me to / Those kids you've been hanging around," she reads. Olivia dissects it so that Viola is repeating only "Anyone can see you prefer me." "You said it." Olivia asserts. The pattern continues. When Viola reappears with another letter, she seems to have read it or heard it from Orson, because she comments that the words aren't persuasive. Here the adaptors have Viola speak a version of her original's line in the first act of *Twelfth Night*: "If I did love you with dea[r] Orson's flame." "What would you do?" asks Olivia, and Viola responds, "Make me a willow cabin at your gate / And call upon my soul within the house, / Write loyal cantons of contemned love / And sing them loud, even in the dead of night" (p. 332). The adaptors have slightly altered Shakespeare's lines, but captured their essence. These lines win Olivia.

The denouement occurs as Sebastian reenters and makes a date with Olivia. He then leaves, and his sister arrives with yet another letter for Olivia while the stage manager presses her for the W4 form. Once again Olivia asks "Charlie" to read the letter aloud. But this time it carries a new and unexpected message: "I give you back your freedom / I cannot love you" (p. 359). It overwhelms and surprises Olivia but delights Viola, who quickly explains, "He doesn't love you anymore." Now she has a chance with Orson. She then runs out, but not before Olivia says she'll meet him (Charlie/Viola) at dinner, confirming the date she just made with Sebastian. The sister quickly, if abruptly, explains that this is purely a job, attempting to disabuse Olivia. The scene confirms the close resemblance of the twins. A confused Olivia looks to the audience, then exits right. The lights go down.

Orson enters with books under his arm. As he reads works on latent homosexuality, he comments, "I'm glad mother is dead." Meanwhile "slides are projected over the entire set showing Viola/Charlie in beguiling poses." Orson begins to sing, "When you're young and in love." The song progresses to "Every bell starts to ring, every season is spring"; he feels "really in love" (p. 361). Slides add an extra dimension as they depict a variety of historical periods, as well as Viola and the Apocalypse.

Combining Orson's fantasies with Viola's story about her father's daughter, the adaptors create a scene where Orson, still fantasizing, tries to tell Charlie to flee, suggesting how harassed homosexuals are, but Viola, smiling, continues telling her story. The cycloramas show Orson being hung, his hands tied behind his back and his neck seeming to search for the noose, dramatizing the fate that may be in store for men who declare themselves gay.[19] Meanwhile, Viola, attempting to tell Orson her name, finally bursts out, "Call me Viola." But Orson can merely answer, "That's not playing this thing very cool," thinking she has made up a name for herself instead of using her real name, Charlie. She hasn't convinced him she's a girl. Finally, in anger, she decides that he only loves her because she appears to be a guy (p. 367).

A broader understanding of the fluidity of sexual identity ultimately results, as Orson concedes that it doesn't matter what Charlie's name is. Once again the conventions of the time intercede. Viola finally takes off her shirt and throws it down, clearly revealing that she is a girl. Nevertheless, Orson seems to have learned from this experience. Like Olivia pleading with Sebastian, Orson too sings, "Don't leave me." The scene must have been a raucous one, with Orson grabbing Charlie's/Sebastian's leg before realizing he has hold of the wrong person and Olivia attempting to protect Charlie/Viola from Orson while Viola pushes the other woman's hand from her shoulder.

In bringing the musical to a close, the adaptors pull out all the stops, combining all the dramatic techniques available to them. In Olivia's dis-

4.4. Convinced of his vulnerability to Charlie/Viola, Orson shields his eyes from looking at her while she aims to prove she is not a he. Shedding her shirt, she reveals her bra. Her body aggressively bends in his direction while Olivia and the laughing Sebastian watch Orson shudder. Although the adaptors ultimately bend to the conventions of the times, their portraits of the confused Orson, the aggressive Olivia, and the uninhibited Apocalypse Quartet suggest the multiple pressures of the rocky, passionate Vietnam years.   *Photo by Frank Derbas, courtesy of Professor Robert Hapgood, retired, University of New Hampshire.*

cotheque, Sebastian and the Apocalypse are dancing the hunca munca. "A completely mad-hatter motion-picture film of bands marching, [and] science-fiction characters" is projected on the screen (p. 369). A kaleido-scope of colors dominates the lighting. Onstage, Orson and Olivia are chasing Viola and Sebastian around the stage. The song is "Don't Leave Me." Only when Viola reenters and gives Olivia back her clothes (left by Sebastian in Olivia's digs, mistaking sister for brother) do brother and sister finally meet. "Vi. Boy, am I glad to see you," the entering Sebastian exclaims (pp. 371–74).

In a concession to accepted patterns, Orson and Viola finally understand each other's true identities and fall in love. On the other hand, Olivia and Sebastian defy accepted patterns, since he is younger than she. The musical takes Shakespeare's play as a jumping-off point but develops its own thesis through a variety of new methods and ideas. The projections embody the multiple voices in the surrounding culture while giving the audience a sense of the narrowmindedness of so many. Although Orson's imaginings of death by hanging and an attack by Goliath may exaggerate what homosexuals of the time were facing, nonetheless they were not yet free to come out of the closet and declare themselves. As Orson suggests to Viola/Charlie, "There's still time for you to get away" (p. 365).

The seventeenth-century dramatist resolves the confusion created by identical twins and offers a comedy that twentieth-century adaptors can use, one that had also appealed to adaptors of other centuries who also altered the play's emphasis. In fact, adaptors frequently cut many of Olivia's more aggressive lines, molding her to fit their own times. The twentieth century, however, seemed to offer a most inviting milieu for her, an aggressive woman on the make.

Your Own Thing won the Critics' Circle Award for best musical in 1968, breaking the unspoken taboo on awarding the prize to a show not on Broadway itself. It had 933 performances in New York and toured simultaneously with seven road companies, in Toronto, Washington, Philadelphia, Boston, Los Angeles, San Francisco, Chicago, and other cities throughout this country as well as in Britain.[20]

Whitney Bolton wrote in the *Morning Telegraph* that although "they call it a rock musical . . . the score is mightily pleasing and often dulcet." He attributed the pace of the production to Donald Driver, who directed and knew a good deal about projection at a time when its use in live theater was very new.[21] Another critic noted the loose reworking of the identity crisis of Shakespeare's twins:

> Throughout this show, squeezed between saucy dances and swinging songs, cracks are made about the imposed polarity of the sexes, the divine-right of government-sponsored wars and the identity crisis of long-haired boys and short-haired girls.[22]

Clive Barnes hailed it in the *New York Times* as "blissfully irreverent to Shakespeare and everything else." He particularly liked "Leland Palmer, kooky and appealing as Viola," who had a "leprechaun's face, a glowing smile, and a sweetly belting voice." And then Barnes hit on the show's greatest strength: "its freshness and unexpectedness."[23] In describing its music, John S. Wilson spoke about the changes in musical theater since *Oklahoma!* but he might have gone as far back as 1938, when *The Boys from Syracuse* opened:

> The underlying rhythms, the phrasing of the singers and the modes of the melodic lines are consonant with the popular music that surrounds us today from the hard core rock of the hot 100 hits to the gentler sounds on the "easy listening" charts.[24]

Wilson called "The Middle Years" a song Richard Rodgers might very well have written, and even compared some of the music to Shakespearean madrigals.

The impact *Your Own Thing* had on the contemporary American theatrical scene led Joe Papp, director of the New York Shakespeare Festival, to observe that the work marked a new direction for musicalizing Shakespeare.[25] Papp tried a rock *Hamlet*, which was not successful,[26] but then he hit gold with *The Two Gentlemen of Verona*. With that production, the American musical was incorporated into a Shakespeare play, rather than the two forms mutually influencing each other. After thirty years of trying, here was a work that transformed American musical theater even as it reimagined Shakespeare as a popular American playwright.

FIVE

The Persistence of Love
Two Gentlemen of Verona

With a snap to their steps despite the midsummer heat, the audience are making their way to the Delacorte Theater in New York's Central Park. They wend their way through the park's paths, cross an open road, and glimpse the amphitheater ahead. An actor serenades them as they wait on the slightly damp paths for the doors to open. Jugglers, too, perform for their amusement. They set the tone for the musical version of *Two Gentlemen of Verona*. It's July 27, 1971, a steamy rain-threatening night in Central Park. Ticket holders hope the threat of rain will subside. Workers confidently begin wiping the seats as patrons breathe a sigh of relief. Restless but patient, the audience will finally be permitted to enter. It's a weekday night but it feels like a weekend. A gay spirit pervades the group as Joe Papp's Shakespeare in the Park opens this musical.

For the first time, people of all colors and sizes fill the stage. These are the people you sit next to on the bus. Suddenly they're alive. Their multiple backgrounds overwhelm the audience. In his preface to the play, John Guare had written that he believed the text could be a metaphor for New York City life in the 1970s, or rather

> the idea of the Big City itself, the megalopolis that forces the kaleidoscope of races and colors and cultures to come in constant friction with one another, to deal with each other, betray each other, love each other, hate each other, in the deepest sense, live with each other and ultimately, hopefully, celebrate each other.[1]

This was not the city of *West Side Story,* with its hatred and bias. Rather, this was the exciting city where people of all races managed to live together.

When the musical starts, the performers are exploding joyously on stage in dance and song. Through the open, skeletal stage set, one sees the park and its lake. One absorbs nature's shifting light as the production moves from dusk to nighttime. A sense of joyousness pervades the stage. Clothes hang on some of the structural beams of the set as people of all colors are dancing, jumping rope, and seeming to celebrate.

Entering through wide-arched passageways, the audience confronts an imaginative three-tiered stage set. Its skeletal outline forms a frame for the setting sun and the lake in the background. Strategically placed lights are ready to illuminate the stage when the natural light disappears.

John Guare said in an interview that what he loved was the review of the musical that spoke about it sounding like the mixture of sounds coming from open windows when going through the Barrio.[2] As if to emphasize this melding of sounds, the musical opens with a character dressed in white "running out on stage. Bird calls begin. Whistles. Crows. Roosters. Doves cooing." He chortles a song to Love, identifying it as far beyond the usual spring-like qualities of gentle breezes and birds singing. It's pervasive and sets the tone of the play's opening: Love's persistence.[3] The general gaiety on stage overwhelms the audience as Cupid shoots arrows and another character, later identified as Lucetta, scatters red tissue-paper hearts on everyone from her perch in the uppermost balcony. The high-pitched singer, later revealed as Thurio, Silvia's suitor, here represents the spirit of Love. After his song, he dances off, replaced by Cupid at center stage, followed by an ensemble.

The music immediately sets the mood, both humorous and modern, for what is to come. The orchestra, highly reduced from those in the early musicals, appears on stage on the second level, occasionally highlighted, then fading into the background as the characters in the major plot take over the stage. At this moment, the ensemble sings about Summer, Autumn, Winter, and Spring while Cupid aims his arrows at everyone. Shakespeare's mockeries of the Petrarchan lover take a twentieth-century turn, this time in Cupid's actions on stage. Moments later the two gentlemen of Verona, Proteus and Valentine, stroll onto the bottommost tier, while Speed, one of their servants, laughingly announces "*Two Gentlemen of Verona* / A play by William Shakespeare."

5.1. The multiethnic cast of *Two Gentlemen of Verona*, joyously singing of love in this opening scene, contrasts vividly with the all-white cast of *The Boys from Syracuse* and even the tentative steps toward multiethnic casting of *Kiss Me, Kate*. On a three-tiered open stage, characters are jumping rope, blowing bubbles, and distributing hearts, while musicians are playing on the center level and Proteus is celebrating his dedication to love. *Friedman-Abeles, Billy Rose Theatre Division, New York Public Library for the Performing Arts, Astor, Lenox, and Tilden Foundations.*

The set, as Clive Barnes observed, is "a special triumph for . . . the set designer, Ming Cho Lee, who has given scaffolding a new chic."[4] Lee created a three-level set that resembled the scaffolding for a new building going up. Most of the action occurs on the first level, the largest playing area, while the other two levels function dramatically to differentiate a series of acting and dancing spaces. Later these offer areas for characters to hide and overhear the plots of others.

As Thurio and Cupid, with their singing and dancing ensemble, recede from view, the action shifts to the major playing space below. There Proteus and Valentine, the two gentlemen of Verona, are debating the virtues of staying at home in Verona versus venturing forth to Milan. Like Shakespeare's pair of gentlemen, Proteus plans to remain in Verona, pursuing Julia, his love interest, whereas Valentine is headed for Milan.

Finally, unable to convince Proteus to join him, Valentine asks his friend, "What do you want to do with the rest of your life?" Astonished, Proteus gropes for an answer. He hadn't thought of that.

> That's a very interesting question
> No one ever asked me that question
> Would you mind repeating that question
> Say that question once again. (1.1, p. 13)

Proteus's response indicates his lack of commitment, a failing which he will later exhibit. The director then focuses audience attention on that third tier of the stage. This time Julia, a beautiful young woman, also present in Shakespeare's play, passes across the stage. Distracting Proteus, she offers an easy answer to Valentine's question. Proteus sings, "I'd like to be a rose / That hangs on Julia's breast." His friend immediately counters, "I'd like to be that oak tree / That one that towers above the rest." As the song continues, each can't understand the other's choice. "Oh, for a night with Julia," Proteus exclaims. "Twenty days of wooing for one night of cooing," Valentine teases. His ambition is greater: "There's a million wonderful people in the world / I want to know them all." He thinks, "Verona is too small for me, / Milan is the place to be." However, they agree on one thing: "We are brothers / We are friends / Up until the day that eternity ends" (1.1, pp. 13–16). Their vow is quickly forgotten when Proteus, aware that he is forsworn, reveals his friend's secrets later in the play. As one critic noted, Guare's rhymes are strange and not always spectacular, but he and MacDermot are refashioning the story in the vernacular of the '70s and maintaining a constant musical line.[5]

This musical Shakespeare was a new phenomenon in the history of the development of the form. Not only was the staging different from that of anything previously done, since it occurred outdoors in the park, but also the role of the Public Theater's producer, Joe Papp, had no equivalent among producers of other musical Shakespeares. He had long brought Shakespeare to the masses. However, ever since *Your Own Thing,* three years earlier, Joe Papp had decided he would present his own "rock musical" in the park. He viewed this performance space as a perfect medium for Shakespeare because he considered Shakespeare a contemporary. What better way to convince his fellow New Yorkers of Shakespeare's popular appeal than through just such a rock musical?

The city owned the park. It had to give Papp permission to use the space, but the story behind the contest between the Parks Department and Papp developed into a long contest about whether to charge for seats. Papp wanted admission to be free. Robert Moses, the Parks Commissioner, wanted the theater to charge for admission, citing the extra expenses the Parks Department would have to pay. Eventually they even battled in court. Papp won. And so citizens of New York had free Shakespeare in the Park.

As well as producing Shakespeare in the Park during the summer, Papp also had developed an indoor theater, the Public Theater, for non-Shakespearean original works. Among these plays was *Hair*. Brought to him by its creators, two self-proclaimed hippies, Gerome Ragni and James Rado, it appealed to Papp and his assistant, Gerald Freedman, whose only concern was finding a composer. They did.

His name was Galt MacDermot. He was as square as they were hip, but his musical background was vast; not only had he written oratorios and other forms of church music, but he had mastered several other musical styles, including pop, swing, jazz, blues, and rock 'n' roll. In addition to working as a church organist for seven years, he had been a prominent jazz musician for much longer. His father had been the Canadian high commissioner to South Africa, where the young man had absorbed South African music, especially Quala. "Disco kinda killed rhythm for a while in the '70s and rap brought it back. To me that's what music's all about," he said in 2001.[6] Unlike Ragni and Rado, MacDermot had no experience in theater. Nevertheless, he became part of the team behind the musical *Hair*.

Hair opened in October 1968 at the Public Theater. Although the critics disliked it, it became a hit, and Papp later moved it uptown to Broadway. According to Helen Epstein, Papp's biographer, the musical became a symbol of pacifism, and its songs turned out to be very popular. The play itself seemed structureless. Nevertheless, this absence of structure marked an innovation that *Hair* brought to the American musical. Just as critics initially saw *West Side Story* as merely a picture of the ugliness of street life, missing its poetry, so they misread the form of *Hair*. According to Epstein, the critics "did not grasp this radical shift nor did they appreciate the amplified beat of the six-piece rock band situated ten feet above the stage." Papp answered the critics and critical audience response with an open letter explaining that young people of the time did not trust the existing institutions, sexual mores, and dress codes, and that they were rebelling against "old values, which have produced four wars in the past fifty years." He endorsed their right to speak up.[7]

Following *Hair*'s success, Papp invited MacDermot to write the music for a version of Shakespeare's *Two Gentlemen of Verona*. "Joe Papp called me," MacDermot explained,

> and asked me to do a song, so I wrote "Who Is Sylvia?" Next thing that happened was that Mel Shapiro, who was called on to direct the musical, decided he didn't want to just do a play but wanted to have some fun. So he called John Guare (who was to write the adaptation). His idea was to have a song, written in the vernacular, in each scene. During a run-through, they discovered how very long that was. So they began cutting and just kept the major incidents with their accompanying songs.[8]

This was an important decision. It led to a musical rich in song and outspokenly critical of the Vietnam War, but with an abbreviated plot line. Nevertheless, the central story line remained more or less faithful to Shakespeare.

Unlike MacDermot, who was a comparative newcomer to the Public Theater, John Guare and Mel Shapiro had worked with Papp before. Guare, a playwright, had written several off-Broadway plays, many produced by Papp. A New Yorker, born on February 5, 1938, Guare attended Georgetown University. While there, he not only edited the school's literary magazine but also wrote three one-act plays. Later, pursuing that interest, he attended the Yale School of Drama from 1960 to 1963, where he honed his playwriting skills. He wrote several plays that were produced off-Broadway, some of them by Papp. In 1971 his *House of Blue Leaves,* directed by Shapiro, opened off-Broadway, where it won awards and was seen as the work of a promising new dramatist. That summer *The Two Gentlemen of Verona* opened in Central Park. In fact, *Blue Leaves* was being performed on the night when the musical opened.

Until this time, the major twentieth-century American musicals based on Shakespeare had originated with their adaptors. Rodgers and Hart were already a team when they thought about working on a Shakespeare play and asked George Abbott to join them. Bernstein and Robbins had also worked together and, it appears, were good friends by the time they thought of using the Romeo and Juliet story to extend the musical into the realm of tragedy. Spewack and Porter, too, had collaborated before they joined forces on *Kiss Me, Kate*. And Hal Hester and Danny Apolinar had worked together in other venues, such as nightclubs, and had even co-owned one. They invited Donald Driver to join them because they had been advised by friends to strengthen the writing in *Your Own Thing*. But the case of *Two Gentlemen of Verona* was different. Although Guare, Shapiro, and MacDermot were ultimately responsible for the musical, making major decisions along the way, the original impetus came from Joe Papp. He brought the adaptors together, believing that rock was here to stay and that the Public Theater's Shakespeare in the Park should be part of this new movement.

According to John Guare, Shapiro was skeptical that *Two Gentlemen of Verona* could successfully tour the city, as Shakespeare in the Park productions normally did. He found it incongruous for a play about courtly love to be performed before people suffering through ninety-degree days in the African American slums of Bedford Stuyvesant, Brooklyn, especially in light of the racial unrest in the city the previous summer. "So Galt MacDermot . . . and I began writing songs for *Two Gentlemen*," Guare observed, always with the dual audience in mind.[9]

In the musical, after the two friends part, Proteus is momentarily depressed by Valentine's departure but quickly recovers. Noting, "He after honour hunts, I after love," he sprawls on the floor, with his writing pad before him, and starts penning a love letter to Julia. He continues quoting Shakespeare: "Thou, Julia, thou hast metamorphosed me / Made me neglect my studies, lose my time, / War with good counsel, set the world at nought / Made wit with musing weak, heart sick with thought." This speech leads into his next song, "Thou Has Metamorphosed Me," which not only expresses his feelings but also offers a clue to his name—Proteus—which reflects how his quick shifts of affection and loyalty dot the musical. When one looks at these lines one realizes Shakespeare's contribution. Proteus is already aware of his own weakness: his inability to take advice. He also realizes he has thought too much about things like love. Moreover, Valentine's question, "What do you want to do with the rest of your life?" finds its answer in Shakespeare's text. The dramatist is aware of the foibles and weaknesses of youth and has put them into words for this love-sick young man. As one critic noted, "It is . . . one thing to go in for crowd pleasing and quite another to do it with style and genius. And, while Guare, Shapiro et al. can lay claim to plenty of style, it is still Shakespeare who supplies the genius."[10]

The persistence of love, which defines Proteus, also spreads to Julia and eventually Valentine as each is pierced by Cupid's arrows that opened the musical. While Proteus is writing his love letter, Julia and her servant Lucetta enter the bottommost tier with rakes, hoes, and burlap bags. (And the audience realizes that it was Lucetta who scattered the tissue-paper hearts at the show's beginning.) Proteus quickly moves away, reacting to the women's presence. (According to the text of the play, they scare off Proteus, who is "terrified at their proximity" [1.1, p. 17], but his subsequent actions hardly support the word "terrified.") The women's transformation to farm girls by the adaptors adds not only a laugh but also a new dimension to the differences between Julia and Proteus. In Shakespeare's text, no class differences between the two lovers exist. Rather, Proteus's father thinks his son is too preoccupied with women and wants him to be more cosmopolitan.

"Wouldst thou then counsel me to fall in love?" Julia asks Lucetta when they are alone (1.2.2).[11] A rather foolish question, it betrays Julia's naivete. Lucetta's answer is a qualified "Yes," if you don't stumble. Shakespeare's Julia, when alone, later scolds herself for being so unkind to Proteus by refusing to accept the letter his servant had passed to Lucetta to give to her, then blames Lucetta for allowing her to do so:

> What, fool is she, that knows I am a maid,
> And would not force the letter to my view!
> Since maids, in modesty, say "no" to that
> Which they would have the profferer construe "ay." (1.2.53–56)

Said aloud after Lucetta leaves, the lines reveal Julia's play-acting and Shakespeare's insights. Julia would like Lucetta to work at convincing her young mistress to accept Proteus's note. But Lucetta appears to be fed up with her. Julia must figure out the solution to her own problem. Shakespeare creates in Julia a young woman who has taught herself to dissemble. "How churlishly I chid Lucetta hence, / When willingly I would have had her here!" she admits. "How angerly I taught my brow to frown, / When inward joy enforced my heart to smile" (60–63). Shakespeare, even in this early comedy, has captured a flirtatious young woman who follows the dictates of society although they contradict her true feelings.

Shakespeare's play ranges back and forth between Verona and Milan, but otherwise does not have the flexibility of place that the modern musical has. *Two Gentlemen of Verona* takes advantage of variety in lighting and space. The adaptation relies on the set, with its three levels and the division of each level by lighting, to create various playing areas. Once the musical moves to Milan, it does not return to Verona. Instead, the set provides the variety of places necessary to move the action. Each of the three tiers has three sections easily marked. Red, yellow, and blue colors contribute to the range and intensity of the lights. Sometimes these areas are connected with one another. At other times they help shift the action. Suddenly the pillar in the center of the set takes on new importance. Not only does it define the edges of an area, but it also later becomes a prop behind which to hide. Psychedelic lighting, a feature of rock performances, is also used.

Determined to bring *Two Gentlemen of Verona* to the stage, the adaptors focused on retaining its story but capturing a twentieth-century tone in their adaptation. Like Shakespeare's play, the musical revolves around two young men, friends from Verona, who choose different paths to maturity. Although Proteus intends to stay behind and court Julia, his father, believing his son needs broadening, sends the young man after his friend Valentine to Milan. Before Proteus leaves, however, he wins Julia and promises to be faithful to her. Once in Milan he discovers that his friend has fallen in love with a woman named Silvia, whose father, the Duke, has betrothed her to a wealthy and stupid suitor, Thurio. To prevent her from running away, the Duke locks Silvia up nightly in a tower.

Thus love exists in both young men's lives. But, despite his long farewell to Julia and his promise of everlasting loyalty, Proteus quickly forgets his vows and falls in love with Silvia too. Perfidiously, he informs the Duke of Valentine's plan to elope with Silvia, stealing her from her locked chamber. Shakespeare creates a wonderful scene in which the Duke discovers Valentine's secret, finds the rope ladder hidden beneath his cloak, and banishes the young man to the forest. And here the adaptation deviates from the original.

Whereas the Renaissance dramatist fashions a most unlikely group of outlaws who reside in the forest and are taken with Valentine, deciding he would make a perfect leader for them, the adaptors dispense with the outlaws. Instead, Valentine is put on guard duty with the army, a nonexistent subject in the original. The adaptors have introduced a contemporary subject, one on the minds of their audience at this moment: the Vietnam War. Nor does Sir Eglamour's role remain static. A friend of Silvia's in Shakespeare's play, he becomes a former lover in the adaptation. In both, he at first tries to help her escape. Again, the adaptors have created a new alternative and introduce a marvelously original scene with Eglamour responding to the call of his name and the message of a dove sent to him by Silvia as he climbs over the balcony of the theater and runs up the aisle onto the stage with the dove on his shoulder.

The play wouldn't be a Shakespeare comedy without servants: clowns, assistants, or clever slaves. Launce and Speed attend Proteus and Valentine; Lucetta advises Julia. And Shakespeare also gives Launce a silent partner, the dog Crab, who adds delightful humor to the play; this is the only time the dramatist created such a twosome that had such a long partnership in the play.[12]

The musical turns the story and characters into a wonderfully original rock production that moves on three levels of staging and relies on a multiethnic cast. The adaptors of *Two Gentlemen of Verona* not only retained Shakespeare's title (which may have been in deference to the rules for productions of Shakespeare in the Park) but also sought to construct their musical within the bounds of the original text. Rather than using another story as a metaphor for the broader meaning of their play, the adaptors have added color and shadings that reflected contemporary events and attitudes while maintaining the framework of Shakespeare's *Two Gentlemen of Verona*.

The adaptors wanted to capture the multinational character of Shakespeare's play—an English Renaissance comedy based on a Spanish source that took place in Italian cities imagined by an English dramatist four centuries earlier—with happy melding of people in such a place as New York City. Their vision helps explain the polyglot nature of the show, replete with Spanish outbursts in the text, the use of Calypso rhythms, and even the references to other countries. The adaptors bring this idea to life through casting—the actual appearance of the actors and the sounds of their voices—along with the decision that a specifically English accent would not override these native inflections. No longer is it merely the language, or the songs, or the beat of the music, but casting and speech together help produce an integrated form. As Guare explains,

> For the original production, we cast a Puerto Rican for Proteus and Speed, a Cuban for Julia, Valentine and Silvia and the Duke and occasionally Lucetta were played by Blacks, Launce was originally done in Yiddish, then went country western in a cast change, Eglamour was Chinese, Thurio was an Irishman, Lucetta a Russian-Danish girl. The chorus was every color under the sun. . . . The only secret for producers of subsequent productions of this version of Shakespeare's play is to look around their city and see who lives here and get them upon this stage. In the megalopolis of the 70s, it's so easy not to be noticed, but no longer can anyone be ignored.[13]

These casting choices reflected those of the Public Theater and of Joe Papp, who supported and encouraged the careers of a range of playwrights and performers without regard to their ethnic background.

This ambitious aim of the adaptors expressed their idealism. It contradicted the period's venomous racial hatred, with white backlash directed at calls for Black Power. The aim was obvious to those who attended the show. As Peter Schjeldahl observed, "The nerviest coup of this production is . . . its interracial casting." He was aware of the way members of the cast worked together, not as members of a particular racial group but simply as people, most especially as performers in a Shakespeare play. Those who saw the original production in the park (or listened to its soundtrack) could not miss the Spanish lilt in Raul Julia's speech and in Diane Davila's rendition of Julia's songs. As she spits them out, a touch of Spanish gives an added twist to the music. Nor could one overlook the talents of the performers sent from New York to Melbourne: the strong warm voice of Gilbert Price as Valentine—one of the gentlemen—who established an immediate rapport with the audience; or the intensity of Gail Boggs as Silvia, who "is the hottest property Melbourne has seen for years."[14]

The musical made a star of Raul Julia. In his short career in the theater, he not only soared but revealed a wonderful sense of humor and fun, which was first uncovered in *Two Gentlemen of Verona*. His talents shone throughout. Movements of his body accompanied the slight inflections and deceptive twists of his voice. Tom Prideaux, writing in

Life, described him as "a tall, scowling newcomer named Raul Julia, who glares through his spectacles like a sullen trout, recites Shakespeare with wonderful clarity, sings with near-operatic richness and is the freshest comedian in years."[15]

Having escaped from the women in that early scene, Proteus continues penning his love letter on the topmost tier, where the spotlight now focuses on him. Darkness has taken over Central Park. The opening set slowly disappears, visible only through lighting. The spotlight shifts to the third tier, less often used but highly effective, where Proteus continues his wooing with a solo. "Would you mind if I made you immortal," he sings, and then continues in march time. Of course, he won't write this symphony unless she agrees. "If you will not love me forever . . . then I will leave you alone" (1.1, p. 18). The adaptors capture Proteus's pretentiousness and pomposity in this song. After writing his love letter, he hands it to the chorus members, who are dancing up and down the stairs between the levels and who pass it downward until it reaches Launce, Proteus's servant, who is at the base, where Julia and Lucetta are standing. He hands the letter to Lucetta, who in turn passes it to Julia, who tears it up. Shock ripples through the bystanders.

Accompanied by a guitar and drums playing in march time, Julia indignantly responds, singing in a high, squeaky voice, "I am not interested in poetry / Poetry's another word for love / I am not interested in music / Music is another word for love . . . I find love alarming / I'm happier farming" (1.1, p. 20). The adaptors then give the scene a new twist. While she is responding to Proteus, Thurio reappears. Once more the sound of birdcalls fills the air. Next a soprano, who also enjoys "love, love, love," appears. The adaptors provide the background to overwhelm Julia. Once more, Thurio chortles his dedication to "love," being specific:

> Love is that you
> That fills my ears
> That fills my nose
> That fills my heart. (1.1, p. 20)

Guare interweaves the prosaic and the romantic in this verse: love fills the nose as well as the heart. In other words, love is everywhere. In this musical, it persists despite all obstacles. Addressing the surrounding world, Thurio continues. Love is personified. "Speak up / Speak up / Don't be so shy," the singer insists, then "crosses to Soprano," throwing confetti at her as well as Julia. After flitting around the stage and preparing to chase one another, Thurio and the soprano are, according to the stage directions, deliriously happy "as cupids on a rape" (p. 21). What exactly are we to infer from this phrase? Do they act in a particular way, or is this merely a preface to what occurs later in the scene, since another of the stage directions informs the reader, "Julia has been metamorphosed"? Seemingly hypnotized by Thurio and Cupid, she begins picking up the torn pieces of Proteus's letter, kissing them, and stuffing them into her bosom. Furthermore, following the pattern of Shakespeare's comedy, she then sends Proteus an unexpected letter, which he mentions: "Here is her hand, the agent of her heart; / Here is her oath for love, her honor's pawn" (1.3.46–47). (The dramatist will, in later comedies, be more subtle in contrasting a young woman's socially expected responses and her actual feelings.)

When Thurio throws the confetti at the soprano as well as Julia, his action looks almost like someone casting a spell. The first result is the soprano with Thurio being deliriously happy "as cupids on a rape." This is followed at once by Julia's action of handing Proteus a letter where she expresses her feelings—"I love you"—but also by her "taking Proteus' hand," leading him down left, and lying on the floor. At this point, Launce takes over. He begins to describe in detail what is occurring on the floor. As if recording in his master's voice, he begins, "You leaned down to kiss me / And your pearls got in my mouth," then continues, becoming ever more vivid. "So I brushed back the pearls / And I kissed your mouth." The pearls are pushed aside, and the song culminates with "You just said you loved me, / And the pearls came out of your mouth" (1.1, p. 27). The ending is clear. The next time Julia appears, the audience hears that she is pregnant.[16]

As so often occurs in Shakespeare adaptations, the dramatist's complex sequence of scenes falls before a simpler and more direct order, losing some of its subtlety in the process. In Shakespeare's comedy, after parting from Proteus, Valentine next appears in Milan at the Duke's palace. Proteus, on the other hand, has not yet left Verona and is still deeply involved with Julia. In a short scene between Proteus and his father, his father decides that Proteus could use some broadening of his horizon. He will be sent to Milan, despite the young man's protestations. The adaptors omit this scene and instead introduce Proteus's father for a brief moment to tell the youth he is to head for Milan. Anything he leaves behind will be sent after him.

Shakespeare has two scenes surrounding Proteus's being sent to Milan. The first shows his father, Antonio, speaking with his servant Pantino and discussing the idea of sending his son abroad, then breaking the news to Proteus. The second, a very brief scene of farewell between the youth and Julia where they pledge everlasting loyalty to one another, ends with Pantino's announcement "Sir Proteus, you are stay'd for" (2.2.18). Between the two Shakespeare takes us to Milan, where Valentine meets the Duke and is overwhelmed by Silvia. He is even teased by his servant, Speed, that he has all the signs of a lover:

> First, you have learned (like Sir Proteus) . . . to walk alone, like one that had the pestilence; to sigh, like a schoolboy that had lost his ABC; to weep, like a young wench that had buried her grandam; . . . and now you are metamorphos'd with a mistress, when I look on you, I can hardly think you my master. (2.1.18–32)

Thus Speed pinpoints Valentine's many resemblances to his lover friend, Proteus. The speech is an early attempt by the dramatist to depict the growth of a character. Only after this does Shakespeare return the audience briefly to Verona, long enough to witness the brief parting scene between Proteus and Julia. They exchange rings and he pledges eternal fealty; if he stops thinking of her, "may some foul mischance / Torment [him]" (2.2.11–12). Humor and satire mark this scene of their parting.

The musical, however, never leaves Verona, showing Proteus bidding his long farewell to Julia. Supported by an ensemble, Proteus sings "What Does a Lover Pack?" in which he exaggeratedly enumerates: "one thousand love letters" that he never mailed, as well as "Pictures of Julia / Portraits of Julia / Albums of Julia / Cameos of Julia / Statues of Julia." The adaptors have captured the impassioned verbiage of the Petrarchan lover in twentieth-century style. Guare's lines interweave two sets of voices. "What does a lover pack?" and the comment "Pack in his sack that he'll stack upon his back." The next chorus again asks "What does a lover pack?" answered with "Bring in his sling that he'll swing beneath his wing." Repetition of a phrase followed by a swift move to another idea characterizes the form. "What does a lover pack?" invokes the new rock music. Accompanied by the repetition of the beat, whether of drums or a bass guitar, MacDermot creates a contemporary sound and pattern in his song (1.1, p. 26).

Additionally, the parting scene between the lovers takes a twentieth-century twist. First, Proteus has difficulty fitting Julia's ring on his pinkie. Then, as they're about to kiss, her pearls once more get in the way, so she throws them onto her back. Finally, the two lovers make the same promise their Shakespearean counterparts do: he pledges constancy and invokes the heavens to curse him should he forget his promise. With that, he leaves for Milan, where his friend Valentine will welcome him with open arms. This shift of place is the only one in the musical; once Proteus and Launce arrive in Milan, the rest of the action takes place in and around that city.

Before that, however, the adaptors achieve a scene shift before our eyes, while we're still in Verona. Proteus and Launce mime sailing away, with Launce paddling and Proteus singing one of his more famous songs, titled "I Love My Father." Actually, the song is about loving oneself. After listing all the people he loves—"my father," "my mother," "my sister," and "my brother"—Proteus develops at length his love of himself.

> I love my mirror
> I want to tell me
> I want to love me
> You can't love another
> Without loving yourself. (1.1, pp. 12, 30; 2.1, pp. 82, 85)

Proteus had opened the play with the song. He sings it again at this moment of leaving Verona, while he and his servant mime their departure. The speed of the change of scenes takes us back to Verona, where "working women enter," two scarecrows appear at the top level, and a very dejected Julia and Lucetta enter, singing, "It's very lonely for two ladies in Verona / It's very nice to be a man / And sail off to Milan" (1.1, p. 31). But their song doesn't end here. The audience's attention is redirected from the bottom level, where Lucetta and Julia are, to the scarecrows on the top level. Then Julia continues, "If I were a young man, / I wouldn't be preg*nant*." The lyricist reveals his creativity by forcing an unusual stress on the final syllable, adding emphasis and humor with the false rhyme of "man" and "preg*nant*." Moreover, the introduction of a pregnant Julia helps stress the theme of betrayal to a 1971 audience who might otherwise not have been concerned by a Julia discarded for a new woman. English interlarded with Spanish provides the patterned rhythm of their song, and the chorus sings,

> Take the clothes right off that scarecrow
> And if that scarecrow dare crow
> Tell him he is dealing with
> Two gentlemen
> Two gentlemen of Verona. (1.1, p. 32)

The song is telling a story, a characteristic of rock, and not worrying too much about lyric beat and strong rhyme. The other women strip the scarecrows to provide masculine clothes for Julia and Lucetta. Disguised as youths—actually as somewhat disreputable farm boys—they head for Milan, singing Proteus and Valentine's first song:

> We are brothers, we are friends
> Up until the day that eternity ends. (1.1, p. 16)

As Guare explained, these two women are the "two gentlemen of Verona" at this point.[17] In Shakespeare's comedy, Lucetta disappears from the text after having dressed Julia for the trip to Milan, disguised as a youth traveling alone.

Despite the twentieth-century musical's close resemblance to Shakespeare's comedy, differences between them do occur. Shakespeare's omission of Lucetta for the rest of the comedy is one example. Guare decided against Julia's traveling alone. His point of reference was Shakespeare's *As You Like It,* that later forest play in which Rosalind and Celia travel together, providing companionship and solace to one another.[18]

Pregnancy was a hot political issue in 1971. Fierce debates raged over a woman's right to an abortion, a subject referred to later in the musical. By 1973, in *Roe v. Wade,* the Supreme Court would vote in favor of a woman's right to choose and abortion would become legal. Later in the play, after Proteus's rejection of Julia, many different voices offer her advice. At this moment in the musical, however, she is off to Milan, full of hope and optimism.

An imaginative conjuring of what travel between Verona and Milan might mean follows. The audience floats in a time capsule of sorts. Descriptions of the many places they see and the hazards they must chance challenge the travelers. Although Proteus and Launce had already mimed their departure, and Valentine and Speed are believed ensconced in Milan, they all participate in this scene. The technique borrows from the rock performers of the day, who tended to expound their stories in song, creating brief ballads of personal adventure. The music and lyrics for the travel section exemplify this technique.

Journeying in pairs, Valentine and Speed, Proteus and Launce, and Julia and Lucetta go through mysterious areas and see a rainbow. For the first time, "the chorus appears in black capes and black masks and forces the travelers to weave in and out of its path." Lighting as well as poetry and music intensify the experience. Valentine sings first, referring to the surrounding scene: "Follow the rainbow / Then turn right at the sun / Which you see going down." His closing word leads to the opening of the next triplet, this time sung by Speed: "Down in the valley / Then underneath the waterfall / And mountain (pass)." Valentine picks it up from here: "Pass by the pine trees / The moss is always growing / On the northern (side)" (1.1, p. 33). The images suggest the range of places they see. Alliteration of "pass" and "pine" further stresses the imagery. The next line includes both alliteration and internal rhyme: "Sidesaddle, we'll straddle / Rattlesnakes and fiddle / While we paddle (down)." The repetition of the "ddle" and "ttle" offers a great sound package as the travelers sing of their adventures. While it's hard to visualize straddling rattlesnakes, it's easy to visualize fiddling "while we paddle." Moving on different levels of the stage set, they seem on utterly unlike paths without fear, or hope, of running into one another. This scene appeared on the stage when *Two Gentlemen of Verona* moved to Broadway.[19]

In the park, however, the size of the amphitheater permitted the travelers to pop up in the darkness, lit for a moment by a spotlight, as they wove through a darkened theater illuminated only occasionally by moonlight. Valentine again sings of hazards that confront him. "Down through the rapids / And somersault the waterfall / And whirling (pool)" (1.1, p. 33). In the line "somersault the waterfall," Guare again reveals his poet's ear. The song evokes the hardships they face as they steer toward Milan, avoiding the black-cloaked characters blocking their path. After

Valentine and Speed exit, Proteus and Launce enter, the latter exclaiming in song, "How can we ever be found?" Their exit then paves the way for the reentry of Valentine and Speed, who appear on the third level. All the characters and their adventures contribute to a sense of the difficulties and hazards of the trip. This is especially true when Lucetta and Julia enter and voice their fears that "rajahs and bloodthirsty sheiks / Cause those shrieks / Girls being forced / We are lost" (1.1, p. 33). The short lines, the off-center rhyme add to the excitement, humor, and delight of this interlude.

This is no straight telling of the story but a series of new impressionistic inventions related to rock, through which the characters record their adventures. Moving on different levels of the set, Valentine and Speed then reappear. Suddenly they look up and "the whole scene changes. It's Milan and it looks wonderful and inviting." Valentine bursts out,

Milan, we finally got here
Where's fame
How do I apply? (1.1, p. 34)

The set is alive with light and color. Once again, casting plays an important role. On the topmost tier stands a large black man with a booming voice who is dressed like a Black Panther, a member of the radical Black Power group. He announces himself as the Duke: "I'm the boss here / Silvia / This is my little girl" (p. 34). And standing next to them, all in white, is Thurio, whom we met before at the musical's opening. The Duke introduces Thurio as the man who is to wed his daughter. Meanwhile, further filling the stage, a group of girls are dancing on the main floor below.

Whereas Shakespeare's Duke was an arbitrary leader intent on marrying his daughter to the wealthy Thurio, this Duke is a political figure with a definite message. Presented as a leader who took his people to war, he is now campaigning for reelection, promising to bring the troops back home. "When I got into office / There was too much peace," he proclaims, so he sent his troops all over. "Since I've been elected / I've put troops from here to Rome," he asserts, and then promises, "And if I'm reelected / I'll bring all the boys back home." The chorus sings, "Bring 'em home, / Bring 'em home / Bring all the boys back home." The adaptors are satirizing those promising to "bring the troops back home" from Vietnam.

As the song develops, it becomes more and more bitter and direct. "You should be proud / And feel all warm," the Duke continues; "A shroud's / A lovely uniform" (1.1, pp. 36–37). The United States was involved in a war many of its youth abhorred; some even fled to Canada rather than face the draft and be sent to Vietnam. The quagmire of Vietnam was fueling protests at home.

Nineteen-seventy-one was a turbulent time in American history. Under Lyndon Johnson, the Vietnam War had escalated over the years since John F. Kennedy, then president, had sent American "advisors" to Southeast Asia. Popular dissatisfaction as the war continued, however, led Johnson not to stand for a second term. Americans were dying in combat, and those at home increasingly were voicing their disapproval of the policy that sent U.S. soldiers into the Vietnam quagmire. Richard Nixon, with his running mate, Spiro Agnew, won the election in 1968, promising to bring the troops home. Nothing much happened, although by 1970 the Paris peace talks on Vietnam took place. The Vietnam War was, however, a civil war, and the American presence was not wanted. Nevertheless, American troops remained. In 1971 the secret Pentagon Papers on Vietnam were published, revealing the opposite of what the generals had declared. There was no progress in Vietnam; the U.S. was losing the war. In the meanwhile, in 1970 students at Kent State protested the extension of the war into Cambodia and were fired on by the National Guard. Four students were killed. This dreadful period was capped in 1972 by the Watergate break-in, an attempt by Nixon and his men to find the plans of the Democratic National Committee and steal them.

The adaptors were also satirizing those promising to "bring the troops back home" from Vietnam, by noting how many soldiers were being returned in body bags. The song becomes increasingly bitter and direct as it attacks an administration bent on continuing a worthless war, so costly in human life. The mood in the United States in 1971 confirmed the antiwar sentiment expressed in this song. It also revealed revulsion against those perpetuating the Vietnam War. The organic musical succeeded in integrating a contemporary political topic within its broader scope.[20]

Meanwhile, dressed in white with gold trimmings and half the Duke's size, Thurio not only accompanies the Duke but acts as a drill sergeant, giving the troops orders. Thurio's passivity despite his assigned role suggests the complicity of those supporting the war. Because he is the same character who opens the musical singing a song about love, he hardly appears to be threatening even while ordering troops around. Even at his most unpleasant, he is somehow distant, not well defined, and reactive. As Guare pointed out, "He's a fool."[21]

Moving from this bitter antiwar section to one full of excitement, the adaptors take us to "Valentine's Letter Writing Shoppe" on the bottom tier of the stage, where Valentine is composing a letter to Silvia. Suddenly she appears above, on the third tier, and begins singing "Who Is Silvia?" from Shakespeare's play. Originally designed to describe the young woman as a paragon of virtue, the song later changes in the hands of the adaptors and describes an earthy, flesh-and-blood woman. Shakespeare's song begins,

> Who is Silvia? What is she?
> That all our swains commend her?
> Holy, fair, and wise is she,
> The heavens such grace did lend her,
> That she might admired be. (4.2.39–43)

In the musical Valentine, looking up from his desk, joins Silvia in the song. But then Speed calls her name and she disappears, to Valentine's annoyance (1.1, p. 38). Shortly thereafter, however, she reappears, this time in disguise, at the young lover's shop. Her face partially covered by a red scarf and wearing sunglasses, she asks Valentine to write a letter for her to her love, Eglamour. It begins "To Whom It May Concern" and details the physical attractions of her love, but somewhere in the middle, it becomes a letter to Valentine. Acting seductively, and stretched out on his desk, she shows little resemblance to Shakespeare's Silvia. In fact, later she rejects that portrait when she insists to those who would keep her trapped in the tower, "Release me / From your fantasy / . . . Let me go / Set me free / Love me / I am not solid gold / Touch me / I am flesh and blood and bone" (2.1, p. 70).

This scene in the musical grows out of an exchange between Speed and Valentine in Shakespeare's play where the servant attempts to convince his master that the letter Silvia has dictated for Valentine to write down is in fact intended for him. She tries to hand it back to him, but he's far too literal to understand. "If it please you, take it for your labor," she finally directs. Only the servant, Speed, understands: "O jest unseen, inscrutable, invisible / As a nose on a man's face" (2.1.133–36).

From this scene the adaptors create "Valentine's Letter Writing Shoppe." They erase all obscurity, so that the scene becomes a direct exchange between Silvia and Valentine. Later on, in act 2, her song suggests, "Look at me, feel me, I'm real" (2.1, p. 69). Here is an outright plea for people to look at her and touch her.

This flesh-and-blood Silvia comes to life first in "Night Letter." Having arrived at his letter-writing shop in disguise, she explains that she wants him to write a letter for her and asks his rates. Well, Valentine answers, "We have day rates and night rates." The night rates are cheaper. Her song "Night Letter" follows. As she dictates the letter, she explains, "I have a secret lover / That I do adore / But my pappy / Sent him off to war." His name is Eglamour, and her letter to him becomes very explicit: "My arms and legs and fingers and knees / Long to wrap around your chest and neck and back and legs." Clearly, she is passionately longing for him. Valentine attempts to take dictation. But he slips. When repeating her dictation back to her, he sings "Save me, Silvia" instead of "Save me, Eglamour" (1.1, pp. 40–42). Suddenly she looks at him. Perhaps he can save her. After asking his name, she muses, "I came in here to write to my lover Eglamour. / Instead I found a truer love": Valentine (p. 40). Thus the adaptation bridges the gap between Shakespeare's play and the twentieth-century musical.

Silvia's song, "Night Letter," develops into a wonderful duet between her and Valentine. "Night letter / So divine / Night letter / Come be mine / Nothing better than a / Hot night letter." She continues, "Hear me drool / Nothing wetter than a hot night letter." The double entendres explode from the page as she continues to dictate her letter. Explaining her dilemma of being betrothed to Thurio but hoping to be saved by Eglamour, she begs Valentine to help her. "Help me . . ." but she forgets his name. "Valentine," he volunteers. The song develops into a rich song and dance number between them as they arrange for him to save her from her father and Thurio. She mounts his desk, ready to cajole him. Sexually writhing before going into a dance, she chooses to send this letter not as a day letter but as a night letter. She and Valentine begin dancing to "Night Letter." The song was a smash hit. As they continue to work out details in

5.2. In Valentine's Letter Writing Shoppe, Silvia (Jonelle Allen) announces, "I'm real, not your idea of me," inviting Valentine (Clifton Davis) to help her. Their song "Night Letter," a sensation at the time, mixes rock and island music. Forward and earthy, this twentieth-century Silvia differs from Shakespeare's idealized character. *Friedman-Abeles, Billy Rose Theatre Division, New York Public Library for the Performing Arts, Astor, Lenox, and Tilden Foundations.*

song of how he will save her, "Night Letter" morphs into "Night Ladder." "It's a high tower." "Think baby, think think baby" they repeat responsively in song until he thinks of a "night ladder." Once again they use the pattern of rock. "Let me think," he sings; "think baby, think baby" she responds over and over again. "I got to get my thoughts together," he declares, "I got to get organized." As they build up this musical conversation, he declares, "I think I got it," and later "Talkin' 'bout a night ladder / Night ladder / Good and strong," then together they sing, "Night ladder / Ten feet long," and eventually conclude, "Tonight at eight / Will be just great." Having resolved their difficulties with him going in search of a strong night ladder, they part ecstatically (1.1, pp. 42–44). Galt MacDermot's music had captured the beat of the times. His versatility invested these songs with exhilaration, rhythm, and humor.

Explaining what happened, Jonelle Allen, who played Silvia, recollected, "'When we first went into *Verona* in the park, we felt, "This is a nice job for the summer." Then we heard the music and we knew it was about us loving each other.' . . . Out of improvisation by Miss Allen and Mr. Davis, with the enthusiastic urging of Mr. MacDermot, came the fiery, almost soul-style performance of 'Night Letter,' one of the showstoppers."[22] While they are singing, a guard enters and carries Silvia off. A reprise of Valentine's solo, "Love's Revenge," now includes Proteus and the two servants as countervoices to Valentine's. Whereas Shakespeare has Valentine tell Proteus about his plans, the adaptors translate this to the wonderfully intense song "Night Ladder." But they also compress the information by adding another section of Shakespeare's play, Silvia's appeal to Eglamour after all else has failed.

Once again Shakespeare's play offers the framework of the plot. There too, Silvia is being held in a high tower inaccessible to rescuers. There too, Valentine devises a plan to find a long night ladder woven of strong rope to save her. However, whereas Shakespeare includes a scene with the Duke, who mentions the imminent arrival of Proteus, the musical omits that section and instead has Proteus suddenly appear. When Valentine asks his friend about Julia, Proteus replies, "I know you joy not in love discourse" (2.4.127). Valentine protests, praises his new love, and discloses his intention to elope with her. Their meeting triggers Proteus's decision to disregard his pledge to Julia and betray Valentine. Proteus soliloquizes, "I to myself am dearer than a friend, / For love is still most precious in itself, / And Silvia (witness heaven that made her fair) / Shows Julia but a swarthy Ethiope" (2.6.23–26).

Shakespeare is a true partner in this musical. His knowledge of the ease with which men break their vows has a long record in his plays, particularly in his comedies. In the tragedies, like *Romeo and Juliet*, Juliet warns Romeo and in fact notes that no vows can hold, even as the moon changes shape over time. In *Two Gentlemen of Verona*, Proteus takes only a brief look back at the promises he has made, then rationalizes breaking them. "Even as one heat another heat expels," he generalizes, "So the remembrance of my former love / Is by a newer object quite forgotten" (2.4.192–95). In the musical version the songs help to emphasize these lapses. By placing the ideas within the context of rock music, the adaptors have made them relevant to their audience. Rock not only uses repetition and the constant beat of drums or bass guitars, it also tells a story, often more than one story, as do the Beatles' songs and ballads, where they interject their own observations. This is a new style for American musical comedy music. It expresses a universal point of view against a strong background beat in the music.

Celebrating his decision to betray both Julia and Valentine, Proteus bounces into a song: a fast rumba. "I'm very happy / For my best friend / He found a wonderful girl / She's a calla lily lady / She's a water lily lady," and then, exuberantly, he simply repeats "La la la la la la." He declares, "I assume she knows he's thrifty / What I mean to say is cheap." Then he literally bounces with glee, capturing the island rhythm: "So I'm very happy for my best friend," and he wants that friend to be happy, "But not happier than me / Once again now / But not happier than me" (1.1, pp. 49–50). Spanish words and phrases weave throughout the song, and then Proteus picks up Shakespeare's text. The adaptors have brilliantly used the dramatist's words to expand their portrait of Proteus as he wonders about his "three-fold perjury" in shifting his allegiance from "a twinkling star" (Julia) to "a celestial moon" (Silvia) (2.6.9–10; 1.1, p. 50). He has already made up his mind; his heart is set on Silvia. He even vows, "I will forget that Julia is alive, / Rememb'ring that my love to her is dead" (2.6.27–28; 1.1, p. 51). But Julia is very much alive, and she and Lucetta, disguised as farm boys, will soon confront him.

Once again, the set plays a decisive role. Alone on stage, Proteus stands near the center pole, to which various Renaissance telephones have been attached, to put his plan to betray his friend into action. Alone on stage, he breathes heavily into his Renaissance telephone as he tries contacting the Duke. Annoyed, Thurio replies, "Who is this?" He too is using a telephone, a Baroque one, replying from the balcony above. Here the adaptors rely on anachronisms. More heavy breathing answers him. "It's for you," Thurio asserts, handing the Duke the phone. Proteus, pretending concern that the old ruler's heart might break if his daughter were kidnapped, reveals his friend's plans.

While he's standing there reporting to the Duke, the two disguised women—Julia and Lucetta—enter. They react in horror to Proteus's praise of the pictures of Silvia that flood the stage. "Silvia, Silvia," he rhapsodizes, and quotes Shakespeare's text: "Even as one heat another heat expels / Or as one nail by strength drives out another / So the remembrance of my former love / Is by a newer object quite forgotten, / Silvia, Silvia." Meanwhile, his former love stands aghast before him. "Who are you?" he challenges. As the women attempt to sneak out, he grabs them, asking where they come from. "We come from the land of betrayal," they sing, accompanied by a single instrument pounding out the song. "Our principal export is lying / Truth, youth, and beauty we ban / Our principal pastime is loving / The kind they stamp 'made in Japan'" (implying that it is cheap and easily discardable) (2.1, pp. 54–55). Laced with irony, the song expresses their disgust with Proteus. They include references to the town that changed its name to Everywhere, and describe its inhabitants, who smile all the time there. Angrily they exaggerate the elements in the land they and Proteus come from. He then assigns them their jobs—to serve the Lady Silvia.

In this new world of Milan, Proteus reprises his song "Thou Has Metamorphosed Me," originally addressed to Julia, now to Silvia. With the same seeming sincerity that earlier characterized his passion for Julia, he again turns to Shakespeare's words. This time it is Silvia's influence on him that, he says, "Made me neglect my studies, lose my mind / War with good counsel, set the world at nought." Then, returning to his scheme to trick Valentine, Proteus exclaims, "Love, lend me wings to make my purpose swift, / As thou hast lent me wit to plot this drift" (2.1, p. 53). His plan to betray Valentine and Silvia succeeds.

Valentine, on a bike, pedals hurriedly in to rescue Silvia, only to be intercepted by the Duke and Thurio. The Duke tells him a story that

5.3. The Duke (in black) and Thurio (in white) intercept Valentine on his Renaissance-decorated bike as he goes to rescue Silvia. The Duke tricks the naive youth into revealing his plot, leading Thurio immediately to induct the young lover into the army. Silvia seeks help elsewhere, calling Eglamour, her former lover, and sending a dove to find him in the forest. *Friedman-Abeles, Billy Rose Theatre Division, New York Public Library for the Performing Arts, Astor, Lenox, and Tilden Foundations.*

parallels his own. Like him, the Duke is supposedly courting a lady. Like Valentine's beloved, she too is kept locked in a high tower. Patiently answering all the Duke's questions as to how he might gain access to her, the naive young man even suggests hiding a strong rope ladder under a long cloak. Without much ceremony, the Duke pulls off Valentine's cloak, revealing his own such ladder and a note to Silvia. Troops move in, and Valentine is drafted into the army and banished. "No need to look so quizzical / You just passed your physical," the Duke sings in yet another development of the war theme. Thurio adds to this by handing the young lover a uniform (2.1, p. 59).

Moving seamlessly into quotations from Shakespeare, Valentine bemoans his fate. "And why not death, rather than living torment? / To die is to be banished from myself, / And Silvia is myself; banish'd from her / Is self from self" (3.1.70–73). Silvia bemoans his fate, and Thurio, to his credit, notes, "She takes his going grievously." "No, no," the Duke responds; he tells Thurio that Silvia praised him, calling him a poet. None of this is true, but Thurio wants to hear more. "What did she say to my nose? . . . What did she say to my clothes?" Persistently, he exclaims, "Please don't fake it / I can take it." Unable to improvise further, the Duke sings a song that is fairly unintelligible when heard in the theater, or even on a recording. The rhythm of his answer can be made out, but the words are unintelligible. From the script, however, we can see that the Duke answers with a series of scatological lines:

> She said
> > Boom chicka chicka chicka
> > Fuck fucka wucka wucka
> > Cock cocka wocka wocka (2.1, pp. 61–63)

What should we make of this outburst? Should we understand it as anti-woman propaganda? To what extent can the audience even hear it, and how much does it affect their response?

When I asked John Guare about this exchange between Thurio and the Duke, he explained that, first of all, Thurio is a fool, and secondly, this musical was playing primarily to an audience for its traveling theater.[23] The language would be understandable to that audience. They would recognize it as gibberish spoken to a fool by someone intent on winning points and convincing a rich suitor to continue to pursue his daughter. Guare explained that this musical's primary audience was in the boroughs, not the park. The mobile theater unit of the New York Shakespeare Festival played mainly before the many different communities that make up New York City. It moved into Bedford Stuyvesant and Harlem, where African Americans lived, and performed in Queens before mostly Hispanic and Asian audiences.

Thurio's song, known as "Thurio's Samba," continues in much the same vein. The audiences for which it was intended would not only find this language acceptable, but also recognize it as meaningless. Primarily, it provides a rhythm and implies Thurio's mindlessness as the Duke continues to respond to his queries. Finally, the Duke says, "I may throw up," then sings, "She said / Boom chicka chicka chicka. / Fuck, fucka, wucka, wucka." Satisfied at last, Thurio declares, "Love, I made you lucky / Love / You lucky ducky." The lyricist picks up the language of his time, and suggests its childishness in "lucky ducky." Moreover, when the Duke attempts to claim that Silvia said something quite different, Thurio rejects the change. Quoting Cleopatra's speech after Antony's death in *Antony and Cleopatra,* the Duke tells Thurio that she said, "His legs bestride the ocean. His reared arm / Crested the world. . . . His delights / Were dolphin like." But Thurio objects, "Oh no, she didn't." He turns to the ensemble and maintains, "She said, 'Boom, chicka chicka chicka'" (2.1, pp. 62–63). The repetition of profanity in this song, which is similar to its use in contemporary rock music, finally convinces him that Silvia loves him.[24]

As Thurio and the Duke exit from this scene, the focus shifts to Launce and Speed, who also crave love. They note that "Young folks spend their time lovin' / Rich folks can afford lovin' / I've been / Dog catcher, bartender, log roller / truck driver / But not lover." They then sing, "I want to be a hot lover," alternating their lines (2.1, p. 65). The rhythm of the lines emphasizes the range of jobs Launce has held; he's been everything but a hot lover. He too craves love. As he and Speed make their drunken way offstage, Proteus reappears, intent on wooing Silvia now that Valentine is banished.

His two new employees—the disguised Julia and Lucetta—accompany the dishonest Proteus, who plans to lead a group in singing "Who Is Silvia?" to the Duke's daughter. But first, he decides, he will send her a gift. With that he removes the ring given him by Julia, and instructs the disguised young woman to deliver it to Silvia. "She is dead, belike?" ventures Julia. "Not so; I think she lives." "Alas," shouts Lucetta, speaking a line that was Julia's in Shakespeare's play. Her outcry rocks the audience with laughter. Julia then weaves a lengthy series of excuses for Lucetta's "Alas," illustrating the advantages of dividing the lines that were originally Julia's between the two women (2.1, p. 66).

A different kind of division next surfaces between the two major women characters, Julia and Silvia. Julia sings longingly of her wish to still be beloved by Proteus. "If I could be her," she speculates, "Just for a moment / When he was holding her / I would insult him." Then deliciously she would comfort him. "What a nice idea / What a sweet idea / But easier said than done." As she continues this torch song to a rumba melody, she progresses to "If I could be him," thinking only of wishing to get him to realize his mistake. That, too, is "easier said than done" (2.1, p. 68). Silvia, on the other hand, is interested in owning herself and having freedom. The adaptors join the two women, offering two very different versions of the woman of the seventies. Both illustrate the emerging women's movement: Julia claims sexual freedom, leading to her pregnancy, and Silvia wishes for freedom from family domination and societal pressure to conform to approved patterns of behavior. No longer is she the paragon of virtue that she is in Shakespeare's play; she is more like the women in his later works, who are freer to think for themselves. The musical thus becomes a vehicle for illuminating aspects of contemporary society. This portrait of Silvia conforms to new perspectives on women introduced by the women's movement of the 1970s, just as Julia's behavior also reflects modern approval of sexual freedom.

Proteus enters again, with a chorus of singers called the Black Passion Girls, with whom he reprises "Who is Silvia?" Silvia responds forcefully, "Stop it. Who the hell is Silvia?" and continues in song. "Love me, / Not your idea of me," she pleads; "Release me / From your fantasy . . . Let me go / Let me go." Running to the top tier of the set in an attempt to evade her bodyguards, she finally sends for Eglamour (2.1, pp. 69–70).

In Shakespeare's plot, the exiled Valentine finds himself confronted by a band of outlaws. In a zany scene, they ask why he was banished. When he invents a story of having killed a man, which he now regrets, the outlaws think he would make a wonderful king for them. This lie not only saves his life, so that he can eventually come to Silvia's defense, but also allows him to forgive his friend Proteus. It also leads to Julia's unmasking. However, it has baffled scholars, who wonder why he relinquishes Silvia after having so strongly and passionately wanted her. Since, ultimately, he never gives her up, this may have been an ad hoc decision by a young dramatist still searching for plot devices.

Like Shakespeare, Guare and MacDermot too create a zany scene, but they excise the outlaws. Instead, they concentrate on Eglamour, who appears only briefly in Shakespeare's comedy. Moreover, they change him from a friend of Silvia's to her lover, who was sent to war by her "pappy." Because the adaptors also insisted on multiracial casting, they enlarged Eglamour's role. Silvia sends for him in a highly theatrical scene in which a dove flies over the heads of the audience to Silvia. She puts a note in its beak, and it returns to its keeper. "This magic dove /

5.4. In the multiethnic spirit of this production, Eglamour, an Asian, responds to Silvia's call for help, the dove she sent him perched on his shoulder as he strides down the aisle after boasting of how they outwitted her father. But he is only a temporary stopgap. Proteus is still chasing Silvia; Julia, in disguise, is mooning for Proteus, who has gotten her pregnant; and Valentine can think only of Silvia. The adaptors have a chance to explore the meaning of abortion in those years preceding *Roe v. Wade* even while celebrating love, love, love. A multilingual exchange follows between Julia and Proteus in Spanish and English, before the couples finally pair off in this last of the major musicals based on a Shakespeare play. *Friedman-Abeles, Billy Rose Theatre Division, New York Public Library for the Performing Arts, Astor, Lenox, and Tilden Foundations.*

THE PERSISTENCE OF LOVE · 181

Will find my love / In his jungle destination," she sings. Meanwhile the chorus continues her previous song, "Let Me Go." Finally, she calls out, "Eglamour." From the rear of the balcony, a thrilling baritone sings, "Did I hear someone call my name?" (2.1, pp. 71–72).

A handsome Asian man strides through the audience, having climbed down a ladder from the balcony to the orchestra. He is wearing an army uniform and carrying the magic dove on his shoulder. Once onstage, he tranquilizes those who intercept him by tapping them on the shoulder. A mixture of pure fiction and magic, he flies to Silvia's rescue, using his tap to paralyze all those who would stand in his way. The song, sung responsively by Silvia and Eglamour—"Lucky you," "Lucky me"—suggests an egocentric Eglamour as he repeats, "Lucky you." A strange beat permeates his song as he sings, "Your father sent me off to war / I think your father thought / That I'd be killed / No luck / Here I am / Lucky you." And then together in chorus, they sing, "Lucky me," eventually ending up together in a pup tent decorated with doves (2.1, pp. 72–74).

Although the outlaws have been eliminated from the adaptation, the forest, where all things unfold, has not. Again lighting works the magic, as green permeates the stage. The multilevel outdoor stage allows Silvia and Eglamour to enter the pup tent on the ground level while Valentine, unaware of their presence, stands on guard duty on the third level. He speaks Shakespeare's lines as he contemplates the forest:

> This shadowy desert, unfrequented woods,
> I better brook than flourishing peopled towns. (5.4.2–3)

Then, breaking into song, he invokes Silvia, who lives "in the mansion / I call my heart." Meanwhile Proteus, the Duke, and Thurio are searching for her. Again merging the two plots, Proteus is the first to find her. She's in the pup tent with Eglamour. For the first time, he loses his equanimity, furious at being bested. And, displaying the masculine attitude characterized primarily by force, he decides to go in after her. "What's a nice girl like her / Doing in this place?" he demands in song. "Why are nice lips like hers / Kissing his?" Infuriated, he jumps into the tent. Eglamour flees, leaving Silvia at Proteus's mercy. Like his prototype in Shakespeare's play, he tries to force himself upon her. At this moment Valentine comes to the rescue, swearing, "Proteus, I must never trust thee more" (2.1, pp. 75–77).

With that Eglamour returns with a large paper Chinese dragon with lighted eyes and breathing fire and smoke. The two former friends fight the dragon, who then turns on Eglamour. Once again he runs.

Quoting Shakespeare's play for the last time, Proteus begs to be forgiven and Valentine says the infamous line, "All that was mine in Silvia I give thee." Julia swoons. "Look to the boy," Valentine commands, and Proteus recognizes the ring he gave to Julia. "And Julia herself hath brought it hither," she announces (5.4.83–85; 2.1, p. 78). Like Shakespeare's Julia, she pulls off her cap to reveal her hair, then with an added gesture, puts her hand on her stomach. "And pregnant too," he observes. A debate over abortion follows. "Don't have the baby," Lucetta sings, explaining, "we have too many babies." But Speed disagrees, insisting she not only have the baby, but "tell the baby his father / Was a terrible man." Launce follows his friend and recommends, "Tell the baby his father / Was Emperor of Milan." Finally, Julia asserts she will have the baby because, when they made him, "oh how his father loved me" (p. 79).

The debate on abortion that was raging at the time focused on a woman's right to control her body. Shakespeare once again has the last word on this subject. Julia, reprimanding Proteus, asserts,

> It is the lesser blot modesty finds,
> Women to change their shapes, than men their minds.

and this speech is followed by Proteus's rather mild defense:

> Than men their minds? 'Tis true: O heaven, were man
> But constant, he were perfect.

Clearly, even in this early play the dramatist has created an interesting male character who doesn't really change—here at the end he is still vain, still insisting on his near perfection. But then beginning to realize his error, he continues,

> What is in Sylvia's face, but I may spy
> More fresh in Julia's with a constant eye?

In Shakespeare's comedy Valentine, with a slight reproach, joins Julia's and Proteus's hands, saying, "Come, come, a hand from either." Then, asserting his role:

Let me be blest to make this happy close.
'Twere pity two such friends should be long foes.

With that, Proteus and Julia pledge eternal faithfulness to one another (5.4.108–18).

The musical reaches the conclusion in a different fashion. It adds a conversation in Spanish between Julia and Proteus: "Sinverguenza!" ("Shameless one"), exclaims Julia, then continues, "A buena hora se te occure que—" ("In good time it will occur to you, what—"). "Si," he immediately replies. She asks, "Me quieres?" ("You love me?"). Proteus says, "OK." "Because you didn't think it before," she accuses in Spanish: "Porque no pensaste antes?" Again his answer is reduced to "Si." Julia pursues her theme. They are no longer using single Spanish words or phrases but couching their argument in Spanish sentences. "You got involved with her," Julia says, deciding this is a real problem. Through all of this Proteus is reduced to "Si" and "Okay." Finally she concludes, "Because I don't know whether to forgive you or not" ("Porque no se si perdonarte o no"). At this, his multiple, enthusiastic "Si"s convince her to forgive him, and they leave hand in hand.

For his part, Valentine, too, changes. Although only moments earlier he had offered Silvia to Proteus—"what was mine in Silvia I give thee"—clearly he didn't mean it, because shortly after Proteus and Julia are reunited, Valentine challenges Thurio to a duel over Silvia. "Come not within the measure of my wrath," the young gentleman of Verona exclaims to his rival. Unfazed, Thurio immediately withdraws: "I care not for her, I: / I hold him but a fool that will endanger / His body for a girl that loves him not" (5.4.132–34; 2.1, p. 80). Disappointed in such a weak-kneed suitor, the Duke alters his stance, giving his blessing to Silvia and Valentine. Once again the adaptors have incorporated Shakespeare's play into their musical, wedding the musical form to the Renaissance comedy. With the blessing of the Duke, Valentine then bursts out, "Come on, baby," as they exit together.

Retaining the organic form of the musical while introducing a new kind of music, the collaborators have created yet another expression of a Shakespeare play, uniting plot, music, lyrics, and dance to reflect the culture of the time. Moreover, they have superimposed a breadth of vision not present earlier by plunging into contemporary events. Even more importantly, they have insisted on casting their work with actors representing the range of peoples that populate New York City. And they have urged these varied men and women to love each other, as Jonelle Allen astutely observed.[25] When it was performed in London at the Phoenix in 1973, reference was again made to its mixed casting:

> White and coloured mingle, in love and fun and enmity; the streets of Verona and Milan reflect something of the streets evoked by Shakespeare's play, but also, with some force, modern streets in cities like New York and San Juan, where race and social standing, sex and freedom are motivations in the battle for every day survival.[26]

Your Own Thing innovatively combined slides and film to introduce a three-dimensional quality to the musical where abstract twentieth-century commentators observe and discuss the story unfolding before them. But in his production of *Two Gentlemen of Verona*, the director, Mel Shapiro, uses all kinds of stage tricks, including black-masked characters whose presence suggests the obstacles the travelers encounter as they come from Verona to Milan. His visual methods in *Two Gentlemen of Verona* reflect the new importance of lighting in productions. Characters could be lighted from behind or silhouetted against moving screens suggesting their movement from one place to another. As Clive Barnes, in his review, observed,

> Mr Shapiro keeps the whole musical going as if it were a merry-go-round that had got slightly drunk wherever it is that merry-go-rounds go when they need to celebrate.[27]

Despite this joyous quality of *Two Gentlemen of Verona*, contemporary problems impinge on and enrich the musical. The adaptors have increased Julia's vulnerability by having her "preg*nant*" even as Proteus alters his allegiance. And they have politicized Milan's leader so that he resembles a Black Panther chieftain. Dark glasses and a beret distinguish his outfit, while a deep baritone characterizes his speech.

The adaptors also retain some of Shakespeare's more insightful speeches and capture his humor. Thus they include Valentine's passionate outburst expressing his love for Silvia along with his sudden relinquishing of his right to her. And they develop the humor of Proteus's repetition of "You have metamorphosed me," which he says to each of the two women he loves in turn, and find humor in Julia's uncertainty about how to behave. Does she follow the dictates of her society or of her heart? The adaptors recognize this and imbue her torch song, "If I Could Be Her," with her sense of confusion.

Although MacDermot didn't consider this a musical in the vein of *Hair*, *Two Gentlemen of Verona* certainly brought rock music to Shakespeare's play, making it the last in a line of twentieth-century American musical Shakespeares. The score includes rock, jazz, blues, and even a few ballads, and features a rock band on the second tier of the stage. It also retains the organic organization so characteristic of the American musical form of the time. Most important, it gives a multiethnic feel to the action, as the adaptors point out in their preface to the printed edition. Critics found it an amazing addition to American musical comedy, which had been largely performed by white casts for white audiences, and its revival in 2005, more than thirty years after its first production, proves that the book and score still draw an appreciative audience.

This musical adaptation of *Two Gentlemen of Verona* focused on the theme of love that pervades Shakespeare's comedy and extended it to include the characters in their relationship with one another as well as the cast members. The adaptors had discovered hints of this love in the play. When they transposed it to the form of a musical, relying on contemporary rock music, they found an abundance of love that seemed to extend the play's borders. The play expanded to consider not just the challenges facing two adolescent youths, but also those facing the two women they love. And love expanded to incorporate the servants Speed and Launce, who link up with Lucetta and Cupid. In the process of adapting the play, the adaptors realized, perhaps in response to the music, that only through a multiracial musical could they convey the range in Shakespeare's play. Although *Two Gentlemen of Verona* was the last of the major twentieth-century American musical productions of Shakespeare, these productions and their innovations continued to influence subsequent productions of Shakespeare, taking the dramatist to the masses through film and video, stimulating fresh interpretations, letting Shakespeare live again in the accents of contemporary audiences.

CODA

Shakespeare and the American Musical addresses a particular period in American theater history when the musical and Shakespeare's plays met and developed. It follows the history of those meetings against the constantly changing American scene. More importantly, *Shakespeare and the American Musical* shows how American culture influenced and altered these sixteenth-century plays so that they emerged anew, helping a twentieth-century audience to better understand its own time. In addition, the musicals offered techniques that future producers of Shakespeare's plays could adopt, enriching the plays for the twenty-first century.

At first Shakespeare's texts were merely sources of plot and characterization, but the American Shakespeare musical has come a long way, establishing itself as a force in Shakespeare productions and becoming a voice for political and social change in the twentieth century. It carried Shakespeare's insights into new areas and always remained specifically American. No longer would producers and actor-managers rely on promptbooks from earlier productions for help with a new one. Those marked-up scripts could be discarded. Instead, new twentieth-century voices, dance routines, musical numbers, and adaptations would replace the older forms.

At the same time, these new Shakespeare productions took on a format unlike anything previously known. Older stagings had separated the songs and dances from the events that drove the plot; the music had never been woven into the fabric of the overall production, involving it in the whole work. David Garrick, in the eighteenth century, had incorporated the music of John Christopher Smith as well as songs from Garrick's own earlier opera, *The Fairies,* in his *A Midsummer Night's Dream.*[1] Theodore Komisarjevsky, in the opening years of the twentieth century, had also introduced a good deal of music in his British productions of *The Comedy of Errors* (1938) and *The Taming of the Shrew* (1939).[2] But neither Garrick nor Komisarjevsky perceived music, song, and dance as part of the play's overall scheme. In contrast, twentieth-century American Shakespeare musicals integrated all the elements of the performance with the Renaissance plays. Music, song, dance, and plot development united to move the story forward.

While remaining true to Shakespeare's plays, these American musicals had adopted the newest musical form. Although the adaptors tended to revise these sixteenth-century plays where necessary or rewrite them so that they spoke in contemporary vernacular, these musicals still soared with Shakespeare's poetry. All in all, this was an extraordinary accomplishment.

The use of a Shakespeare text expanded American musicals, providing them with a sophistication they had lacked. His plays offered complex, multilayered plots with psychologically credible characters. Even in *The Comedy of Errors,* with its complex story line and comparatively simple characters, the Antipholus twins and their Dromios take on additional individualizing characteristics. In *The Boys from Syracuse* they turn into men with their own personalities, just as the women, despite some stereotypes, express a range of feelings.

In developing a new form, the American musical had left the earlier tradition of Shakespeare productions behind. Lyricists, composers, and choreographers usurped the authority of directors by collaborating to create alternative interpretations of Shakespeare, no longer beholden to the theatrical practices of the past. Shakespeare's induction to *The Taming of the Shrew* inspired Bella Spewack and Cole Porter to take a second look at the play. After initially rebelling against the idea of creating a musical from *The Taming of the Shrew,* because of its seeming prejudice against women, they found their subject not in the relationship of Kate and Petruchio as much as in the idea of the comedy as a play-within-a-play. They too would create a play within a play. And an earlier production of Shakespeare's play, with Alfred Lunt and Lynn Fontanne as the quarreling pair, had left an indelible mark. The adaptors would mine it. Their *Kiss Me, Kate* invents a play-within-a-play out of a backstage story where Shakespeare's Kate and Petruchio double for Lilli and Fred, the formerly married twentieth-century performers. Thus Kate/Lilli is reimagined, placed amid the complexities of American heterosexual politics. This optimistic, rousing musical, born of the post–World War II years, was soon followed by the sober evaluation of human relationships found in *West Side Story*.

The stage history of *Romeo and Juliet* illustrates the older tradition of Shakespeare performance. Seventeenth- and eighteenth-century audiences disliked Shakespeare's original ending, in which Romeo takes poison beside Juliet's apparent corpse, she awakens to find him dead, and, with no poison remaining, stabs herself with his sword. They preferred the revised ending of Theophilus Cibber's adaptation, which allowed the lovers to meet for a moment before Romeo is overcome by the poison.[3] David Garrick, the eighteenth-century actor, manager, and producer, tried to restore the original ending, but was unable to make it succeed, and returned to Cibber's version.[4] The adaptors of the musical *West Side Story* also wrestled with the ending, and came up with a new, twentieth-century version. A sleeping potion that would put Juliet/Maria into a deathlike trance seemed too simplistic and outlandish a concept for a twentieth-century audience to accept. So the adaptors, as we have seen, decided to have Maria survive, recognizing that survivors of trauma endure a kind of death.

The adaptors of this show ambitiously faced an even greater challenge. They would transform a medium formerly reserved for comedy—the musical—for tragedy. They were not concerned with character development or intricacies of plot, but sought something more from their work: a thematic center. Although the Shakespeare tragedy they settled on was the tragic love story *Romeo and Juliet,* they read it primarily as an example of unfounded bias. The hatreds and antipathies of Shakespeare's play evolved into the contemporary prejudices of two groups of ghetto residents, the Sharks and the Jets—Puerto Rican immigrants and the poor residents of the same urban space who call themselves Americans.

That team of adaptors left an important mark on the American musical by combining classical and popular in both music and dance. Headed by Leonard Bernstein and Jerome Robbins and assisted by Arthur Laurents in the critical role of scriptwriter, they were also joined by Stephen Sondheim, who composed some of the lyrics. As Robbins later noted in the 1985 symposium on *West Side Story,* illustrating just how difficult it is to capture as well as to paraphrase Shakespeare's language,

> Lenny, Steve and I had nothing to put our work against. Arthur had that text by Mr. William S all the time. We could make our poetry out of the music, the dancing, the song lyrics, but Arthur had the burden of making his text go along with *Romeo and Juliet* and still communicate some of the poetry, the argot, the drives and passions of the 1950s, while trying to match, somehow, the style we were creating as we went along.[5]

And they all succeeded.

In the next successful American Shakespeare musical, *Your Own Thing,* the genre of popular music changed to rock. A small onstage orchestra replaced the traditional large band in the pit. Hidden from audience view, those bands had helped create the illusion of a single unity of music, song, and story. Now a new intimacy was created between the audience and the visible music-makers. Not only were performers extensively miked, but the performance took on a deliberate theatrical quality. Sounds were mixed on a mixing board at the rear of the orchestra. Audiences no longer heard sounds that came just from the stage. All reveled in the openness of the technology that pervaded *Your Own Thing.* Film clips, screen projections, and onstage performers were interwoven in an original off-Broadway production. Film clips dramatize the fate of the ship and its occupants. Then slide projections allow diverse commentators, particularly Buddha, to discuss the brother and sister pair.

Danny Apolinar, Hal Hester, and Donald Driver were inventing a new way of seeing. They brought a fresh perspective to the musical as they approached Shakespeare's *Twelfth Night* and its hidden messages with a new, twentieth-century directness. The homosexuality suggested by the appeal of Viola to Olivia and Sebastian to Antonio in *Twelfth Night* becomes explicit. Orson falls for Viola, who is masquerading as her brother, and wrestles with his demons. He dreams of being hanged by shadows of cowboys, seen on slides, for being unmanly. Although the musical ultimately backs away from its subject, it raises an important and provocative topic of the time as its performers do their own thing. It also addresses a question often overlooked in the sexual relations of men and women, the apparent requirement that a woman be younger than the man she pairs off with. "He's twenty, I'm thirty, does it matter?" Olivia sings, then resignedly, "Well, let it be." Samuel Johnson said that we need not find a totally new way of looking at a work. It is enough to bring a new insight to a previously familiar work.[6] American musical Shakespeare has been responsible for such a shift in perspective. More than ever, Shakespeare remained exciting. By becoming Americanized and musical, he became accessible to the twentieth and twenty-first centuries and popular among diverse audiences once again.

The themes of the works capture elements in the human life cycle, subjects covered in Shakespeare's plays—birth, death, marriage, love, hate, fear, same-sex friendships, scheming, jealousy. The adaptors translated these subjects into the twentieth-century vernacular. While childbirth may no longer be as threatening as it was in Shakespeare's times, childbearing outside of marriage carried a great stigma until recently. *Two Gentlemen of Verona* explores Julia's options when she reveals she's pregnant. The characters debate the question of abortion. The perennial scheming by a friend to steal his friend's girlfriend also pops up in that musical. But other preoccupations also engage the characters: the cost of war, the duplicity of a ruler, and the corruption that surrounds him. The Vietnam War and the divisions it caused spilled over onto the stage as the Duke sang of bringing the troops home in body bags.

New technology also affected *Two Gentlemen of Verona*. When Joseph Papp, the great entrepreneur of twentieth-century Shakespeare in New York City, launched his production in Central Park, he determined to exhibit the sounds and sights of the rock musical. To do so, he assembled a talented group of adaptors; this was the first time the adaptors hadn't decided of their own accord to collaborate on developing a musical. Once assembled by Papp, these men evolved a vision of what they would do that was different from his.

For them, *Two Gentlemen of Verona* glorified the city and its inhabitants. The Milan and Verona of the original were transformed into New York and San Juan.[7] The adaptors knew that the city included all races, so Blacks, Hispanics, and Asians found a place in their musical. Drawing on the mixed population of this city, the adaptors broke the color line so prevalent in the musical theater and insisted that their practice continue in overseas productions. This revolutionized theater. As Guare said when asked about the casting of Eglamour, "Well, we had every other racial group but Chinese. We wanted an Asian, and what better way than an Asian white-knight?"[8]

The city, considered as a specific place, changes shape and meaning in each of these musicals. In *Your Own Thing,* it's the place where Viola first comes ashore, and Mayor Lindsay's voice and image welcome her. "Illyria is a fun city," he coughs from his place on the screen. Looking at a film of New York, she observes, "So much glass, so much steel, . . . Can I ever call this place home?" Soon enough she does. From another perspective, Anita in *West Side Story* sings, "I like the island Manhattan / Smoke on your pipe and put that in." She heads a group of Puerto Rican girls who also like America, especially their particular locale, New York City. In *Two Gentlemen of Verona,* New York City becomes Milan, the city of excitement where everything happens, and the sounds of the show are the sounds of the barrio.

That same sense of place marks *Kiss Me, Kate.* There the place is Baltimore, the hot southern city on the edge of Washington. Although distant from New York, here musicals live or die before hitting the Great White Way. They try out, hoping to eliminate the wrinkles. In the case of *Kiss Me, Kate,* those wrinkles are due to the hostility and love between the main characters. In tryout cities, dreams are made and possibilities explored. "Another op'nin', another show," the actors sing, hoping for a hit. Later they sing, "It's too darn hot," complaining that the heat saps sexual energy. Gone is the abstractness of place in Shakespeare's plays.

The theater of the twentieth century differed from the theater of the Renaissance in its lighting, stage conditions, performers, and means of sound projection. Only men and boys could work as actors, and sound projection from the stage relied on the design of the theater: the shape of the stage and the make-up of the building's floors, seats, and walls.[9] In contrast, a twentieth-century production draws on the skill of the sound engineers who can amplify or diminish a voice, and of the lighting designers who can change a place or a costume merely through lighting.

Shakespeare's resources were more limited, but he had language. And what language it was. Words informed the audience of the time of day, described the setting, and conveyed the personalities of the characters. And through his poetry, the dramatist could alter the relationships between characters. In *Romeo and Juliet,* Romeo declaims, "What light through yonder window breaks? / It is the east and Juliet is the sun." In *West Side Story,* we see Maria peering through the darkness for a glimpse of Tony.

On the other hand, Shakespeare's language could also puzzle the twentieth-century audience. Jokes that once evoked immediate laughter now needed footnotes. Whereas Shakespeare's Capulet servants could pun on "collier" and "choler" in the opening lines of *Romeo and Juliet,* today's audiences don't even know what the words mean. In scripting the conversations of the Sharks and Jets, Arthur Laurents said, "I had to invent language." He chose "cool" as slang since the word was comparatively unknown. "Now it's used for everything," he asserted.[10]

These new musicals altered Shakespeare's language, making it easier to understand, and they inspired a host of other versions of Shakespeare's plays. They captivated their audiences. They danced their way into movie theaters and onto television screens. Shakespeare won applause both in new works, such as *Shakespeare in Love* (1998), and in new film versions of his comedies, such as *Much Ado about Nothing* (1993). Music accompanies that movie's opening as young women of the town anticipate the men's return from war. No pall of disaster hangs over their heads; both men and women look forward to laughter and dancing. The mixed-race casting that was so celebrated in *Two Gentlemen of Verona* does not even elicit comment in this film, in which Denzel Washington as Don Pedro, dramatically costumed in a white uniform, heads the team of mounted soldiers. The youthfulness of the lovers and the substitution of a tenement fire escape for a balcony in *West Side Story* similarly left their imprint on subsequent adaptations of *Romeo and Juliet.* In Buz Lehrmann's 1996 film adaptation, Leonardo DiCaprio and Claire Danes meet and woo in the swimming pool of her parents' home.

The forty-year period from the 1930s to the 1970s marked a golden age of the American musical and of Shakespeare's vital place in its development. After that, musical imports from Britain replaced homegrown works. Nevertheless, the lasting effect of this breakthrough could be seen in the Shakespeare productions that followed. That distinctively American musical sound carries on, as Shakespeare continues to move us.

American musical Shakespeare broadened interpretations of the plays to give them a life for our time. In a larger world, they showed the artist's breadth and humanity. As John Guare observed, taking Proteus's line from *Two Gentlemen of Verona,* "Shakespeare metamorphosed me." He meant that the Renaissance dramatist had a profound effect on the voice within the modern playwright.[11] For it is Shakespeare's amazing strength to understand the human heart and record it with insight and sensitivity, to dramatize human interaction among all classes, and to recognize the insecurities and failures of human beings even while sympathizing with their plight. In the several plays, mainly comedies, that they borrowed from this master craftsman, the twentieth-century musical adaptors acknowledged his greatness while translating his insights for their own worlds.

NOTES

Abbreviations

ABC — Friedman clipping file, Australian Broadcasting Corporation archives, Sydney

BRTD — Billy Rose Theatre Division, New York Public Library for the Performing Arts

JRDD — Jerome Robbins Dance Division, New York Public Library for the Performing Arts

MDLC — Music Division, Library of Congress

RB&MLCU — Rare Book and Manuscript Library, Columbia University

Introduction

1. "Chasing the *Boys from Syracuse*," in *Popular Balanchine Dossiers,* JRDD.

2. Brooks Atkinson, *Broadway* (New York: Macmillan, 1970), 335.

3. Ethan Mordden, *Better Foot Forward: The History of American Musical Theatre* (New York: Grossman, 1976), 143.

4. Atkinson, *Broadway,* 336.

5. Ethan Mordden, *Sing for Your Supper: The Broadway Musical in the 1930s* (New York: Palgrave, 2005), 244.

6. Bernstein's papers include a copy of Kittredge's 1940 edition of *Romeo and Juliet* with a handwritten note beside the prologue: "Should be prologue interrupted by street fight." Across the top of the page and above the title appears "An out and out plea for racial tolerance." Writings, 1954–55, box 73, folder 9, Leonard Bernstein Collection, MDLC.

7. Amanda Vaill, *Somewhere: The Life of Jerome Robbins* (New York: Broadway Books, 2006), 5–9, 15–16.

8. Arthur Laurents, "*West Side Story* at 50," lecture at Bruno Walter Auditorium, New York Public Library for the Performing Arts, September 20, 2007.

9. Telephone interview with John Guare, August 10, 2007.

10. Telephone interview with John Guare, August 24, 2007.

11. Philip Edwards, "Beginnings and Continuities," *Shakespeare Survey* 51 (1998): 146.

1. A Bold Adventure

1. Quotations are from the typescript of *The Boys from Syracuse,* by George Abbott, with music by Richard Rodgers, lyrics by Lorenz Hart, and choreography by George Balanchine, which opened at the Alvin Theatre, New York, on November 23, 1938, BRTD. References in the text are to act, scene, and page number in that typescript. A few typographical errors have been corrected. A printed version, "Brushing Up on Kate's Dates," also appeared in *Theatre Arts* 39 (January 1955): 33–57.

2. "Chasing the *Boys from Syracuse,*" in *Popular Balanchine Dossiers,* JRDD.

3. William Shakespeare, *The Comedy of Errors,* in *The Riverside Shakespeare,* ed. G. Blakemore Evans and J. J. Tobin, 2nd ed. (Boston: Houghton, 1997). All references to the text are to this edition. Scholars are uncertain of the exact date for *The Comedy of Errors* and date it 1594–95.

4. Although the play (following its Plautine original, *The Menaechmi*) calls the Dromios slaves, their relationship with their masters more closely resembles that of servants.

5. Frederick Nolan, *Lorenz Hart: A Poet on Broadway* (New York: Oxford University Press, 1994), 9–10.

6. Richard Rodgers, *Musical Stages: An Autobiography* (New York: Random House, 2002), 53.

7. Nolan, *Lorenz Hart,* 18.

8. Letters discussing *Mixed Company* are in *T-MSS-1993-002, series 4, box 26, folder 1 and series 2, box 4, folder 4, Jo Mielziner Papers, BRTD.

9. Both quotations are from Frederick Russell, "He Brought Ballet to Broadway," *American Dancer,* April 1939, 15, 37.

10. Burns Mantle, "*The Boys from Syracuse* Scores More Hits Than Errors," *New York Daily News,* November 24, 1938, *Popular Balanchine Dossiers.*

11. Arthur M. Schlesinger, Jr., ed., *The Almanac of American History* (New York: G. P. Putnam's Sons, 1983), 461.

12. John Woods, "Wow," *Yale News,* November 4, 1938, in *Popular Balanchine Dossiers,* JRDD.

13. *Popular Balanchine Dossiers,* compiled by Camille Hardy, book 1 of 2, 13. JRDD. The male dancer was George Church, who also played the Dancing Policeman; the women were Heidi Vosseler (Secretary to the Courtesan), who danced ballet, and Betty Bruce (Courtesan), who danced tap.

14. Jack Gould, "Rodgers and Hart Do the Words and Music," *New York Times,* December 4, 1938.

15. Tetsuo Kishi, "Shakespeare and the Musical," in *Shakespeare and the Twentieth Century: Proceedings of the International Shakespeare Association World Congress, Los Angeles, 1996,* ed. Jonathan Bate, Jill L. Levinson, and Dieter Mehl (Newark: University of Delaware Press, 1998), 157–67.

16. Brooks Atkinson, "The Boys from Syracuse," *New York Times,* November 24, 1938, *Popular Balanchine Dossiers,* JRDD. My description of the staging is based on a handwritten copy of the music of the finale of act 1 in box 2, folder 27 of the Richard Rodgers Collection, MDLC; *Playbill,* a program for *The Boys from Syracuse,* BRTD; and the 1938 typescript. Camille Hardy describes the scene: "The sung demand begins with the policemen (Lawrence, Wilkinson, and Church) and Dromio E. (Hart). The Tailor's apprentice (Ives) joins in as a crowd gathers. The courtesans enter to special music. Still chanting, some of the male ensemble kneel in supplication. Others beat on the

walls of the house. There is a dance solo for Bruce (the courtesan) as she enters and lets Antipholus E. know that he can come home with her for the night. Building frenetically to a climax, the score indicates twenty measures for the first 'run around'—part of the chorus encircles the house singing and thumping—and sixteen for the second that ends as the curtain falls." "Chasing the *Boys from Syracuse,*" in *Popular Balanchine Dossiers.* The 1997 studio CD, although recorded long after the original production, gives a sense of Antipholus's verve, annoyance, and then anger as his repeated knocking fails to gain him entrance.

17. Rosamond Gilder, "Song and Dance: Broadway in Review," *Theatre Arts Monthly,* January 1939, 11. The biographical note to the Jo Mielziner Papers, BRTD, says that Mielziner was an assistant and apprentice to Robert Edmond Jones and Lee Simonson, both exponents of the New Stagecraft, which insisted "on making the designer a full collaborator in the production process." Mielziner believed in the importance of scenery in the interpretation of a play or musical.

18. *Playbill,* program for *The Boys from Syracuse,* BRTD, 41.

19. *Oklahoma!* opened on March 31, 1943, at the St. James Theatre in New York.

20. Libretto for *The Boys from Syracuse* (first produced on April 15, 1963, at Theatre Four, New York), 55. Rodgers and Hammerstein Theatre Library, New York.

2. Double Vision

1. Quotations are from the typescript of *Kiss Me, Kate,* by Cole Porter and Bella Spewack, which opened at the New Century Theatre, New York, on December 30, 1948; the typescript is held in the Cole Porter Collection, Library of Congress. All references in the text are to this edition unless otherwise noted. A few typographical errors have been corrected. (This typescript, the one in the Samuel and Bella Spewack Papers, RB&MLCU, and the copy in the Lord Chamberlain's Office at the British Library all contain the attribution "by Cole Porter and Bella Spewack." In contrast, the printed version of 1953 has "book by Samuel and Bella Spewack, lyrics by Cole Porter." The copy in the Lord Chamberlain's Office is dated 1950 rather than 1948; this may be when it was licensed.)

2. William Shakespeare, *The Taming of the Shrew,* in *The Riverside Shakespeare,* ed. G. Blakemore Evans and J. J. M. Tobin, 2nd ed. (Boston: Houghton, 1997). All references in the text are to this edition.

3. Lawrence Stone, *The Family, Sex and Marriage in England, 1500–1800* (New York: Harper, 1977), 182.

4. Ibid., 136. Stone quotes Robert Cleaver and J. Dod, *A Godlye Forme of Householde Government* (London, 1614).

5. Act 2, scene 5, p. 31 in *Kiss Me, Kate,* script C "Final" (October 30, 1948), box 27, Spewack Papers.

6. David Garrick, *Catharine and Petruchio: A Comedy, in Three Acts* (London: J. and R. Tonson and S. Draper, 1756). For a full discussion of this version and its influence, see "Challenging Patterns" in Irene Dash, *Wooing, Wedding, and Power: Women in Shakespeare's Plays* (New York: Columbia University Press, 1984), 33–64.

7. *Taming of the Shrew: A Comedy by William Shakspere as Arranged by Augustin Daly. First produced at Daly's Theatre, January 18, 1887, receiving its One Hundredth Representation April 13, 1887 and here printed from the*

Prompter's Copy. Daly Collection, Folger Shakespeare Library.

8. Garrick, *Catharine and Petruchio,* 17.

9. Act 1, scene 7, pp. 37–39 in *Kiss Me, Kate,* script B with notes, box 27, Spewack Papers.

10. Spewack later noted that she had sought to write "a mature story to run parallel with the Shrew and at a certain point to go on one track." Dated April 22, the note begins, "This is the story of show business. It is a musical love story of the eternal serio-comic battle of male and female played against the events of an opening night of the tryout of a musical version of Shakespeare's *Taming of the Shrew* at Ford's Theatre in Baltimore." "Backstage," box 26, "Production: *Kiss Me, Kate,*" notes and worksheets, folder 1, Spewack Papers.

11. Typescript of *The Taming of the Shrew,* by William Shakespeare, produced by the Theatre Guild at the Guild Theatre, New York, September 30, 1935, copy 1, BRTD.

12. "A *Shrew* with Flourish," *Call Bulletin,* a press release in advance of the arrival of the Lunt-Fontanne *Shrew,* San Francisco, October 28, 1939. William Shakespeare, *Taming of the Shrew* (1935) clippings file, BRTD.

13. Brooks Atkinson, "The Play," *New York Times,* October 1, 1935, BRTD.

14. Hancock is another example of a woman artist in the theater who has been forgotten. Only her husband, Lee Simonson, is now remembered, although she preceded him in the field. Her designs for the sets, together with illustrations of the production, are in the Vandamm Collection, BRTD. Her copy of the play's typescript (labeled "copy 2" and with the name "Carolyn Simonson" on the title page) is also in the BRTD file; it has tabs on every page

where a change of set occurs, but includes no stage directions. Thus it differs from the acting typescript, copy 1, and provides additional information on her perceptions of the scenes.

15. Porter to Spewack, June 16, 1948, box E, Spewack Papers.

16. "Copyright 1948 by Bella Spewack. Revisions and Introduction copyright 1953 by Samuel and Bella Spewack." "Brushing Up on Kate's Dates," *Theatre Arts* 39 (January 1955).

17. The *Current Biography Yearbook of 1954,* s.v. "Holm, Hanya," says that she had one son, Klaus Holm, a stage designer and lighting expert.

18. Like Kate, a defiant Lilli responds but her options are limited. To emphasize that defiance, Cole Porter wrote "I Hate Men" for Lilli/Kate and a lyrical comic song for Fred/Petruchio, "Were Thine That Special Face." In the former, she is basically singing the idea of Shakespeare's play: her great dislike, disrelish, distaste for men indicated by the text. As each refrain opens with "I hate men," Porter moves from the single virgin, to the traveling salesman who sweet-talks a woman. "Their worth upon this earth I dinna ken," Kate sings, then progresses to the old man: "Though roosters they, I will not play the hen." Here "men," "dinna ken," and "hen" all rhyme. Her loud banging of a drinking cup on the table emphasizes her hate. By contrast, Petruchio's "Were Thine That Special Face" lyrically and romantically describes the kind of a face he would love to find in Kate, then ends with the reality "When all these charms are thine / Then you'll be mine, all mine." Between the two songs, however, Lilli has read the note "not meant for me" and ad libs her lines as she throws the bouquet at him and tears up the note. Although its words cap-

ture the irony implicit in the plot, they take on additional meaning when Kate/Lilli responds as one voice to Fred's Petruchio.

19. Walter Terry, "Dance: Miss Holm and Her Fine 'Kiss Me, Kate' Choreography," *New York Herald Tribune,* January 9, 1949. The dance Holm created here did not belong to a specific model, but rather carried her ideas onto the stage. Reviewing her work in *Kiss Me, Kate,* Walter Terry observed that she always put the entire play first rather than showcasing her own talents in a particular form. Her dances did not interrupt the course of the show. Instead, she created

> arresting dance passages, movement details of wit and beauty, and an amazing array of styles. . . . At appropriate moments [Holm and her assistant, Ray Harrison] provided the show with classic ballet, modern dance, jitterbugging, softshoe, acrobatics, court dance, folk dance and episodes which might be described as rhythmic playfulness.

She usually concealed "her enormous talents in the classroom," but in this musical, although there was no ballet as such, "there [was] dancing, all of it firmly integrated into the show to contribute to the achieving of a total theatrical impression." Praising her aim of integrating the dance into the whole, he then went on to try to decide which of the dances he liked best, and had a difficult time. Of "Another Op'nin'" he observed that it "permitted the dancing ensemble to enliven a backstage scene with spurts of practice-action, fragments of formal dance and a good deal of frolic."

In another review, Arthur Todd ("A Brace of Musicals," *Dance,* March 1949, 28–29) praised Holm as someone who "assume[d] an eminent position in the contemporary theatre and one in which she may well play a major role in the future of the Broadway musical and lyric theatre." And she did. She later choreographed *My Fair Lady, Where's Charley,* and *Camelot,* among other works.

Todd gave readers an idea of what the dance accompanying "Another Op'nin'" looked like:

> Danced by the twelve ensemble dancers, this work is performed in rehearsal clothes in a backstage setting. It is enriched by marvelous serpentine and diagonal formations and groupings.

The power and originality of Holm's choreography here led her to copyright, a first in the field of dance. Praise for Hanya Holm and familiarity with her work permeated the criticism of the time.

20. For the film, Harrison Howell, the advisor to presidents who called Lilli from the White House, was transformed into Tex, a wealthy rancher, and also the name originally of one of Lois's lovers. Politics, too, was eliminated from the film, as the telephone conversation between Tex and Lilli was interrupted by Fred asking about the price of beef rather than borscht.

21. Letter from Lars Schmidt of Lars Schmidt & Co. to Bella Spewack, August 26, 1952, box 21, folder 1952, Spewack Papers.

22. Porter did, however, receive much correspondence from abroad, from managers as well as agents. Also, his lawyers were very involved in all the contracts signed on *Kiss Me, Kate,* as becomes apparent from his correspondence in the Cole Porter Musical and Literary Property Trusts as well as in the Spewack Papers.

23. Spewack to Porter, May 30, 1961, Cole Porter Letters, box E, Spewack Papers.

24. Spewack to Russian Ministry of Culture, August 3, 1968, box 24, Spewack Papers.

25. The parallel isn't exact, since Kate meets hostility from those around her and Lilli does not. Nevertheless, Lilli meets internal hostility. Having the freedom to choose does not always mean having the freedom to say "no." It may also mean reevaluating a situation. Here is where Fred's request and his statement "But I came back" fits in. If she initiated the reunion with Fred, then Fred's contention that he "came back" must also be considered.

26. See "Challenging Patterns" in Dash, *Wooing, Wedding, and Power*.

27. Typescript, *Taming of the Shrew*, 1935, 2–46, BRTD.

3. The Challenge of Tragedy

1. Leonard Bernstein, "Excerpts from a West Side Story Log," Writings, box 75, folder 7, Leonard Bernstein Collection, MDLC (article published in *Playbill*, September 1957); Leonard Bernstein, *Findings* (New York: Anchor, 1982), 147; Deborah Jowitt, *Jerome Robbins: His Life, His Theater, His Dance* (New York: Simon and Shuster, 2004) 267; Humphrey Burton, *Leonard Bernstein* (New York: Doubleday, 1994), 187. According to both Jowitt and Burton, the log was fabricated.

2. Anna Kisselgoff, "Jerome Robbins, 79, Is Dead; Giant of Ballet and Broadway," *New York Times*, July 30, 1998. The words are Robbins's own.

3. Burton, *Leonard Bernstein*, 114–15.

4. Arthur Laurents, *Home of the Brave*, acting edition (New York: Dramatists Play Service, 1945).

5. Craig Zadan, *Sondheim & Co.*, 2nd ed. (New York: Harper, 1986), 14.

6. Ibid., 11.

7. "Landmark Symposium," transcript of a conversation among Laurents, Bernstein, Robbins, and Sondheim, moderated by Terrence McNally, *Dramatists' Guild Quarterly*, Autumn 1985, 13. Original transcripts of the symposium are in box 563, folder 7, Leonard Bernstein Collection, MDLC, and in the Jerome Robbins Papers, JRDD.

8. Bernstein's papers include a copy of Kittredge's 1940 edition of *Romeo and Juliet* with a handwritten note beside the prologue: "Should be prologue interrupted by street fight." Across the top of the page and above the title appears "An out and out plea for racial tolerance." Writings, 1954–55, box 73, folder 9, Leonard Bernstein Collection, MDLC.

9. Burton, *Leonard Bernstein*, 102.

10. Amanda Vaill, *Somewhere: The Life of Jerome Robbins* (New York: Broadway Books, 2006), 14–16, 319.

11. Jowitt, *Jerome Robbins*, 106.

12. Zadan, *Sondheim & Co.*, 14. According to Zadan, Flora Roberts, Sondheim's agent, said he used every excuse not to do the show, including that he had never been that poor.

13. Literally, this means "the going out of the Sabbath."

14. File labeled "Typescript: Act 1 of *Romeo and Juliet*," box 73, folder 10, Leonard Bernstein Collection, MDLC. The typescript is labeled "Tonio and Dorrie" in pencil. The quotation is from 1.2, p. 6. The Robbins Papers, JRDD, also have several short scripts. One includes a Jewish gang, with Bernard as gang chief who meets Mercutio as gang chief. Another script, called "Romeo," gives scene 1 where "against music we see two or three shadowy figures beat-

ing up a boy." Others in box 81, folder 1, *MGXMD130 indicate the attempts by Robbins and Bernstein to develop this script. There is even a reference to dropping Paris, Juliet's principal suitor, since the ending must differ from that of Shakespeare's play. Other folders in this box testify to the several attempts to pull together a plot line.

15. Typescript in Writings, 1954–55, box 73, folder 10, Leonard Bernstein Collection, MDLC.

16. "Typescript: Act 1 of *Romeo and Juliet*," 1.2, p. 6.

17. *South Pacific* opened at the Majestic Theatre, New York, on April 7, 1949, with music by Richard Rodgers, lyrics by Oscar Hammerstein II, and book by Hammerstein and Joshua Logan.

18. Quotations are from the typescript of *West Side Story* (based on a conception by Jerome Robbins, book by Arthur Laurents, music by Leonard Bernstein, lyrics by Stephen Sondheim and Leonard Bernstein, direction and choreography by Jerome Robbins), RM #138, BRTD. All references in the text are to this edition unless otherwise noted. A few typographical errors have been corrected.

19. Laurence Urdang, ed., *Timetables of American History,* millennial ed. (New York: Simon and Schuster, 1996), 360.

20. Jowitt, *Jerome Robbins,* 151.

21. Julia L. Foulkes, "Angels 'Rewolt!': Jewish Women in Modern Dance in the 1930s," *American Jewish History* 88 (June 2000): 233–52.

22. "I took a crack at an outline for what I entitled 'East Side Story,' but the Catholic—Jewish Romeo and Juliet concept seemed curiously familiar. For good reason. . . . In the Twenties, there was a long-running hit play called *Ab-*

ie's Irish Rose. 'East Side Story' was *Abie's Irish Rose* set to music. I bowed out." Arthur Laurents, *Original Story By: A Memoir of Broadway and Hollywood* (New York: Alfred A. Knopf, 2000), 330.

23. Incomplete scripts in the Bernstein collection at the Library of Congress indicate that several attempts were made. In his autobiography, Laurents writes that he sent the other two collaborators a script for *East Side Story.* As the men said in a 1985 interview, their recollections differ and one could call this a "Rashomon" on the play. Bernstein commented, "Arthur wrote some sketched-out scenes, one of which was pretty complete." "Landmark Symposium," 13.

24. Zadan, *Sondheim & Co.,* 15.

25. "Gang Bang" (a working title that may have been an inside joke), box 73, folder 10, Leonard Bernstein Collection, MDLC.

26. Joan Peyser, *Bernstein, A Biography: Revised and Updated* (New York: Billboard, 1998), p. 264.

27. Deborah Dash Moore, *To the Golden Cities: Pursuing the American Jewish Dream in Miami and L.A.* (Cambridge, Mass.: Harvard University Press, 1996), and talks with the author.

28. William Shakespeare, *Romeo and Juliet,* in *The Riverside Shakespeare,* ed. G. Blakemore Evans and J. J. Tobin, 2nd ed. (Boston: Houghton, 1997). All references to the text are to this edition.

29. Walter Kerr, "Theater: *West Side Story* Sharks and Jets Battle in Dance," *New York Herald Tribune,* October 6, 1957.

30. Peter Brinson, "The New Kind of Dancer," *London Times,* December 7, 1958.

31. Letter from Robbins to Laurents and Bernstein, October 18, 1955, Writings, 1954–55, box 73, folder 7 labeled

"West Side Story," Leonard Bernstein Collection, MDLC.

32. "Robbins, the Legend Who Was Human," *New York Times*, August 9, 1998.

33. Jowitt, *Jerome Robbins*, 270; letter from Robbins to Laurents and Bernstein, October 18, 1955.

34. "Landmark Symposium," 18.

35. Leonard Bernstein, *West Side Story*, score (New York: Jalni Publications, Boosey and Hawkes, 1994), ix.

36. Laurents, *Original Story By*, 356.

37. Annotated script excerpts, 1.1, p. 1, box 81, folder 2, Jerome Robbins Papers, JRDD.

38. Raphael Mostel, "When the Ram's Horn Sounds," *Forward*, September 6, 2002: 14.

39. Laurents, *Original Story By*, 356.

40. Bernstein, *West Side Story* score, 94.

41. Quoted in Jowitt, *Jerome Robbins*, 275.

42. Bernstein, *West Side Story* score, 86–134. The dance in the gym is divided into several numbers.

43. Mark Eden Horowitz, *Sondheim on Music: Minor Details and Major Decisions* (Lanham, Md., and Oxford: Scarecrow Press in association with the Library of Congress, 2003), 12.

44. Bernstein, *West Side Story* score, 168–205.

45. "Robbins, the Legend Who Was Human."

46. James F. Short, Jr., and Fred L. Strodtbeck, *Group Process and Gang Delinquency* (Chicago: University of Chicago Press, 1965).

47. Arthur M. Schlesinger, Jr., ed., *The Almanac of American History* (New York: G. P. Putnam's Sons, 1983), 541–49.

48. Elliot Norton, "Cheers for *West Side*," review of film, Leonard Bernstein Collection, MDLC.

49. Laurents, *Original Story By*, 362.

50. "Landmark Symposium," 21.

51. I own a copy of the subcommittee's interim report, published in 1954.

52. Zadan, *Sondheim & Co.*, 26.

53. Brooks Atkinson, "*West Side*: Moving Music Drama on Callous Theme," *New York Times*, October 6, 1957.

54. Jay Carmody, "New Theatre Season Has Dazzling Start," *Evening Star*, August 20, 1957.

55. Zadan, *Sondheim & Co.*, 26.

56. Brooks Atkinson, "Theatre: Musical Is Back," *New York Times*, April 28, 1960.

57. "Landmark Symposium," 17.

58. Ibid., 14.

4. Out of the Closet

1. Anthony Mancini, "Closeup: His Own Thing," interview with Donald Driver, *New York Post*, February 2, 1968.

2. Doris Hering, "Broadway . . . On and Off," *Dance Magazine*, April 1968, 26ff.

3. Danny Apolinar's copy of the script of *Your Own Thing* is in series 2, box 3, folder 12, Danny Apolinar Papers, BRTD; see also *Your Own Thing*, by Hal Hester and Danny Apolinar, book by Donald Driver, in Stanley Richards, ed., *Great Rock Musicals*, (New York: Stein and Day, 1979), 289–377. References in the text are to this edition, which has no act or scene divisions.

4. They met at the Five Oaks Restaurant on Grove Street in Greenwich Village. Elenore Lester, "Is This Where It's At?" *New York Times*, February 25, 1968.

5. Richards, *Great Rock Musicals*, 289–91.

6. Ibid.

7. Danny Apolinar Papers, BRTD.

8. Mancini, "Closeup: His Own Thing."

9. Scott Warfield, "From *Hair* to *Rent*: Is 'Rock' a Four-Letter Word on Broadway?" in *The Cambridge Companion to the Musical*, ed. William A. Everett and Paul R. Laird (Cambridge: Cambridge University Press, 2002), 231, 243.

10. Series 2, box 3, folders 1–3, 11, Danny Apolinar Papers, BRTD.

11. Series 3, box 8, folder 16, Danny Apolinar Papers, BRTD.

12. Series 3, box 8, folder 10, Danny Apolinar Papers, BRTD.

13. Richard P. Cooke, "Swinging with Shakespeare," review of *Your Own Thing*, *Wall Street Journal*, January 16, 1968.

14. Stuart H. Benedict, introduction to *Your Own Thing*, music and lyrics by Hal Hester and Danny Apolinar, book by Donald Driver (New York: Dell, 1970), 125; also in series 2, box 3, folder 10, Danny Apolinar Papers, BRTD.

15. According to Janet Sovey, "the notes from Buddha were in an actor's hand that appeared and disappeared."

16. Series 2, box 3, folder 11, Danny Apolinar Papers, BRTD.

17. Clive Barnes, "A Rocking *Twelfth Night: Your Own Thing* Is Blissfully Irreverent," *New York Times*, January 15, 1968.

18. According to Janet Sovey, the actors had great difficulty with the dance.

19. An illustration of a scene from the play in *Vogue* shows Orson looking at himself being strung up. Cowboys surround him. They are also projected on the screens surrounding the central scene. The critic, Anthony West, commends the imaginative staging that allows the designer to relieve the visual boredom that accompanies a static set and permits a range of imaginative images. "*Vogue's* Spotlight: Theatre. *Your Own Thing*," *Vogue*, April 15, 1968, 46, Danny Apolinar Papers, BRTD.

20. Copy of letter from Norman Rothstein to Peter Filichia, September 9, 1998, series 1, box 1, folder 5, Danny Apolinar Papers, BRTD.

21. Whitney Bolton, "*Your Own Thing*: A Rock Musical," *Morning Telegraph*, January 16, 1968.

22. Daphne Kraft, "*Your Own Thing* Bows at Orpheum," *Newark Evening News*, January 15, 1968.

23. Barnes, "A Rocking *Twelfth Night*."

24. John S. Wilson, "Doing *Your Own Thing*," *New York Times*, March 24, 1968.

25. Lewis Funke, "News of the Rialto: Will B'way Rock?" *New York Times*, December 10, 1967. This article was written before the January 1968 opening of *Your Own Thing*. Papp had produced *Hair*, which was described as a tribal rock 'n' roll musical. Funke notes that eventually rock will take over, and quotes Driver as saying, "This new music allows us to get closer to where we are at in the world today in terms of political concepts, sexual concepts, protests against the Establishment. It has meaning and is about the way we live." All references to *Twelfth Night* are to *The Riverside Shakespeare*, ed. G. Blakemore Evans and J. J. Tobin, 2nd ed. (1997).

26. It included such songs as "Tomorrow Is Saint Valentine's Day," "How Should I My True Love Know," and "He's Dead and Buried."

5. The Persistence of Love

1. *Two Gentlemen of Verona: A Grand New Musical*, adapted by John Guare and Mel Shapiro with lyrics by John Guare and music by Galt MacDermot, produced by Joseph Papp, Delacorte Theatre, New York, July 28,

1971, and St. James Theater, New York, December 1, 1971, typescript, p. 1 (now missing). I saw this typescript in the archives of the Public Theater before they were disbanded and most of their holdings transferred to the BRTD. The following quotations are from the manifesto that opened it, which has now unfortunately vanished.

2. Telephone interview, August 24, 2007.

3. *Two Gentlemen of Verona, Adapted from the Shakespeare Play by John Guare and Mel Shapiro,* lyrics by John Guare, music by Galt MacDermot (New York: Holt, Rinehart and Winston, 1973), 1.1, p. 11. All references in the text are to this edition. The play also appears in *Great Rock Musicals,* ed. Stanley Richards (New York: Stein and Day, 1979). In the performance in the park, the song was "It's Love in Bloom," with music by Leo Robin and words by Ralph Rainer. It was the theme song for Jack Benny's radio program. According to Guare, when the play moved to Broadway the opening song was changed to "Love, Is That You?" and the change was retained in the 2005 Central Park revival.

4. Clive Barnes, "*Two Gentlemen of Verona:* Musical Is Adaptation by Guare and Shapiro, Most of Papp Retained in St. James Version," *New York Times,* December 2, 1971. The article is a review of the Broadway production, which ran for eighteen months. Dinitia Smith, "Age of Aquarius Returns in Shakespearean Romp," *New York Times,* August 16, 2005.

5. Barnes, "*Two Gentlemen of Verona.*"

6. *Village Voice,* July 3, 2001.

7. Epstein's comments and Papp's response to the critics are both in Helen Epstein, *Joe Papp: An American Life* (Boston: Little, Brown, 1994), 214.

8. Galt MacDermot, "The Music Man: Galt MacDermot Talks to P & P," *Plays and Players* 20, no. 9 (June 1973): 22.

9. Guare and Shapiro, *Two Gentlemen of Verona,* 5. Public Theater productions played in Central Park for three weeks and then toured the city for a month, before audiences that were more raucous.

10. Peter Schjeldahl, "An Up-to-Date and Sexy *Verona,*" *New York Times,* August 8, 1971.

11. The line is quoted from William Shakespeare, *Two Gentlemen of Verona,* in *The Riverside Shakespeare,* ed. G. Blakemore Evans and J. J. Tobin, 2nd ed. (Boston: Houghton, 1997). All references to the text are to this edition.

12. In *A Midsummer Night's Dream,* Starveling, as Moonshine, also has a dog. However, he makes only a momentary appearance and does not join his master in what appear to be several lengthy exchanges, as occurs between Launce and Crab.

13. In fact, when the musical played Melbourne, Australia, a trio of black performers sent from New York joined the Australian actors, so that the multiracial effect so important to the adaptors would be retained. "What distinguishes the show from most we get is the professional finish of the import principals, Gail Boggs, Gilbert Price and Judd Jones," wrote Howard Palmer in the April 2, 1973, *Melbourne Review* ("2 Gentlemen of Laughter"). Another critic, Laurie Landry, didn't understand why the adaptors had sent these performers abroad, and wrote, "How to get by in a big city despite the frictions of mixed cultures and races, is the idea behind the rock-beat musical version of Shakespeare's *Two Gentlemen of Verona* at her majesty's. . . . The show is full of topnotch performances by singing actors from home and abroad, in

particular three blacks from New York.
Don't bother to work out why blacks are
playing the roles, just sit back and enjoy
their superb singing and dancing." Laurie Landry, "Lots of Love from *Verona*,"
Your Guide to the Shows, April 7–13,
1973, BRTD. But, of course, the adaptors
did have a reason: they wanted to capture the many voices of those in the city
and in their audience when they toured
the boroughs.

14. Schjeldahl, "An Up-to-Date and
Sexy *Verona*"; Palmer, "2 Gentlemen of
Laughter."

15. Tom Prideaux, "Vaudeville from
Verona: *Two Gentlemen of Verona*,"
Life, February 11, 1972[?], Collection
of Newspaper Clippings of Dramatic
Criticism, 1971–72, New York Public Library. Raul Julia died on October 24,
1994, at the age of fifty-four. By then he
had played a range of roles in the theater, including Othello, Petruchio, and
Mack the Knife in *The Threepenny Opera*, and had played in films, among
them *The Kiss of the Spider Woman* and
The Addams Family.

16. In this scene, Proteus first looks
up to heaven as if thanking the powers
above, then, fully clothed, lies on top of
Julia, who is also fully clothed.

17. Telephone interview with John
Guare, August 24, 2007.

18. Ibid.

19. Ibid.

20. At the revival of *Two Gentlemen of Verona* in 2005, the audience
applauded, revealing the enduring relevance of the line "Bring all the troops
back home," although this time everyone thought about the Iraq War, instead
of Vietnam.

21. Telephone interview, August 24,
2007.

22. Richard F. Shepard, "They Put
Verona on Broadway Map," *New York
Times,* December 3, 1971.

23. Telephone interview, August 10,
2007.

24. Frances Teague observes, "*Two
Gents* is plain-spoken about sex." She
describes these lyrics as celebrating love
and belonging to the age of Aquarius,
yet she faults the musical as being more
conservative than Shakespeare's comedy in its development of outspoken
women. *Shakespeare and the American
Popular Stage* (Cambridge: Cambridge
University Press, 2006), 161.

25. Shepard, "They Put *Verona* on
Broadway Map."

26. R. B. Marriott, "Musical 'Verona' Is a Joyous Hit at the Phoenix,"
Stage and Television Today, May 3, 1973,
19. He also observed, "the action of the
heart and the hope of happiness are the
dominating strands," and specifically
noted the skillful integration of book,
music, dance, and development of the
story, characteristics of the organic musical, as well as the "human elements."

27. Barnes, "*Two Gentlemen of
Verona.*"

Coda

1. David Garrick, *The Plays of David
Garrick,* ed. Harry William Pedicord
and Frederick Louis Bergmann (Carbondale: Southern Illinois University
Press, 1981), vols. 1, 3, and 4. See especially 3:418–23, 4:420–31.

2. Tori Haring-Smith, *From Farce
to Metadrama: A Stage History of The
Taming of the Shrew,* Contributions in
Drama and Theatre Studies 16 (Westport, Conn.: Greenwood, 1985).

3. Charles Beecher Hogan, *Shakespeare in the Theatre, 1701–1800,* vol. 1
(Oxford: Oxford University Press, 1952),
404–13.

4. *The Plays of David Garrick,* vols.
3 and 4.

5. "Landmark Symposium," transcript of a conversation among Lau-

rents, Bernstein, Robbins, and Sondheim, moderated by Terrence McNally,
Dramatists' Guild Quarterly, Autumn
1985, 15. Original transcripts of the symposium are in box 563, folder 7, Leonard
Bernstein Collection, MDLC, and in
the Jerome Robbins Papers, JRDD.

6. "It is . . . not necessary, that a
man should forbear to write, till he has
discovered some truth unknown before;
he may be sufficiently useful, by only
diversifying the surface of knowledge,
and luring the mind by a new appearance to a second view of those beauties
which it had passed over inattentively
before." *Adventurer* no. 137, February 26, 1754, in *The Yale Edition of the
Works of Samuel Johnson,* ed. Allen T.
Hazen, vol. 2, *The Idler and The Adventurer,* ed. W. J. Bate (New Haven, Conn.:
Yale University Press, 1963), 491.

7. "Verona, in our minds, was San
Juan," Mr. Guare told the interviewer, and "Milan was New York." Dinitia Smith, "Age of Aquarius Returns
in Shakespearean Romp," *New York
Times,* August 16, 2005.

8. Telephone interview with John
Guare, August 24, 2007.

9. Bruce R. Smith, *The Acoustic
World of Early Modern England* (Chicago: University of Chicago Press, 1999).

10. Arthur Laurents, "*West Side Story*
at Fifty," lecture at Bruno Walter Auditorium, New York Public Library for the
Performing Arts, September 20, 2007.

11. John Guare, "He Has Metamorphosed Me," lecture at Bruno Walter
Auditorium, New York Public Library
for the Performing Arts, October 4,
2007.

BIBLIOGRAPHY

Archives and Collections

Some of the more significant items in the archives are listed here.

THE BOYS FROM SYRACUSE

Billy Rose Theatre Division. New York Library for the Performing Arts.

The Boys from Syracuse, typescript, by George Abbott, with music by Richard Rodgers, lyrics by Lorenz Hart, and choreography by George Balanchine. Opened at the Alvin Theatre, New York, on November 23, 1938. Restricted Material NCOF + 1938.

Jo Mielziner Papers.

Jo Mielziner, designs and technical drawings, 1924–1976.

Palmer, Howard. "2 Gentlemen of Laughter." Review of *Two Gentlemen of Verona.* Her Majesty's Theater, Melbourne. *Melbourne Review,* April 2, 1973.

Playbill, program for *The Boys from Syracuse,* opening December 26, 1938, Alvin Theatre, New York, in the George Abbot clippings folder, MWEZ +nc 18,690.

Popular Balanchine Dossiers. Compiled by Camille Hardy. Jerome Robbins Dance Division. New York Public Library for the Performing Arts. (S)*MGZMD 146.

Atkinson, Brooks. "The Boys from Syracuse." Review. Alvin Theatre, New York. *New York Times,* November 24, 1938. In *New York Times Theater Reviews* 4 (1934–41).

"Chasing the *Boys from Syracuse.*"

Mantle, Burns. "*The Boys from Syracuse* Scores More Hits Than Errors." Review. Alvin Theatre, New York. *New York Daily News,* November 24, 1938. Box 15.

Woods, John. "Wow." *Yale News,* November 4, 1938.

Richard Rodgers Collection. Music Division. Library of Congress.

Rodgers and Hammerstein Theatre Library. New York, N.Y.

Libretto for *The Boys from Syracuse.* First produced on April 15, 1963, at Theatre Four, New York.

Billy Rose Theatre Division. New York Public Library for the Performing Arts.

KISS ME, KATE

Lord Chamberlain's Office. British
Library.
> Kiss Me, Kate, typescript, #2329,
> Department of Manuscripts.

Clifford Collection. Music Division.
Library of Congress.

Daly Collection. Folger Shakespeare
Library.

Alan M. and Saliann Kriegsman
Collection. Music Division. Library
of Congress.

Cole Porter Collection. Music Division.
Library of Congress.
> Kiss Me, Kate, typescript (identi-
> fied as "Cole Porter, Waldorf
> Tower, 41c), ML 50.P8 K5 1948b
> (Case), by Cole Porter and Bella
> Spewack. Opened at the New
> Century Theatre, New York, on
> December 30, 1948.

Cole Porter Musical and Literary
Property Trusts. New York, N.Y.

Billy Rose Theatre Division. New York
Public Library for the Performing
Arts.
> Atkinson, Brooks. "The Play."
> Review of The Taming of the
> Shrew. Guild Theatre, New York.
> New York Times, October 1,
> 1935. In New York Times Theater
> Reviews 4 (1934–41).
> Kiss Me, Kate, typescript, October
> 30, 1948. Includes "We Shall
> Never Be Younger." Restricted
> Material #1831.
> "A Shrew with Flourish." Call
> Bulletin, October 28, 1939.
> Taming of the Shrew (1935) clip-
> pings file.
> The Taming of the Shrew, type-
> script, by William Shakespeare.
> Produced by the Theatre Guild
> at the Guild Theatre, New York,
> September 30, 1935. Copies la-
> beled 1 and 2; the second bears

the name of the set designer,
> Carolyn Simonson.
> Vandamm Collection.

Samuel and Bella Spewack Papers.
Rare Book and Manuscript Library.
Columbia University.
> Kiss Me, Kate, scripts labeled A, B,
> B with notes, C, C with notes,
> and C "Final." Box 27.

Vandamm Collection. Billy Rose
Theatre Division. New York Public
Library for the Performing Arts.

WEST SIDE STORY

Leonard Bernstein Collection. Music
Division. Library of Congress.
> Norton, Elliot. "Cheers for West
> Side." Review.

Lord Chamberlain's Office. British
Library.

Cheryl Crawford Collection. Billy Rose
Theatre Division. New York Public
Library for the Performing Arts.

Jerome Robbins Papers. Jerome Robbins
Dance Division. New York Public
Library for the Performing Arts.

Billy Rose Theatre Division. New York
Public Library for the Performing
Arts.
> West Side Story, typescript, based
> on a conception by Jerome
> Robbins, book by Arthur
> Laurents, music by Leonard
> Bernstein, lyrics by Stephen
> Sondheim and Leonard
> Bernstein, direction and cho-
> reography by Jerome Robbins.
> RM #138.

Theatre on Film and Tape Archive.

YOUR OWN THING

Danny Apolinar Papers. Billy Rose
Theatre Division. New York Public
Library for the Performing Arts.

Your Own Thing. Apolinar's copy of the script. Series 2, box 3, folder 12.

West, Anthony. "*Vogue's* Spotlight: Theatre. *Your Own Thing.*" Review. Orpheum Theater, New York. *Vogue,* April 15, 1968, 46. MWEZ +nc 21,578.

TWO GENTLEMEN OF VERONA

Archives. Public Theater, New York. (Now dissolved; most holdings transferred to the Billy Rose Theatre Division, New York Public Library for the Performing Arts.)

New York Public Library for the Performing Arts.

Prideaux, Tom. "Vaudeville from Verona: *Two Gentlemen of Verona.*" *Life,* February 11, 1972. In Collection of Newspaper Clippings of Dramatic Criticism, 1971–72, T-U *T-NBL+(collection). The date is handwritten and appears to be in error.

Billy Rose Theatre Division. New York Public Library for the Performing Arts.

New York Shakespeare Festival Records.

Printed Works

Allen, Michael J. B., and Kenneth Muir, eds. *Shakespeare's Plays in Quarto.* Berkeley: University of California Press, 1981.

Allen, Shirley S. *Samuel Phelps and Sadler's Wells Theatre.* Middletown, Conn.: Wesleyan University Press, 1971.

Anderegg, Michael. *Orson Welles, Shakespeare, and Popular Culture.* New York: Columbia University Press, 1999.

Atkinson, Brooks. *Broadway.* New York: Macmillan, 1970.

———. "Theatre: Musical Is Back." Review of *West Side Story.* Winter Garden, New York. *New York Times,* April 28, 1960.

———. "*West Side:* Moving Music Drama on Callous Theme." Review. Winter Garden, New York. *New York Times,* October 6, 1957.

———. "Words and Music: From Padua to Gotham in *Kiss Me, Kate.*" *New York Times,* January 16, 1949.

Auerbach, Nina. *Ellen Terry: Player in Her Time.* New York: W. W. Norton, 1987.

Bamber, Linda. *Comic Women, Tragic Men: A Study of Gender and Genre in Shakespeare.* Stanford, Calif.: Stanford University Press, 1982.

Barber, C. L. *Shakespeare's Festive Comedy.* Princeton, N.J.: Princeton University Press, 1959.

Barnes, Clive. "A Rocking *Twelfth Night: Your Own Thing* Is Blissfully Irreverent." Review. Orpheum Theater, New York. *New York Times,* January 15, 1968.

———. "*Two Gentlemen of Verona:* Musical Is Adaptation by Guare and Shapiro, Most of Papp Retained in St. James Version." Review. St. James Theatre, New York. *New York Times,* December 2, 1971.

Barnes, Howard. "A Kiss to Remember." Review of *Kiss Me, Kate.* New Century Theatre, New York. *New York Herald Tribune,* December 31, 1948. *New York Theatre Critics' Reviews,* 1948, volume 9.

———. "Shakespeare is Advanced to Musical Comedy Rank." Sunday Column on *Kiss Me, Kate.* New Century Theatre, New York. *New York Herald Tribune,* January 2, 1949.

Barranger, Milly S. *Margaret Webster: A Life in the Theater*. Ann Arbor: University of Michigan Press, 2004.

Beauvoir, Simone de. *The Second Sex*. Translated and edited by H. M. Parshley. New York: Knopf, 1953. Reprint, New York: Bantam, 1961.

Bellafante, Ginia. "In the Heartland and Out of the Closet." *New York Times*, December 28, 2006.

Benbow, Taryn, ed. *International Dictionary of Modern Dance*. Detroit, Mich.: St. James Press, 1998.

Benedict, Stuart H. Introduction to *Your Own Thing*, music and lyrics by Hal Hester and Danny Apolinar, book by Donald Driver. New York: Dell, 1970.

Berkowitz, Joel. *Shakespeare on the American Yiddish Stage*. Iowa City: University of Iowa Press, 2002.

Bernstein, Leonard. *Findings*. New York: Anchor, 1982.

———. *The Unanswered Question: Six Talks at Harvard*. Cambridge, Mass.: Harvard University Press, 1976.

———. *West Side Story*. Score. New York: Jalni Publications, Boosey and Hawkes, 1994.

Bolton, Whitney. "*Your Own Thing*: A Rock Musical." Review. Orpheum Theater, New York. *Morning Telegraph*, January 16, 1968.

Bordman, Gerald. *American Musical Theatre: A Chronicle*. 2nd ed. New York: Oxford University Press, 1992.

Borgzinner, Jon. "Whang! The Rock Musicals." *Life*, March 22, 1968, 84–85.

Bradbury, Malcolm, and David Palmer, eds. *Shakespearian Comedy*. Stratford-upon-Avon Studies 14. London: Edward Arnold Ltd., 1972.

Bradley, A. C. *Shakespearean Tragedy*. 1904. Reprint, New York: Fawcett, 1965.

Brinson, Peter. "The New Kind of Dancer." *London Times*, December 7, 1958.

Bristol, Michael D. *Big Time Shakespeare*. London: Routledge, 1996.

Brook, Peter. *Peter Brook's Production of William Shakespeare's "A Midsummer Night's Dream" for the Royal Shakespeare Company*. Edited and with interviews by Glenn Loney. Chicago: Dramatic Publishing Co., 1974.

Brownmiller, Susan. *Against Our Will: Men, Women, and Rape*. New York: Simon and Schuster, 1975.

Bryer, Jackson R., and Richard A. Davison. *The Art of the American Musical: Conversations with the Creators*. New Brunswick: Rutgers University Press, 2005.

Bullough, Geoffrey, ed. *Narrative and Dramatic Sources of Shakespeare*. 8 vols. New York: Columbia University Press, 1957–75.

Burnim, Kalman A. *David Garrick: Director*. 1961. Reprint, Carbondale and Edwardsville: Southern Illinois University Press, 1973.

Burton, Humphrey. *Leonard Bernstein*. New York: Doubleday, 1994.

Campbell, Oscar James, and Edward G. Quinn. *The Reader's Encyclopedia of Shakespeare*. New York: Crowell, 1966.

Carlisle, Carol Jones. *Helen Faucit: Fire and Ice on the Victorian Stage*. London: Society for Theatre Research, 2000.

———. *Shakespeare from the Greenroom: Actors' Criticisms of Four Major Tragedies*. Chapel Hill: University of North Carolina Press, 1969.

Carmody, Jay. "New Theatre Season Has Dazzling Start." Review of *West Side Story*. National Theatre, Washington, D.C. *Evening Star*, August 20, 1957.

Carroll, William C. *The Metamorphoses of Shakespearean Comedy*. Princeton, N.J.: Princeton University Press, 1985.

Carter, Tim. *"Oklahoma!" The Making of an American Musical*. New Haven, Conn.: Yale University Press, 2007.

Champion, Larry S. *The Evolution of Shakespeare's Comedy: A Study of Dramatic Perspective*. Cambridge, Mass.: Harvard University Press, 1970.

Chapman, John. "*West Side Story* a Splendid and Super-Modern Musical Drama." Winter Garden Theatre, New York. *New York Daily News* September 27, 1957. *New York Theatre Critics' Reviews*, 1957, volume 18.

——. "*Kiss Me, Kate* Is Cole Porter's Sprightliest and Best Musical." Review of *Kiss Me, Kate*. Century Theater, New York. *Daily News*, December 31, 1948. *New York Theatre Critics' Reviews*, 1948, volume 9.

Cibber, Theophilus. *Romeo and Juliet*. London: C. Corbett, 1748.

Coe, Richard L. "*West Side* Has That Beat." Review of *West Side Story*. National Theatre, Washington, D.C. *Washington Post*, August 20, 1957.

——. "A Zestful Musical for Off-Broadway." Review of *Your Own Thing*. Orpheum Theater, New York. *Washington Post*, March 17, 1968.

——. "Everybody's Own Thing." Review of *Your Own Thing*. National Theatre, Washington, D.C. *Washington Post*, April 30, 1969.

Coleman, Robert. "*Kiss Me, Kate* Porter's Best, A Terrific Hit." Review of *Kiss Me, Kate*. Century Theatre, New York. *Daily Mirror,* December 31, 1948. *New York Theatre Critics' Reviews*, 1948, volume 9.

——. "Robert Coleman's Theatre: *West Side Story* A Sensational Hit!" Review of *West Side Story*. Winter Garden Theatre, New York. *Daily Mirror,* September 27, 1957.

Coleridge, Samuel Taylor. *Coleridge's Shakespearean Criticism*. Edited by Thomas Middleton Raysor. 2 vols. London: Constable, 1930.

Cooke, Richard P. "Swinging with Shakespeare." Review of *Your Own Thing*. Orpheum Theater, New York. *Wall Street Journal*, January 16, 1968.

Cristofori, Marilyn. "Hanya Holm." *American National Biography,* vol. 11. New York: Oxford University Press, 1999.

Current Biography Yearbook of 1954. Bronx, N.Y.: H. W. Wilson Co., 1954.

Dash, Irene G. "Double Vision: *Kiss Me, Kate*." *Shakespeare Newsletter* (Iona College) 55, no. 264 (Spring 2005): 3–4, 19, 22–31.

——. "*Hamlet* at the Public." *Shakespeare Bulletin* 8, no. 4 (1990): 22–24.

——. "Holliday, Judy." In *Jewish Women in America: An Historical Encyclopedia,* ed. Paula E. Hyman and Deborah Dash Moore, vol. 1. New York: Routledge, 1997.

——. "*Macbeth* at the Public." *Shakespeare Bulletin* 8, no. 1 (1990): 10–11.

——. "A Penchant for Perdita on the Eighteenth-Century Stage." In *The Woman's Part,* ed. Carolyn Ruth Swift Lenz, Gayle Greene, and Carol Thomas Neely, 271–84. Urbana: University of Illinois Press, 1980.

——. "Peter Hall's *Merchant of Venice*." *Shakespeare Bulletin* 8, no. 2 (1990): 10–11.

——. "Shakespeare and the American Musical." In *Shakespeare in American Life,* by the Folger Shakespeare Library, compiled and edited by Virginia Mason Vaughan and Alden T. Vaughan, 63–74. Washington, D.C.: Folger Shakespeare Library, 2007.

——. *Women's Worlds in Shakespeare's Plays*. Delaware: University of Delaware Press, 1997.

———. *Wooing, Wedding, and Power: Women in Shakespeare's Plays.* New York: Columbia University Press, 1984. First published 1981.

Dessen, Alan C. *Elizabethan Stage Conventions and Modern Interpreters.* Cambridge: Cambridge University Press, 1984.

Downer, Alan S. *The Eminent Tragedian: William Charles Macready.* Cambridge, Mass.: Harvard University Press, 1966.

Dusinberre, Juliet. *Shakespeare and the Nature of Women.* 2nd ed. New York: St. Martin's, 1996.

Eagleton, Terry. *William Shakespeare.* Oxford: Blackwell, 1986.

Edwards, Philip. "Beginnings and Continuities." *Shakespeare Survey* 51 (1998): 141–46.

Engel, Lehman. *The American Musical Theater: A Consideration.* With an introduction by Brooks Atkinson. New York: Macmillan, 1967.

Epstein, Helen. *Joe Papp: An American Life.* Boston: Little, Brown, 1994.

Ewen, David. *The Complete Book of the American Musical Theater.* Rev. ed. New York: Henry Holt, 1958.

———. *The Life and Death of Tin Pan Alley: The Golden Age of American Popular Music.* New York: Funk and Wagnalls, 1965.

Farrell, Kirby, Elizabeth H. Hageman, and Arthur F. Kinney, eds. *Women in the Renaissance.* Amherst: University of Massachusetts Press, 1988.

Felheim, Marvin. *The Theater of Augustin Daly.* Cambridge, Mass.: Harvard University Press, 1956.

Fisher, Barbara Milberg. *In Balanchine's Company: A Dancer's Memoir.* Middletown, Conn.: Wesleyan University Press, 2006.

Fitz, L. T. "'What Says the Married Woman?': Marriage Theory and Feminism in the English Renaissance." *Mosaic* 13, no. 2 (1980): 1–22.

Flinn, Denny Martin. *Musical! A Grand Tour: The Rise, Glory, and Fall of an American Institution.* New York: Schirmer, 1997.

Foulkes, Julia L. "Angels 'Rewolt!': Jewish Women in Modern Dance in the 1930s." *American Jewish History* 88 (June 2000): 233–52.

Friedan, Betty. *The Feminine Mystique.* 1963. Reprint, New York: Dell, 1975.

Frye, Northrop. *Anatomy of Criticism.* Princeton, N.J.: Princeton University Press, 1957.

Funke, Lewis. "News of the Rialto: Will B'way Rock?" *New York Times,* December 10, 1967.

Funke, Phyllis. "A Classic Comedy That's Funny." Review of *Two Gentlemen of Verona.* Delacorte Theater, New York. *Morning Telegraph,* July 29, 1971.

Furia, Philip. *The Poets of Tin Pan Alley: A History of America's Great Lyricists.* New York: Oxford University Press, 1990.

Garber, Marjorie. *Dream in Shakespeare.* New Haven, Conn.: Yale University Press, 1974.

Garland, Robert. "A Musical Comedy That Has Everything." Review of *Kiss Me, Kate.* Century Theater, New York. *New York Journal American,* December 31, 1948. *New York Theatre Critics' Reviews,* 1948, volume 9.

Garrick, David. *Catharine and Petruchio: A Comedy, in Three Acts.* London: J. and R. Tonson and S. Draper, 1756.

———. *The Plays of David Garrick.* Edited by Harry William Pedicord and Frederick Louis Bergmann. Vols. 1, 3, and 4. Carbondale: Southern Illinois University Press, 1981.

Gilder, Rosamond. *John Gielgud's Hamlet, 1937: A Record of Performances.* New York: Oxford University Press, 1937.

———. "Song and Dance: Broadway in Review." *Theatre Arts Monthly* 23, no. 1 (January 1939): 6–17.

Goldberg, Isaac. *Tin Pan Alley: A Chronicle of American Popular Music.* 1930. Reprint, with a supplement by Edward Jablonski, New York: Ungar, 1961.

Goldman, William. *The Season.* New York: Harcourt, Brace, and World, 1969.

Gould, Jack. "Rodgers and Hart Do the Words and Music." Review of *The Boys from Syracuse.* Alvin Theatre, New York. *New York Times,* December 4, 1938.

Granville-Barker, Harley. *More Prefaces to Shakespeare.* Edited by Edward M. Moore. Princeton, N.J.: Princeton University Press, 1974.

Green, Stanley. *Ring Bells! Sing Songs.* New Rochelle, N.Y.: Arlington House, 1971.

———. *The World of Musical Comedy.* 3rd ed. New York: Barnes and Noble, 1974.

Greenblatt, Stephen. *Will in the World.* New York: W. W. Norton, 2004.

Greg, W. W. *The Shakespeare First Folio.* 1955. Reprint, London: Oxford University Press, 1969.

Guare, John. "He Has Metamorphosed Me." Lecture at Bruno Walter Auditorium, New York Public Library for the Performing Arts, October 4, 2007.

Guare, John, and Mel Shapiro. *Two Gentlemen of Verona, Adapted from the Shakespeare Play by John Guare and Mel Shapiro.* Lyrics by John Guare. Music by Galt MacDermot. New York: Holt, Rinehart and Winston, 1973.

Hagood, Thomas K. *History of Dance in American Higher Education: Dance and the American University.* Lewiston, N.Y.: E. Mellen, 2000.

Harding, D. W. "Women's Fantasy of Manhood: A Shakespearian Theme." *Shakespeare Quarterly* 20 (1969): 245–53.

Haring-Smith, Tori. *From Farce to Metadrama: A Stage History of The Taming of the Shrew.* Contributions in Drama and Theatre Studies 16. Westport, Conn.: Greenwood, 1985.

Hart, Dorothy, and Robert Kimball, eds. *The Complete Lyrics of Lorenz Hart.* New York: Knopf, 1986.

Hastings, Ronald. "*Twelfth Night* Rock." Review of *Your Own Thing.* Comedy Theatre, London. *Daily Telegraph,* January 25, 1969.

Hering, Doris. "Broadway . . . On and Off." *Dance Magazine* 42, no. 4 (April 1968): 26–31.

Hogan, Charles Beecher. *Shakespeare in the Theatre, 1701–1800.* 2 vols. Oxford: Oxford University Press, 1952–57.

Horner, Matina. "Fail: Bright Women." *Psychology Today* 3, no. 6 (November 1969): 36–39.

Horowitz, Mark Eden. *Sondheim and Music: Minor Details and Major Decisions.* Lanham, Md., and Oxford: Scarecrow Press in Association with the Library of Congress, 2003.

Hotaling, Edward A. *Shakespeare and the Musical Stage.* Boston: G. K. Hall, 1990.

Howard, Jean E., and Phyllis Rackin. *Engendering a Nation.* London: Routledge, 1997.

Hughes, Alan. *Henry Irving, Shakespearean.* Cambridge: Cambridge University Press, 1981.

International Dictionary of Modern Dance. Edited by Taryn Benbow-Pfalzgraf. Detroit, Mich.: St. James Press, 1998.

Jackson, Russell. *Shakespeare Films in the Making: Vision, Production, and Reception.* Cambridge: Cambridge University Press, 2007.

———. Introduction to *Two Gentlemen of Verona,* by William Shakespeare. London: Penguin Shakespeare Series, 2005.

Jackson, Russell, and Robert Smallwood, eds. *Players of Shakespeare 2.* Cambridge: Cambridge University Press, 1989.

Jensen, Ejner J. *Shakespeare and the Ends of Comedy.* Drama and Performance Studies Series. Bloomington: Indiana University Press, 1991.

Johnson, Samuel. *The Yale Edition of the Works of Samuel Johnson.* Edited by Allen T. Hazen. Vol. 2, *The Idler and The Adventurer,* edited by W. J. Bate. New Haven, Conn.: Yale University Press, 1963.

Jowitt, Deborah. *Jerome Robbins: His Life, His Theater, His Dance.* New York: Simon and Schuster, 2004.

Keller, Evelyn Fox. *Reflections on Gender and Science.* New Haven, Conn.: Yale University Press, 1985.

Kerr, Walter. "Theater: *West Side Story* Sharks and Jets Battle in Dance." Review. Winter Garden, New York. *New York Herald Tribune,* October 6, 1957.

———. "Kerr Has a Happier Time at *Your Own Thing.*" Review. Orpheum Theater, New York. *New York Times,* January 28, 1968.

———. "Theater: *West Side Story.*" Review. Winter Garden, New York. *New York Herald Tribune,* September 27, 1957. *New York Theatre Critics' Reviews,* 1957, volume 18.

Kimball, Robert, Brendan Gill, and Bea Feitler. *Cole.* New York: Holt Rinehart, 1971.

Kimbrough, Robert. "Androgyny Seen through Shakespeare's Disguise." *Shakespeare Quarterly* 33 (1982): 17–33.

Kishi, Tetsuo. "Shakespeare and the Musical." In *Shakespeare and the Twentieth Century: Proceedings of the International Shakespeare Association World Congress, Los Angeles, 1996,* edited by Jonathan Bate, Jill L. Levinson, and Dieter Mehl, 157–67. Newark: University of Delaware Press, 1998.

Kisselgoff, Anna. "Jerome Robbins, 79, Is Dead; Giant of Ballet and Broadway." *New York Times,* July 30, 1998.

Komisarjevsky, Theodore. *Settings and Costumes of the Modern Stage.* New York: Studio Publications, 1933.

Kott, Jan. *Shakespeare Our Contemporary.* Translated by Boleslaw Taborski. Preface by Peter Brook. London: Methuen, 1965. Reprint. New York: Norton, 1974.

Kraft, Daphne. "*Your Own Thing* Bows at Orpheum." Review. Orpheum Theater, New York. *Newark Evening News,* January 15, 1968.

"Landmark Symposium." Transcript of a conversation among Arthur Laurents, Leonard Bernstein, Jerome Robbins, and Stephen Sondheim, moderated by Terrence McNally. *Dramatists' Guild Quarterly* 22 (Autumn 1985): 11–25.

Landry, Laurie. "Lots of Love from Verona." Review of *Two Gentlemen of Verona.* Live Theatre: *Your Guide to the Shows,* April 7–13, 1973. Her Majesty's Theatre, Melbourne, Australia.

Lardner, John. "Of Sweet Kate and Mr. Porter." Review of *Kiss Me, Kate.* Century Theater, New York. *New York Star.* January 2, 1948. *New York Critics' Theatre Reviews,* 1948, volume 9.

Laurents, Arthur. *Home of the Brave.* New York: Dramatists Play Service, 1945.

———. *Original Story By: A Memoir of Broadway and Hollywood*. New York: Knopf, 2000.

———, book. *West Side Story, a Musical.* Music by Leonard Bernstein, lyrics by Stephen Sondheim, production directed and choreographed by Jerome Robbins. New York: Random House, 1958.

———. "*West Side Story* at 50." Lecture at Bruno Walter Auditorium, New York Public Library for the Performing Arts, September 20, 2007.

Lerman, Leo. "Something to Talk About: *Your Own Thing.*" *Mademoiselle,* June 1968.

Lester, Elenore. "Is This Where It's At?" *New York Times,* February 25, 1968.

Levine, Lawrence W. "William Shakespeare and the American People: A Study in Cultural Transformation." *American Historical Review* 89 (February 1984): 34–66. Revised and enlarged in *Highbrow/Lowbrow: The Emergence of Cultural Hierarchy in America* (Cambridge, Mass.: Harvard University Press, 1988).

Loney, Glenn, ed. *Musical Theatre in America*. Westport, Conn.: Greenwood, 1984.

Macaulay, Alastair. "Robbins's Legacy of Anguish and Exuberance." *New York Times,* April 27, 2008.

MacDermot, Galt. "The Music Man: Galt MacDermot Talks to P & P." Interview. *Plays and Players* 20, no. 9 (June 1973): 22–25.

MacLean, Ian. *The Renaissance Notion of Woman*. Cambridge: Cambridge University Press, 1980.

Mancini, Anthony. "Closeup: His Own Thing." Interview with Donald Driver. *New York Post,* February 2, 1968.

Mantle, Burns. Review of *The Boys from Syracuse.* Alvin Theatre, New York. *New York Daily News,* November 24, 1938.

Marriott, R. B. "Musical 'Verona' Is a Joyous Hit at the Phoenix." Review of *Two Gentlemen of Verona.* Phoenix Theatre, London. *Stage and Television Today,* May 3, 1973, 19.

Martin, John. "*West Side Story* as an Experiment in Method." Review. Winter Garden Theater, New York. *New York Times,* October 27, 1957.

Mathews, Jane De Hart. *The Federal Theatre, 1935–1939*. Princeton, N.J.: Princeton University Press, 1967.

Mayhead, Gerald. "Not Such a Bard Night Out." Review of *Two Gentlemen of Verona.* Her Majesty's Theatre. *Herald,* Melbourne, Australia. April 2, 1973.

McBrien, William. *Cole Porter: A Biography*. New York: Knopf, 1998.

McElroy, Bernard. *Shakespeare's Mature Tragedies*. Princeton, N.J.: Princeton University Press, 1973.

McGuire, Philip C. *Speechless Dialect: Shakespeare's Open Silences*. Berkeley: University of California Press, 1985.

Millennium Year by Year: A Chronicle of World History from AD 1000 to the End of 1999. Updated ed. London: Dorling Kindersley, 2000.

Millett, Kate. *Sexual Politics*. New York: Doubleday, 1970.

Miola, Robert S., ed. *The Comedy of Errors: Critical Essays*. New York: Routledge, 1997.

Moore, Deborah Dash. *To the Golden Cities: Pursuing the American Jewish Dream in Miami and L.A.* Cambridge, Mass.: Harvard University Press, 1996.

Mordden, Ethan. *Better Foot Forward: The History of American Musical Theatre*. New York: Grossman, 1976.

———. *Coming Up Roses: The Broadway Musical in the 1950s.* New York: Oxford University Press, 1968.

———. *Open a New Window: The Broadway Musical in the 1960s.* New York: Palgrave, 2001.

———. *Sing for Your Supper: The Broadway Musical in the 1930s.* New York: Palgrave, 2005.

Morley, Henry. *The Journal of a London Playgoer.* London, 1866. Reprint, Leicester: Leicester University Press, 1974.

Most, Andrea. *Making Americans: Jews and the Broadway Musical.* Cambridge, Mass.: Harvard University Press, 2004.

Mostel, Raphael. "When the Ram's Horn Sounds." *Forward,* September 6, 2002: 14.

Mullaney, Steven. *The Place of the Stage: License, Play, and Power in Renaissance England.* Chicago: University of Chicago Press, 1988.

Nevo, Ruth. *Comic Transformations in Shakespeare.* London: Methuen, 1980.

Newman, Karen. *Shakespeare's Rhetoric of Comic Character: Dramatic Convention in Classical and Renaissance Comedy.* New York: Methuen, 1985.

Nicoll, Allardyce. *English Drama, 1900–1930.* Cambridge: Cambridge University Press, 1973.

———. *A History of English Drama, 1660–1900.* 6 vols. 1959. Reprint, Cambridge: Cambridge University Press, 1965.

Nolan, Frederick. *Lorenz Hart: A Poet on Broadway.* New York: Oxford University Press, 1994.

Odell, George C. D. *Annals of the New York Stage.* 15 vols. New York: Columbia University Press, 1927–49.

———. *Shakespeare from Betterton to Irving.* 2 vols. 1920. Reprint, New York: Dover, 1966.

Otway, Thomas. *The History and Fall of Caius Marius.* London, 1680.

Owen, Bobbi. *Costume Design on Broadway: Designers and Their Credits, 1915–1985.* Westport, Conn.: Greenwood, 1987.

Palmer, Howard. "2 Gentlemen of Laughter." Review of *Two Gentlemen of Verona.* Her Majesty's Theatre. Melbourne, Australia. *Melbourne Review,* April 2, 1973.

Peyser, Joan. *Bernstein, A Biography: Revised and Updated.* New York: Billboard, 1998.

Pinciss, Gerald M. *Why Shakespeare: An Introduction to the Playwright's Art.* New York: Continuum, 2003.

Pinciss, Gerald M., and Roger Lockyer, eds. *Shakespeare's World.* New York: Continuum, 1989.

Playbill. Program for *The Boys from Syracuse,* opening December 26, 1938, Alvin Theatre, New York. Held by the Billy Rose Theatre Division, New York Public Library for the Performing Arts.

———. Program for *Two Gentlemen of Verona,* opening August 16, 2005, Shakespeare in the Park. Property of Irene G. Dash.

Pollack, Howard. *George Gershwin: His Life and Work.* Berkeley: University of California Press, 2006.

Rabkin, Norman. *Shakespeare and the Common Understanding.* New York: Free Press, 1967.

———. *Shakespeare and the Problem of Meaning.* Chicago: University of Chicago Press, 1981.

Rackin, Phyllis. *Stages of History: Shakespeare's English Chronicles.* Ithaca, N.Y.: Cornell University Press and Routledge, 1990.

Ranald, Margaret Loftus. *Shakespeare and His Social Context: Essays in Osmotic Knowledge and Literary Interpretation.* New York: AMS, 1987.

Richards, David. "A *Carousel* for the 90s, Full of Grit and Passion." Review. Vivian Beaumont Theater, Lincoln Center, New York. *New York Times,* March 25, 1994.

Richards, Stanley, ed. *Great Rock Musicals.* New York: Stein and Day, 1979.

Ripman, Olive. "Musicals—Then and Now." *Dancing Times,* n.s. 502 (July 1952): 596–98.

"Robbins, the Legend Who Was Human." Remembrances by his friends and colleagues, including Harold Prince and Jennifer Tipton. *New York Times,* August 9, 1998.

Rodgers, Richard. *Musical Stages: An Autobiography.* 1975. New York: Da Capo, 2002.

Rothwell, Kenneth. *A History of Shakespeare on Screen: A Century of Film and Television.* 1999. Reprint, Cambridge: Cambridge University Press, 2001.

Russell, Frederick. "He Brought Ballet to Broadway." *American Dancer,* April 1939, 15, 37.

Rutter, Carol. *Clamorous Voices: Shakespeare's Women Today.* New York: Routledge, 1989.

Schjeldahl, Peter. "An Up-to-Date and Sexy *Verona.*" Review of *Two Gentlemen of Verona.* Delacorte Theater, New York. *New York Times,* August 8, 1971.

Schlesinger, Arthur M., Jr., ed. *The Almanac of American History.* New York: G. P. Putnam's Sons, 1983.

Schwartz, Charles. *Cole Porter: A Biography.* New York: Da Capo Paperback, 1977.

Secrest, Meryle. *Stephen Sondheim: A Life.* New York: Knopf, 1998.

Shakespeare, William. *The Riverside Shakespeare.* Edited by G. Blakemore Evans and J. J. M. Tobin. 2nd ed. Boston: Houghton, 1997.

———. *Shakespeare's Comedy of Twelfth Night: An Acting Edition.* With a producer's preface by Harley Granville-Barker. Produced at the Savoy Theatre, London. Opened November 15, 1912. London: William Heinemann, 1912.

———. *Twelfth Night.* Program for the production by Joseph Papp at the New York Shakespeare Festival. Wilford Leach, director. Delacorte Theatre, Central Park, Summer 1986.

———. *Twelfth Night, or, What You Will . . . As performed at the Theatres Royal, Drury Lane and Covent Garden. Printed under the authority of the managers, from the prompt- book. With remarks by Mrs. Inchbald.* London: Longman, Hurst, Rees, and Orme, 1808.

Shapiro, James. *A Year in the Life of William Shakespeare: 1599.* New York: Harper Collins, 2005.

Shattuck, Charles H. *The Shakespeare Promptbooks: A Descriptive Catalogue.* Urbana: University of Illinois Press, 1965.

Shaw, George Bernard. *Shaw on Shakespeare.* Edited with an intro- duction by Edwin Wilson. New York: Dutton, 1961.

Shepard, Richard F. "They Put *Verona* on Broadway Map." *New York Times,* December 3, 1971.

Short, James F., Jr., and Fred L. Strodtbeck. *Group Process and Gang Delinquency.* Chicago: University of Chicago Press, 1965.

Simas, Rick. *The Musicals No One Came to See.* New York: Garland, 1987.

Smith, Bruce R. *The Acoustic World of Early Modern England.* Chicago: University of Chicago Press, 1999.

Smith, Cecil. *Musical Comedy in America*. New York: Theatre Arts Books, 1950.

Smith, Dinitia. "Age of Aquarius Returns in Shakespearean Romp." Article on *Two Gentlemen of Verona* in anticipation of its revival in Central Park. *New York Times*, August 16, 2005.

Sorell, Walter. *Hanya Holm: The Biography of an Artist*. Middletown, Conn.: Wesleyan University Press, 1969.

Spencer, Christopher, ed. *Five Restoration Adaptations of Shakespeare*. Urbana: University of Illinois Press, 1965.

Spevack, Marvin. *A Complete Concordance to the Works of Shakespeare*. 6 vols. Hildesheim, Germany: George Olms, 1968–70.

Spewack, Samuel and Bella, book. *Kiss Me, Kate*. Lyrics by Cole Porter. New York: Knopf, 1953.

Sternfeld, Jessica. *The Megamusical*. Bloomington: Indiana University Press, 2006.

Stone, George Winchester, Jr. "Garrick's Handling of Shakespeare's Plays and His Influence upon the Changed Attitude of Shakespearian Criticism during the Eighteenth Century." Ph.D. diss., Harvard University, 1940.

Stone, Lawrence. *The Family, Sex, and Marriage in England, 1500–1800*. New York: Harper, 1977.

———. *Road to Divorce: England, 1530–1987*. Oxford: Oxford University Press, 1990.

Taylor, Gary, and John Jowett. *Shakespeare Reshaped, 1606–1623*. Oxford: Clarendon, 1993.

Teague, Frances. *Shakespeare and the American Popular Stage*. Cambridge: Cambridge University Press, 2006.

Terry, Ellen. *Ellen Terry's Memoirs*. Edited by Edith Craig and Christopher St. John. London, 1932. Reprint, New York: Benjamin Blom, 1969.

Terry, Walter. "Dance: Miss Holm and Her Fine 'Kiss Me, Kate' Choreography." *New York Herald Tribune*, January 9, 1949.

Todd, Arthur. "A Brace of Musicals." *Dance* 23, no. 3 (March 1949): 28–29.

Urdang, Laurence, ed. *Timetables of American History*. Millennial ed. New York: Simon and Schuster, 1996.

Vaill, Amanda. *Somewhere: The Life of Jerome Robbins*. New York: Broadway Books, 2006.

Van Lennep, William, et al., eds. *The London Stage, 1660–1800*. 5 parts in 11 vols. Carbondale: Southern Illinois University Press, 1960–68.

Vaughan, Alden T., and Virginia Mason. *Shakespeare's Caliban: A Cultural History*. Cambridge: Cambridge University Press, 1991.

Vaughan, Virginia Mason, and Alden T., comps. and eds. *Shakespeare in American Life*. Washington, D.C.: Folger Shakespeare Library, 2007.

Wardle, Irving. "The Uncommercial Broadway." *London Times Saturday Review*, February 22, 1969.

———. "Viola Transported to Fun City." Review of *Your Own Thing*. Comedy Theatre, London. *London Times*, February 7, 1969.

Warfield, Scott. "From *Hair* to *Rent*: Is 'Rock' a Four-Letter Word on Broadway?" In *The Cambridge Companion to the Musical*, ed. William A. Everett and Paul R. Laird, 231–45. Cambridge: Cambridge University Press, 2002.

Watt, Douglas. "Central Park 'Verona' Rocks, Jumps for Joy." Review of *Two Gentlemen of Verona*. Delacorte Theater, New York. *Daily News*, July 29, 1971.

Watts, Richard, Jr. "New Musical Comedy Lives Up to Promise." Review of *Kiss Me, Kate.* Century Theater, New York. *New York Post,* December 31, 1948. *New York Theatre Critics Reviews,* 1948, volume 9.

——. "Romeo and Juliet in a Gang War." Review of *West Side Story.* Winter Garden Theatre, New York. *New York Post,* September 27, 1957. *New York Theatre Critics' Reviews,* 1957, volume 18.

Webster, Margaret. *Shakespeare without Tears.* Cleveland: World, 1942.

Weiler, A. H. "Jazz Up Your Shakespeare." *New York Times,* April 7, 1968.

Wesker, Arnold. *The Birth of Shylock and the Death of Zero Mostel.* New York: First Fromm International, 1999.

Whitfield, Stephen. "West Side Storied." *Forward,* September 7, 2007, B3.

Williams, George Walton. "Staging the Adulerate Blot in *The Comedy of Errors.*" *Shakespeare Bulletin* 18, no. 3 (Summer 2000): 5–6.

Williamson, Marilyn. *The Patriarchy of Shakespeare's Comedies.* Detroit: Wayne State University Press, 1986.

Wilson, John S. "Doing *Your Own Thing.*" Review of original cast recording of *Your Own Thing* (RCA Victor LOC 1148; LSO 1148). *New York Times,* March 24, 1968.

Wilson, Katharina M., ed. *Women Writers of the Renaissance and Reformation.* Athens: University of Georgia Press, 1987.

Wollman, Elizabeth L. *The Theater Will Rock: A History of the Rock Musical from "Hair" to "Hedwig."* Ann Arbor: University of Michigan Press, 2006.

Woolf, Virginia. *A Room of One's Own.* New York: Harcourt, 1929.

Wylie, Philip. *Generation of Vipers.* New York: Farrar and Rinehart, 1942.

Zadan, Craig. *Sondheim & Co.* 2nd ed. New York: Harper, 1986.

Audio and Video Recordings

The Beatles. *Past Masters,* vol. 2. Original recordings made by EMI Records Ltd., this compilation by Mark Lewisohn. EMI Records Ltd., 1988.

The Boys from Syracuse. Book by George Abbot, music by Richard Rodgers, and lyrics by Lorenz Hart. Studio cast, 1997, new restoration of original orchestration. Produced for Records by Hugh Fordin. DRG 94767.

The Boys from Syracuse. Book by George Abbot, music by Richard Rodgers, and lyrics by Lorenz Hart. Produced by Goddard Lieberson. Columbia Records, 1953. SONY Broadway. SK 53329.

Eye on Dance. "Yesterday Shapes Today: Tracing the Roots." Interview with Hanya Holm and Don Redlich, conducted by Celia Ipiotis. Telecast May 27, 1985. WNYC-TV, *MGZOC 9-2952.

Jerome Robbins' Broadway. Twenty-six-tape set. NCOV 823, Theatre on Film and Tape Archive, Billy Rose Theatre Division, New York Public Library for the Performing Arts.

Kiss Me, Kate. Screenplay by Dorothy Kingsley, play by Samuel Spewack and Bella Spewack, music and lyrics by Cole Porter. Directed by George Sidney. Produced by Jack Cummings. MGM, 1953. DVD Warner Home Video, 2003.

Kiss Me, Kate. Book by Bella Spewack and Samuel Spewack, with Alfred Drake and Patricia Morison, music and lyrics by Cole Porter. January 13, 1949. Columbia Records/CBS, CK4140.

Two Gentlemen of Verona, by William Shakespeare, adapted by John Guare and Mel Shapiro. Lyrics by John Guare, music by Galt MacDermot. A Decca Broadway Original Cast recording, 2002. Universal Music Company 440 017 565-2.

West Side Story. Conducted by Leonard Bernstein. Book by Arthur Laurents, music by Leonard Bernstein, lyrics by Stephen Sondheim, based on a conception by Jerome Robbins. With Kiri Te Kanawa, Jose Carreras, Tatiana Troyanos, Kurt Ollmann, and Marilyn Horne. Polydore International, 1985. Digital Stereo 289 457 1992.

West Side Story. Book by Arthur Laurents, music by Leonard Bernstein, lyrics by Stephen Sondheim, based on a concep-tion by Jerome Robbins. Original Broadway cast recording, 1957, with Carol Lawrence, Larry Kert, Chita Rivera, and Art Smith. Produced by Goddard Lieberson. Columbia Records, CBS, Compact Disc, CK 32603.

West Side Story. Conducted by Leonard Bernstein. Screenplay by Ernest Lehman. Directed by Jerome Robinson and Robert Wise, 1961. Special Edition DVD Collector's Set. Los Angeles: MGM, 2003.

Your Own Thing. Book by Donald Driver, music and lyrics by Hal Hester and Danny Apolinar. Original cast recording. Recorded January 30–31, 1968, in RCA Victor's Studio A, New York, digitally remastered in September 1999 at BMG Studios, New York. 09026-63582-2.

INDEX

Italicized page numbers refer to illustrations.

IRENE G. DASH is author of *Women's Worlds in Shakespeare's Plays,* which won a Choice Best Academic Book Award, and *Wooing, Wedding, and Power: Women in Shakespeare's Plays.* Her most recent publication is a chapter on Shakespeare and the American musical in the Folger Shakespeare Library's edited volume *Shakespeare in American Life.*